LIBRARY OF SECOND TEMPLE STUDIES
78

Formerly the Journal for the Study of the Pseudepigrapha Supplement Series

Editor
Lester L. Grabbe

Editorial Board
Randall D. Chesnutt, Philip R. Davies, Jan Willem van Henten, Judith M. Lieu,
Steven Mason, James R. Mueller, Loren T. Stuckenbruck, James C. VanderKam

Founding Editors
James H. Charlesworth

THE CONCEPT OF THE MESSIAH IN THE SCRIPTURES OF JUDAISM AND CHRISTIANITY

Shirley Lucass

t&t clark

Published by T & T Clark International
A Continuum imprint
80 Maiden Lane, New York, NY 10038
The Tower Building, 11 York Road, London SE1 7NX

www.continuumbooks.com

All rights reserved. No part of this publication may be reproduced or transmitted in any form or by any means, electronic or mechanical, including photocopying, recording or any information storage or retrieval system, without permission in writing from the publishers.

© Shirley Lucass, 2011

Shirley Lucass has asserted her right under the Copyright, Designs and Patents Act, 1988, to be identified as the Author of this work

British Library Cataloguing-in-Publication Date
A catalogue record for this book is available from the British Library

ISBN: HB: 978-0-567-58384-0

Library of Congress Cataloging-in-Publication Data
A catalog record for this book is available from the Library of Congress

Typeset and copy-edited by Forthcoming Publications Ltd. (www.forthpub.com)
Printed and bound in Great Britain

Contents

Preface	ix
Acknowledgments	xiii
Abbreviations	xv
INTRODUCTION	1

Chapter 1
THE QUESTION, THE STATE OF THE QUESTION
AND THE APPROACH 4
- The Question — 4
- The State of the Question — 5
- Recent Approaches to the Question — 8
- Clearing the Ground — 12
- A New Approach — 15

Chapter 2
JEWISH WRITERS IN DIALOGUE 19
- The Jewish Reclamation of Jesus — 19
- The Person of the Messiah — 21
- The Role of the Messiah — 30
- Outcome of the Messiah's Role — 34
- Conclusion — 35

Chapter 3
KINGSHIP IN THE ANCIENT NEAR EAST 37
- Introduction — 37
- The Person of the King — 40
- The Role of the King — 48
- Outcome of the King's Role — 59
- Conclusion — 65

Chapter 4
KINGSHIP IN THE HEBREW SCRIPTURES:
THE PSALMS

	66
Introduction	66
The Person of the King	67
The Role of the King	73
Outcome of the King's Role	91
Conclusion	93

Chapter 5
KINGSHIP IN THE HEBREW SCRIPTURES:
THE PROPHETS

	94
Introduction	94
The Person of the King	95
The Role of the King	106
Outcome of the King's Role	115
Conclusion	120

Chapter 6
THE ANOINTED IN THE SECOND TEMPLE PERIOD:
THE HIGH PRIEST

	122
Introduction	122
The Person of the High Priest	123
The Role of the High Priest	130
The Outcome of the High Priest's Role	140
Conclusion	142

Chapter 7
THE ANOINTED IN THE SECOND TEMPLE PERIOD:
THE SON OF MAN

	144
The Son of Man	144
The Person of the Son of Man	146
The Role of the Son of Man	153
The Outcome of the Son of Man's Role	156
Conclusion	156

Chapter 8
THE MESSIAH IN THE NEW TESTAMENT

	158
Introduction	158
The Person of the Messiah	158
The Role of the Messiah	171
Outcome of the Messiah's Role	182
Conclusion	185

Chapter 9
IMPLICATIONS FOR DIALOGUE 188
    The Person of the Anointed 188
    The Role of the Messiah 196
    The Outcome of the Messiah's Role 201
    Conclusion 208

Bibliography 211

Index of References 221
Index of Authors 234

Preface

As with any work covering such a wide variety of texts over so broad a sweep of time, from Ancient Egypt through to contemporary Jewish–Christian dialogue, I have only been able to engage superficially with contentious issues. It is also not possible to be competent, let alone expert, in so many different areas. However, only a cursory discussion of these areas would have enabled me to take forward the line of argument I offer in the following pages. Furthermore, because of space constraints I am unable to answer objections, particularly in the case of the final chapter, that I can already see may be raised. That does not, however, mean that these cannot be answered. My thinking on this subject has developed over the last fifteen years, yet only a small sample of my thoughts can be reflected here. Again, space constraints have not allowed me to take the argument beyond the first century into post-70 C.E. Jewish messianism (although this task has already been undertaken) in order to demonstrate that sacral kingship does feature as an integral part of this thinking and emerges not only in the mystical tradition but also right in the heart of the orthodox liturgy and festivals.

All that I have hoped to demonstrate here is that, although it fell out of favour with scholarship, sacral kingship "has been walked away from, not disproven," and lies at the heart of messianism. It is only through that lens, that messianism, in all its aspects, can be properly viewed. Once this is understood from its Near Eastern background, it provides the key to understanding much else that otherwise appears opaque. It is universally accepted that the root of the messianic concept is found in the *meshiah Yahweh* or *Ha-melekh ha-mashiah*, and in particular the Davidic kingship. Furthermore, despite the modifications of later eras, the concept of the Anointed king and his enthronement continued to inform all aspects of messianism, even those in which there is no mention of a Davidic Messiah, and where the Messiah has become a heavenly redeemer; the same imagery of kingship and enthronement, and the same ultimate utopian outcomes are expected. Unfortunately for dialogue, the origins of the concept of Messiah and how these origins were understood at the time of the parting of the two major Jewish groups to emerge from the first century is usually ignored. Instead, until the middle of last century it was considered that "the Jews" had missed "the time of their visitation" and "the Christians" had distorted the Jewish Scriptures and fabricated a Hellenized version of the Messiah that had little in common with Judaism. This understanding, coupled with the seemingly anti-Jewish polemic of John's Gospel, played a large part in the formulation of the doctrines which led to the persecution of the Jewish people by Christians in the name of Christianity, finally hardening into the positions which prevailed until the abomination of the Holocaust caused them to be re-assessed. The renunciation of the doctrine of supersessionism by the Church has opened up doorways to dialogue which have been closed for almost 2000 years. In the words of Fisher,

> Today…we are in effect in the second generation of a theological dialogue between the church and the Jewish people made possible by the elimination of Christian claims to have replaced Judaism in God's plan of salvation. We stand in a unique moment of history, reassessing all that has gone before us in a spirit of reconciliation and renewed hope for the future. Much is at stake, for good or ill, in how we today understand and frame Christian–Jewish relations.[1]

What I have attempted to do here is to clear the ground so that a new framework for dialogue can be constructed. Rather than try to unravel the past 2000 years of claim and counter-claim, of doctrines decided, with one eye on what the other was saying, taking a fresh look instead at the origins of the concept allows each party to see how the positions they now hold have been developed. It also allows each party to see that these need not be mutually exclusive positions. Rather than being a barrier, a stumbling block to dialogue, Jesus in fact could be the cornerstone of that new framework (Eph 2:17–22).

Whilst I could have engaged with more recent Jewish scholarship on the question of dialogue, no recent Jewish scholars (to my knowledge) deal directly with Jesus in the same bold way as do the writers I have chosen. Their boldness may be attributed to the post-Holocaust atmosphere prevalent at the time of their writing, a fact which precipitated a movement to reclaim Jesus for Judaism. It was felt that if the Hellenistic accretions were removed it would be possible to get back to a more simple, Jewish Jesus, one who, through no fault of his own, had been made into the Christ of Christianity.

Therefore, although such well-known names as Novak and Neusner have consistently been engaged in dialogue, producing various works on the subject, neither of them deals directly with Christology. As a result,

---

1. Eugene J. Fisher, *Visions of the Other: Jewish and Christian Theologians Assess the Dialogue* (New Jersey: Paulist, 1994), 2.

to my mind, they leave untouched and therefore unanswered the central stumbling block of all Jewish–Christian dialogue: Was Jesus the Messiah? Whilst the ultimate answer to that must be a question of faith, what I have attempted to demonstrate here is simply that he could have been. That is, he could have been the expected Messiah of Judaism, one that fits fully into the Jewish expectations of that period, and not the product of Paul's Hellenistic Judaism mixed with elements of the mystery religions, nor a product of the Church's later theologizing. Neither is it my belief that this understanding of the Messiah was "subsequently transformed as Christianity spread in the Gentile world";[2] rather, I would argue that all that the New Testament writers say about Jesus can be rooted in antecedent Jewish tradition which pre-dates the arrival of Jesus. That is not to say that I think the later Church has been innocent of developing certain New Testament lines of thought in un-Jewish ways. Instead, it is my contention that the fundamentals of the faith, as set forth in the creeds, are to be found within the pages of the Hebrew Scriptures and the New Testament. If it were possible to establish this, then the ground would be cleared and the foundation laid for real dialogue to begin. Initiating this dialogue is the ultimate goal of the present work.

---

2. Adela Yarbro Collins and John J. Collins, *King and Messiah as Son of God* (Grand Rapids: Eerdmans, 2008), xiv.

Acknowledgments

I wish to thank all those who have contributed in some way to enabling me to produce this volume—David Gait, Philip Alexander, Virginia, Linda, Mal, Deni, and most especially my daughters Heather and Beth, whose love has kept me going.

> Sing to the LORD a new song,
>   for he has done marvellous things;
> his right hand and his holy arm
>   have worked salvation for him.
> The LORD has made his salvation known
>   and revealed his righteousness to the nations.
> He has remembered his love
>   and his faithfulness to the house of Israel;
> all the ends of the earth have seen
>   the salvation of our God. (Ps 98:1–3)

ABBREVIATIONS

ANET	*Ancient Near Eastern Texts Relating to the Old Testament*. Edited by J. B. Pritchard. 3d ed. Princeton, 1969
BCOTWP	Baker Commentary on the Old Testament Wisdom and Psalms
CAH	*Cambridge Ancient History*
FAT	Forschungen zum Alten Testament
JSOTSup	Journal for the Study of the Old Testament: Supplement Series
KTU	*Die keilalphabetischen Texte aus Ugarit*. Edited by M. Dietrich, O. Loretz, and J. Sanmartín. AOAT 24/1. Neukirchen–Vluyn, 1976. 2d enlarged ed. of *KTU*: *The Cuneiform Alphabetic Texts from Ugarit, Ras Ibn Hani, and Other Places*. Edited by M. Dietrich, O. Loretz, and J. Sanmartín. Münster, 1995 (= *CTU*)
LXX	Septuagint
MT	Masoretic Text
NIV	New International Version
NRSV	New Revised Standard Version
OTM	Oxford Theological Monographs
RSV	Revised Standard Version
SOTMS	Society for Old Testament Monograph Series
WUNT	Wissenschaftliche Untersuchungen zum Neuen Testament

INTRODUCTION

A fundamental reason Jewish thinkers have rejected the claim that Jesus is the Messiah is the high Christology in which that claim has been expressed. Though many Jews might still have rejected Jesus as Messiah even if it had not been claimed that he was God incarnate (Jewish history furnishes several examples of human Messiahs who were nonetheless rejected), there can be no question that that claim, once made, lies at the heart of the rejection. The classic Jewish argument against the high Christology is threefold: that it is not rooted in Jewish tradition, that it is incompatible with Jewish monotheism and that it finds no support in antecedent Judaism. This argument is presented in a variety of ways. One common form attempts to prove that the high Christology of early Christianity is a secondary development. According to this, Jesus did not regard himself as a supernatural being, nor did the early disciples; instead, that idea developed on pagan soil and was influenced by polytheistic pagan ideas. However, what if this is not, in fact, the case? What if the high Christology pertaining to the earliest Christian understanding of the person of Jesus is as rooted in Judaism as the naturalistic concept of the Messiah? Initially this is a straightforward historical question, open to historical investigation, and one capable, in principle, of historical proof or disproof. There are good historical reasons emerging from scholarly analysis of the primary texts over the past one hundred years, as well as the discovery and publication of new sources of evidence, for accepting that the high Christology of the New Testament is not secondary, but is firmly rooted within Judaism. Nothing can, of course, be proven beyond all possible dispute, but a strong case for this can certainly now be made, a case strong enough to challenge any confident rejection of high early Christian views of Jesus as secondary and "un-Jewish." Most experts on early Judaism would agree with this point: Second Temple Judaism has emerged in recent scholarship as a far more richly complex theological phenomenon than was often supposed. However, it is the implications of this historical fact upon contemporary Jewish–Christian dialogue that ultimately concerns us. Judaism and Christianity are historical religions: both have a strong sense of history, and appeal to tradition, particularly as expressed in the *Tanakh*/Old Testament, to validate their respective positions. They cannot simply assert that they are right. They must demonstrate that they are right. If, then, it can be demonstrated that the high Christology of the New Testament can be grounded in the Hebrew Scriptures and other Jewish texts which precede the first century, what impact would this have on contemporary Jewish–Christian dialogue? This is the question that I propose to explore.

The first step in this enquiry is to carry out an analysis of the work of four Jewish writers in order to assess their views concerning the messiahship of Jesus, and, as a consequence, to ascertain their particular contentions against this claim. I will then explore the origins of the concept of Messiah in order to compare this with the concept of Messiah portrayed in the New Testament as well as with the Jewish writers' contentions concerning the messiahship of Jesus and their assertions concerning the "Jewish" concept of Messiah. Fundamental to the enquiry is the widely acknowledged scholarly opinion that the origins of the concept of Messiah are to be found with the ancient Israelite ideology of kingship. However, it is also widely accepted that this kingship ideology can only be understood within its ancient Near Eastern cultural context. I will, therefore, consider the person and role of the king within four ancient Near Eastern cultures, namely, the Egyptian, Mesopotamian, Hittite and Ugaritic/Canaanite cultures, since these are believed to have influenced the ancient Israelite ideology of kingship.

One particular aspect of the royal ideology that I will examine is the king's role in the New Year/enthronement festivals of these cultures, and the ways in which this idea may have impacted on Israelite theology. Here I have been guided to some extent by the work of the "myth and ritual" school that found prominence in the first half of the last century. Whilst the arguments of this school no longer command the widespread acceptance that they once did, and therefore recent scholarship has tended to steer away from their conclusions, nonetheless I find the position generally convincing and believe it has been sometimes unfairly criticized and unjustly neglected in recent years.[1] Moreover, an acknowledgment of the relevance of the ancient Near Eastern cultic material has been made more recently by writers such as Moshe Idel[2] and Adela Yarbro Collins and John Collins,[3] as well as by commentators on the Hebrew Psalms, such as Eaton and Day.[4]

---

1. I engage with some of the criticism of this theory at the beginning of Chapter 3.
2. See Moshe Idel, *Messianic Mystics* (London: Yale University Press, 1998).
3. See Adela Yarbro Collins and J. J. Collins, *King and Messiah as Son of God* (Grand Rapids: Eerdmans, 2008), xi. Note that in this work only the Egyptian influence on Israel has been considered.
4. The work of both of these scholars is treated in Chapter 4.

Armed with knowledge of this ancient Near Eastern background, the line of enquiry will then move to the Hebrew Scriptures in order to consider the concept of the Anointed within the Psalms and the Prophets. The Psalms have been particularly singled out by a number of scholars as a literature replete with this notion of sacral kingship. However, if sacral kingship does play an important part in the mindset of the ancient Israelites, then it should be apparent in writings other than the Psalms. With this in mind, the Prophetic literature will also be explored in order to ascertain whether a royal ideology can be discerned in this portion of the Hebrew canon. Finally, in this investigation of the roots of the concept, I will examine the inter-testamental literature, paying close attention to the book of Enoch, in order to establish what developments took place in the concept of Messiah during the Second Temple period, focussing particularly on how the role of the Anointed altered post-Exile, following the demise of the monarchy and the assumption of the king's cultic role by the high priest.

Having established the origins of the concept of Messiah in the pre-Christian Jewish texts, I will examine the New Testament itself, in order to determine how the New Testament writers have portrayed the messiahship of Jesus. In this I will argue that the New Testament has an irreducibly high Christology, one which pervades all the documents, from the earliest to the latest. My approach here will be synchronic. There is, of course, diversity within the New Testament writings in their attitude towards the person and work of Christ, yet a synchronic approach is defensible here for two reasons. The first is the often ignored fact that the New Testament view of Christ is remarkably homogeneous: writers of all persuasions unite to express a high Christology. Second, the harmonizing, synchronous approach is the one that Christianity has traditionally taken towards its Scriptures, and it should be respected in the context of dialogue.

Finally, I consider the implications of this historical argument for Jewish–Christian dialogue. If it can be established that the high Christology of the New Testament has its roots in antecedent Jewish tradition, and that it is not merely a creation of the post-Easter Church, where does this leave Jewish–Christian dialogue? Given that normative Rabbinic Judaism is also deeply rooted within early Jewish tradition, it would follow that if both parties in dialogue are genuinely committed to a recognition of historical truth, then they will surely be obliged to acknowledge that *both* their positions are grounded in early Jewish tradition, in the rich and complex theology of biblical and post-biblical Judaism, and, as a consequence, begin to construct their dialogue on the basis of this fact.

Chapter 1

THE QUESTION, THE STATE OF THE QUESTION AND THE APPROACH

The Question

"Is Jesus the Christ? If so, then Judaism falls. If not, then Christianity fails."¹ This stark statement, articulated by Jacob Neusner, penetrates to the heart of the problem which continues to prove the key issue in Jewish–Christian dialogue. Neusner is not alone; the centrality of the question is also recognized by other scholars.² Scholem remarks: "Any discussion of the problems relating to messianism is a delicate matter, for it is here that the essential conflict between Judaism and Christianity has developed and continues to exist."³ What lies behind these statements is the acknowledgment that, whilst, on the one hand, Christianity and Judaism are joint heirs of first-century Judaism, and as such stand in a special relationship with one another, consequently sharing numerous concepts, on the other, it is the shared concept of the Messiah, central to both faiths, which is, in fact, the very root of their division. As the opening quote from Neusner hints, however, it is not just this concept that is problematic; alongside the claim, which Christianity makes, that Jesus is the long-awaited Messiah of Judaism, are two further claims. One, exclusivism, asserts that Christianity, because of its acceptance of Jesus'

---

1. Jacob Neusner, *Jews and Christians: The Myth of a Common Tradition* (London: SPCK, 1991), 49.
2. "At this level, the debate, indeed the only essential debate, is whether or not Jesus of Nazareth is the promised Messiah of the House of Israel. The Christians say yes; the Jews say no. That difference alone has been more than sufficient to keep Jews and Christians in two separate, indeed competing, communities since the first century." David Novak, *Talking with Christians: Musings of a Jewish Theologian* (Grand Rapids: Eerdmans, 2005), 58.
3. Gershom Scholem, *The Messianic Idea in Judaism and Other Essays on Jewish Spirituality* (London: Allen & Unwin, 1971), 1.

messiahship, has become the sole means of access to the God of Israel, making obsolete all other means. The other, supersessionism, states that Christianity, representing the culmination of the Judaism which preceded it, has superseded that Judaism, and thus any subsequent form of Judaism, which is not Christianity, is redundant.[4] This central question of the messiahship of Jesus has been the subject of debate between Jews and Christians from New Testament times through the Patristic era and the great formal disputations of the Middle Ages down to the present day, but little progress appears to have been made. The debate seems rapidly to reach an impasse: it becomes a stark either/or, because at stake is the very theology on which Christianity rests. As its name indicates, Christianity involves the belief that Jesus of Nazareth was the Christ, the Messiah; Judaism's rejection of this is not just the rejection of a particular doctrine of Christianity, it is a rejection of Christianity itself.

The State of the Question

Before considering some of the more recent attempts to break out of this impasse it is important to clarify what is meant by "dialogue," since dialogue can take place on a number of levels. Notably, dialogue may involve joint action by Jews and Christians to tackle social or ethical problems on which they share common perspectives.[5] There is a long history of such joint action to improve the world, going back to Jewish involvement in reform movements in the nineteenth century, and this approach has been particularly favoured in more recent times by the World Council of Churches.[6] However, although this may be commendable in itself, shared action focused on a single (political) issue can hardly be called dialogue, since it does not address key points of difference between the co-operating parties: it ignores "the elephant in the room," in that it deliberately refuses to address the fact that, theologically speaking, for Christianity, Judaism should not exist, and vice versa. The only true dialogue in this case is theological. Dialogue at this level has tended to take place within academia, but even in this sphere it often

---

4. Novak acknowledges how deeply supersessionism is embedded, particularly in Christian doctrine, and comments on the difficulties therefore in renouncing it. Novak, *Talking with Christians*, 8–9.

5. See, for example, Gerhart M. Riegner and Franz von Hammerstein, *Jewish Christian Dialogue* (Geneva: International Jewish Committee on Inter-religious Consultations and the World Council of Churches' Sub-Unit on Dialogue with the People of Living Faiths and Ideologies, 1975), 18.

6. Ibid., 9.

does not involve scholars openly interacting with each other[7] in the manner of the mediaeval disputes.[8] Although there are some attempts at dialogue in this fashion, for example, when scholars from both traditions co-operate to produce a volume such as those by Falk and Harrelson or Lapide and Luz,[9] this is not widespread. What has been more common is the production of single-author volumes from within one tradition, alluding at times consciously, though not explicitly, to other works from the same tradition, but not really engaging in dialogue with scholars from the opposite side. What seems to be happening is that each side (predominantly the Jewish side) is attempting to understand the other, without actually engaging in direct dialogue or dealing with the central issues. Novak, in the Preface to his 2005 volume of essays, a collection which represents the past twenty-five years of his work dealing with Christianity from a Jewish perspective, states that he has engaged in conversations with "serious Christians, especially with some important Christian theologians." Nonetheless, he admits "there are no discussions here of the Incarnation, the Trinity, or Christian ecclesiology. Such topics are not the business of a Jewish theologian to discuss critically."[10]

Unlike other religions, it is the very theological inter-relatedness of Christianity and Judaism which should determine the way forward in dialogue;[11] yet, it is that very theological inter-relatedness which led to the persecution and degradation of the Jewish people that culminated in the Holocaust. Theologians from within both Christianity and Judaism

---

7. There have been numerous works on Christian–Jewish dialogue, particularly post-Holocaust: for an extensive bibliography, see Helen Fry, ed., *Christian–Jewish Dialogue* (Exeter: University of Exeter Press, 1996). A further bibliography and short survey of writers is also available in Peter Ochs, "Judaism and Christian Theology," in *The Modern Theologians* (ed. David F. Ford; 2d ed.; Oxford: Blackwell, 1998), 607–25. See also Edward Kessler and Neil Wenborn, eds., *A Dictionary of Jewish–Christian Relations* (Cambridge: Cambridge University Press, 2005).

8. Cf. Hyam Maccoby, *Judaism on Trial* (London: Associated University Presses, 1982), and William Horbury, *Jews and Christians in Conflict and Controversy* (Edinburgh: T. & T. Clark, 1998).

9. See Walter Harrelson and Randall Falk, *Jews and Christians: A Troubled Family* (Nashville: Abingdon, 1990); Pinchas Lapide and Ulrich Luz, *Jesus in Two Perspectives: A Jewish–Christian Dialogue* (Minneapolis: Augsburg, 1985). See also Leon Klenicki and Geoffrey Wigoder, eds., *A Dictionary of the Jewish–Christian Dialogue* (New York: Paulist, 1995), which looks at the question through individual topics presented alternately by Jewish and Christian writers. See too Eugene J. Fisher, ed., *Visions of the Other: Jewish and Christian Theologians Assess the Dialogue* (New Jersey: Paulist, 1994).

10. Novak, *Talking with Christians*, xii.

11. With the possible exception of Buddhism and Hinduism.

have acknowledged the role that the theology of the New Testament and its perceived anti-Judaism played in laying the groundwork that allowed the racial anti-Semitism of late nineteenth- and early twentieth-century Europe to flourish.[12] This acknowledgment has had a twofold affect. On the positive side, it has given the dialogue impetus.[13] Institutionally, this has resulted in moves made towards reconciliation from within the Christian Churches.[14] Academically, there has been an acceleration of the pre-Holocaust phenomenon of Jewish scholars entering into the, for them, previously uncharted waters of New Testament scholarship. However, on the negative side, perhaps with reconciliation in mind, some Christian scholars have displayed the tendency to make theological concessions, resulting in a lower Christology than that traditionally held.[15] This has proved less helpful than the open polemic of the medieval disputes, and has, arguably, resulted in the stultification of the dialogue, because unless both sides feel free to state and defend their classic beliefs as they see fit, without the pressure of "moral blackmail," dialogue cannot progress.

Furthermore, neither faith is static. Even if the central beliefs are maintained intact, how those beliefs are interpreted and understood will vary from age to age. Thus, although substantial amounts of work have been done in the area of Christology by theologians such as Barth and Bultmann, this has done little to elucidate the problem directly for dialogue. Similarly with the modern diversity within Judaism, messianic beliefs have evolved that further complicate the differences between the

---

12. See, for example, Rosemary Radford Ruether, *Faith or Fratricide: The Theological Roots of Anti-Semitism* (New York: Seabury, 1974).

13. See Michael Wyschogrod, "A Jewish Postscript," in *Encountering Jesus: A Debate on Christology* (ed. Stephen T. Davis; Atlanta: John Knox, 1988), 179.

14. See Ford, ed., *The Modern Theologians*, 611–14; Helga Croner, ed., *Stepping Stones to Further Jewish–Christian Relations* (New York: Stimulus, 1977), and the later Helga Croner, ed., *More Stepping Stones to Jewish–Christian Relations (An Unabridged Collection of Christian Documents 1975–1983)* (New York: Paulist, 1985); Irving Greenberg, *For the Sake of Heaven and Earth: The New Encounter between Judaism and Christianity* (Philadelphia: The Jewish Publication Society of America, 2004), 3–4.

15. "Roy and Alice Eckhardt argue that a belief in the resurrection of Christ is inherently triumphalistic and anti-Judaic. They maintain that this belief must be given up as part of the price to be paid in affirming the validity of Judaism in its own right." Richard Harries, "Judaism and Christianity," in *The Blackwell Encyclopaedia of Modern Christian Thought* (ed. Alister E. McGrath; repr. Oxford: Blackwell, 1996), 284. See also John Hick, ed., *The Myth of God Incarnate* (London: SCM, 1956); James D. G. Dunn, *The Christ and the Spirit* (Grand Rapids: Eerdmans, 1998), 416; N. T. Wright, *Jesus, the Victory of God* (London: SPCK, 1996), 478.

messianic concepts of both faiths, beliefs which lie at the heart of the conflict in dialogue. It is interesting to note, however, that although the interpretation and expression of their theology of the Messiah may fluctuate, according to trends within scholarship, within the framework of dialogue, regardless of which tradition they may belong to, most Jewish scholars are largely in agreement when it comes to the doctrine of the Messiah.[16] That is to say, in opposition to what they perceive to be the Christian concept of the Messiah, these writers form a reasonably united front. Thus, quite elaborate differences are often asserted to exist between the Christian and Jewish understandings of atonement and messiahship, yet these do not always do justice to the complexity and subtlety of either side's real beliefs.[17]

Recent Approaches to the Question

If the concept of Messiah represents the key issue upon which all Christian and Jewish dialogue falters, how can this be overcome? A number of possibilities have been explored. One is to adopt a theological stance which minimizes the conflict. For example, a Christian theologian in dialogue with Jewish writers could adopt the position of the authors of *The Myth of God Incarnate*, who contend that Jesus never claimed to be the son of God, but was promoted to that status by pagan and other influences on early Christians.[18] Again this highlights the complexity of the question: it is not just the claim that Jesus was the Messiah that divides the two faiths, nor the doctrines of exclusivism and supersessionism mentioned above; it is also the *type* of messianism. Christianity claims that Jesus was not just a human figure, but that he was God himself. If this claim were denied, as these Christian authors have done, then this would remove one of the major obstacles to dialogue. However, to do so would result in a Christ that is unrecognizable to the vast majority of the Church, not just considered historically, but in terms of Christian belief today. Such a dialogue might be very satisfactory for the parties concerned, and reach a high level of consensus, but it would be irrelevant for the majority of Christians. It also fails to do justice to the evidence of the New Testament text, which unquestionably has a high Christology, and any attempt at dialogue must engage with that text. The present dialogue simply side-steps the main problem; it does not address it.

---

16. See Eugene B. Borowitz, *Contemporary Christologies: A Jewish Response* (New York: Paulist, 1980), 8.
17. As also acknowledged by ibid., 4.
18. Hick, *The Myth*, ix.

A further possibility would be to ignore the centrality of the concept of Messiah and the inter-relatedness of Christianity and Judaism. This approach has been adopted by the Jewish writer Jacob Neusner, whose contention it is that, to date, no real dialogue has taken place.[19] Notably, though Neusner agrees that religions need to frame a theology of "the other," he also acknowledges the difficulties which this incurs: "The fact that thinking about the other means we have also to rethink the truth about ourselves explains, I think, why we are so reluctant to do so."[20] Although, I would agree with this statement, his further suggestion that we employ the methodology of comparative religion, taking concepts that the two faiths *do* have in common and comparing them, ignoring as it does the central issue of Messiah, would only serve to further dialogue on a superficial level, leaving untouched the main theological issues. Neusner suggests that only when Judaism and Christianity understand themselves as "totally alien to one another" will dialogue be able to begin: "Dialogue will begin with the recognition of difference, with a search for grounds for some form of communication, rather than with the assumption of sameness and the search for commonalties."[21] Even if this method were to prove fruitful on the lines of showing some commonality of thought and aims, this again would tend to be useful only at an institutional level; it would serve little to progress real dialogue.

Another possible approach has been explored by those Jewish writers who form part of the endeavour to reclaim for Judaism a "Jewish Jesus" who is distinct from the "Christ of Christianity." It is their belief that it is possible to strip away the accretions of later Hellenism which resulted in the faith we now know as Christianity and to reach a much simpler, more Judaic faith which had been distorted.[22] A number of writers have attempted to remove the "myth and legend" which they claim has adhered to Jesus, to discover beneath not the "historical Jesus" who formed the quest of late nineteenth-century liberal Christian scholarship, but a genuinely "Jewish" Jesus: Jesus the Rabbi, the Hasid, the Pharisee, the Essene, the Zealot, the miracle worker—dependent upon which particular Jewish persuasion the writer himself was from.[23] However, this produces a similar problem to that outlined above, in that the resultant "Jesus" bears

---

19. Neusner, *Jews and Christians*, ix.
20. Ibid., 112.
21. Ibid., 119.
22. See Geza Vermes, *Jesus the Jew: An Historian's Reading of the New Testament* (London: Fontana, 1976), 9.
23. For example, Klausner's messianism is very much informed by his Zionist views.

little resemblance to the Christ of Christianity and inhibits Christians from entering into dialogue. This problem has been recognized by both Christian and Jewish scholars.[24] Furthermore it is also recognized by Christian scholars that Jesus' teaching and ministry are only understandable within the context of the claims which Christianity makes for his person, that is, his divine status and the claim that he fulfils the messianic prophecies of the Hebrew Scriptures.[25] A variation on this approach, taken by a number of Jewish writers, is to argue that it was Paul, and not Jesus, with whom the fault lies, as the title of one of Hyam Maccoby's works suggests.[26] According to this view Jesus was either an amazing/ordinary Rabbi (again dependent upon the writer's personal persuasion) with no messianic pretensions or, alternatively, he did have a messianic consciousness, one that was either changed by Jesus himself, as he recognized the failure of his mission, or that was changed post-Easter by the emergent Church, and in particular Paul.[27]

Whilst the Jewish reclamation of Jesus may provide interesting and useful insight into first-century Judaism and enlighten both Christians and Jews, it can do little to further Jewish–Christian dialogue. This is because it fails to tackle the stark choice with which we began—the fact that if Jesus is not the Christ, then Christianity *does* fail. To attempt to unpack the key issue in this way, to divest it of its "accretions" and reveal that in fact it is something other than was thought, turns out, therefore, to be as limited and problematic as the other approaches. Suggesting that Jesus is other than the Christ does not allow Christianity any room for manoeuvre and must as a consequence force its withdrawal from the dialogue. This results in a mirror image of Christian supersessionism. If Jesus is not the Christ, then Christianity is obsolete, and Judaism no longer has a partner in dialogue.

Conversely, insisting that Jesus is the Christ does not force the same options onto Judaism—Judaism is not made obsolete because Jesus is the Christ in Christian theology. Obsolescence only comes when this is coupled with the doctrine of supersession. The claim of exclusivism, on the other hand, not only excludes Judaism as a means of salvation, but all

---

24. Cf. Neusner, *Jews and Christians*, 120; Donald Hagner, *The Jewish Reclamation of Jesus* (Grand Rapids: Zondervan, 1993), 227.

25. See, for example, the discussion between Pinchas Lapide and Ulrich Luz in *Jesus in Two Perspectives*.

26. Hyam Maccoby, *The Mythmaker: Paul and the Invention of Christianity* (London: Weidenfield & Nicholson, 1986).

27. These differing responses are explored further in Chapter 2.

else that is not Christianity. Thus exclusivism, whilst it is also problematic in Jewish–Christian dialogue, is a problem with which Christians have to come to terms when in dialogue with all other faiths, not just Judaism, in its formulation of a concept of "the other." Whilst any interpretation of Jesus as other than "the Christ" fails to do justice to the New Testament, both supersessionism and exclusivism may be open to an interpretation which would not only leave Christianity intact, but also could encompass the other form of Judaism which emerged from the first century.[28] Though this would not resolve the question of Jesus' messiahship, nonetheless it would remove two further obstacles to dialogue and reduce the residual problem to the "type" of messiah that Jesus was. What this would mean, therefore, is that if it was possible to demonstrate that the type of messianism claimed by the New Testament for Jesus did in fact derive from antecedent Jewish tradition, and that it was not an alien intrusion into the tradition by New Testament writers, then dialogue would, arguably, be put on a new footing. That is to say, rather than insisting that Jesus did not conform to first-century Jewish expectations of Messiah, as not only Jewish writers, but also some Christian writers claim, which has the effect of bringing dialogue to a standstill, the acceptance of the New Testament concept of Jesus' messiahship as "authentically" Jewish would force dialogue to centre on other issues such as the potential impact of that messiahship on both Jews and Gentiles.

Setting aside for the moment the claims of supersession and exclusivism (to which I shall return in Chapter 9), it would appear, therefore, that a more promising way forward would be to explore the concept of Messiah itself. Rather than adopting any of the above approaches, which arguably ignore or circumvent the central issue, I propose instead to focus on it and to consider the origin of the concept of Messiah. Given that both modern Judaism and Christianity emerged from first-century Judaism and both took forward the concept of Messiah, the probability is that the concept of Messiah they hold was derived from antecedent Jewish tradition. If it proves possible to uncover the origin of that concept, then it may be possible to understand the divergent transmission that has occurred and, furthermore, it may be possible to suggest ways of reconciling that divergence which do not diminish the centrality or the specific understanding of that concept within either tradition.

---

28. How this can be achieved will be considered in the final chapter of the present work.

Clearing the Ground

Two points that have bedevilled previous dialogue need to be clarified. One is a question of language. Although a few scholars are alert to the problem, many more continue to use the terms "Christianity" and "Judaism" when speaking of the first-century groups from which eventually the two faiths crystallized. If challenged, none of them would deny the diversity of the Judaism of this period nor that Christianity at this time was not known as such and was in effect a Second Temple Jewish messianic sect.[29] Nonetheless, the continued use of these terms serves to compound the idea that there already existed at this point two completely separate faiths. It is important that this is highlighted so that the correct perspective is maintained. Thus the perceived anti-Judaism of the Gospels referred to above is shown to be an intra-mural argument between two different Jewish groups—not "Christians" vs. "Jews." Although the term "the Jews" is employed in the New Testament, a usage which would imply that the other group using this term is something other than Jewish, it has been suggested that the term *Ioudaioi* referred to a particular set of Jewish people.[30] Moreover, there were numerous Jewish groups in that period (as today) which were often hostile to the others' ideologies.[31] Sandmel is one of the few Jewish writers to acknowledge this.[32] In this same vein, although axiomatic, it is pertinent to stress that all of Jesus' original followers were Jewish, with no suggestion that they were derived from any previously partisan movement. They were all, rather, from diverse backgrounds. This understanding does not seem evident in some of the work of writers in dialogue, and is exacerbated by the use of anachronistic terms. Again Sandmel is an exception to this:

---

29. A sect known as "the Way" according to the testimony of Acts 9:2; 19:9, 23; 22:4; 24:14.

30. See, for example, D. Moody Smith, "Judaism and the Gospel of John," in *Jews and Christians: Exploring the Past, Present and Future* (ed. James H. Charlesworth, Frank X. Blisard and Jeffrey S. Siker; New York: Crossroads, 1990).

31. See P. D. Hanson, "Messianic Figures in Proto-Apocalypticism," in *The Messiah: Developments in Earliest Judaism and Christianity* (ed. James H. Charlesworth; Minneapolis: Fortress, 1992), 67–75. Bruce comments on John's Gospel: "the Evangelist frequently speaks of 'the Jews' in a way that suggests that he is distancing himself from them, but when he does so, he regularly means 'the other Jews' (as distinct from his and his associates) or else, on occasion, the Judeans (as distinct from the Galileans)." F. F. Bruce, *The Gospel of John* (Grand Rapids: Eerdmans, 1983), 1.

32. See Samuel Sandmel, *We Jews and Jesus* (London: Gallancz, 1965), 33.

> Early Christianity was a Judaism. It acquired its name, Christianity, about a half-century after the time of Jesus. Were it not for the accident of nomenclature, the distinctions between Judaism and Christianity, rooted in theology and fixed by diverse historical experiences, would not support the broad impression which endured so long, that they are total distinctions. They are not; the fact that Christianity was born within Judaism meant that it shared extensive common possessions.[33]

One further point deserves clarification and that is the term *Messiah* itself. Buda, in his discussion of the term, highlights the difficulty of arriving at a definition.[34] One of the main problems in understanding the concept is that too narrow a definition has been applied to the term, as Hays has pointed out: "the image of the messiah and the idea of messianism comprise a broad concept that far outreaches the few instances where the term 'anointed' is used. It is the concept that we are seeking to define, not merely one particular Hebrew word."[35] This is, in fact, the position taken by a number of writers who contend that the term "Messiah" merely translates the term "Anointed," and thus is not a technical term as such, but one used of anyone who is chosen for a special task by God.[36] Conversely, other scholars argue that "*the* Messiah" was in effect a technical term in the first century.[37] There is widespread confusion therefore concerning the concept of Messiah and what constitutes messianism. Becker proposes that there is a "messianic vacuum" with the Old Testament and that the Apocrypha and Pseudepigrapha provide a "no-hope" list for messianism.[38] Other scholars suggest that there is only a "pre-messianism" in the Hebrew Scriptures. However, I believe that in so arguing, not only do scholars ignore the wealth of messianic material in the Hebrew Scriptures,[39] a trove which I hope to

---

33. Ibid., 150.
34. Mark J. Boda, "Figuring the Future: The Prophets and Messiah," in *The Messiah in the Old and New Testaments* (ed. Stanley E. Porter; Grand Rapids: Eerdmans, 2007), 35–45.
35. J. D. Hays cited in ibid., 44.
36. See Charlesworth, ed., *The Messiah*, 11; also Sigmund Mowinckel, *He That Cometh* (trans. G. W. Anderson; Oxford: Blackwell, 1959), 7; also Stuart Rosenberg, *The Christian Problem: A Jewish View* (New York: Hippocrene, 1986), 33–34.
37. See William Horbury, *Jewish Messianism and the Cult of Christ* (London: SCM, 1998), 7; also Paul D. Wegner, *An Examination of Kingship and Messianic Expectation in Isaiah 1–35* (New York: Mellen Biblical, 1992), 6.
38. Cited by Horbury, who considers this question and lists a number of other scholars who also hold this opinion. In addition, Horbury refers to others who see only a minimal messianism within the Second Temple period. Horbury, *Jewish Messianism*, 171 n. 4.
39. See also Wegner, *An Examination of Kingship*, 2–3.

unearth in the following chapters, but they are often guilty of reading back into the first century the Rabbinic doctrine of Messiah for which there is no documentary evidence before the Talmudic period,[40] which post-dates the first century by 300 years.[41] Although messianic ideas can be found in much earlier texts within the rabbinic tradition,[42] according to Alexander "the first clear, full and coherent statement of messianism strictly within the rabbinic tradition" is to be found even later in Saadia Gaon's (882–942) Eighth Treatise of *The Book of Beliefs and Opinions*. Against this some scholars will point to the messianism of the *Amidah*, but not only does this not contain the full Rabbinic doctrine of Messiah,[43] the form in which the *Amidah* now exists cannot be conclusively dated.[44]

However, not only was the Rabbinic doctrine of Messiah fluid for centuries prior to *Saadia*'s statement on messianism, the mystical tradition which existed alongside this brought a further dimension to the concept. In addition, not only was there no consensus on the type and role of the Messiah,[45] but also what constitutes the Messianic Age/Age to Come was a matter of debate:

> The distinction between the Age to Come and the Messianic Age is a comparatively late development and it follows that they were often synonymous terms in early apocalyptic. On the other hand however there are passages where the Messianic Age and the Age to Come are sharply distinguished, of the former it was possible to prophecy but of the latter it was thought that it transcended all human conception.[46]

---

40. Although, as we shall see in Chapter 6, messianism is evident in Jewish texts within the Apocrypha and Pseudepigrapha, these works were not incorporated into the Hebrew Scriptures and were rejected by Rabbinic Judaism.

41. See Neusner, *Jews and Christians*, 54–55.

42. In the Targumim, as well as in the midrashim and aggadot of the Talmud. See Philip S. Alexander, "The King Messiah in Rabbinic Judaism," in *King and Messiah in Israel and the Ancient Near East* (ed. John Day; JSOTSup 270; Sheffield: Sheffield Academic, 1998), 457.

43. Nonetheless, it is suggested that it was the Amidah, forming as it still does an important part of the synagogue liturgy, as well as the Targumim, that kept messianism alive in the earlier Rabbinic period, which otherwise was more concerned with Torah obedience. See ibid., 470–73.

44. Although it is considered to have undergone redaction ca. 100 C.E. Cf. Philip S. Alexander, *Textual Sources for the Study of Judaism* (Manchester: Manchester University Press, 1984), 6–7. Although not Rabbinic in origin, the Amidah was modified under Rabbinic influence. See Alexander, "The King Messiah," 456.

45. Idel, *Messianic Mystics*, 42–43; Julius H. Greenstone, *The Messiah Idea in Jewish History* (Philadelphia: The Jewish Publication Society of America, 1943), 83.

46. W. D. Davies, *Torah in the Messianic Age/Age to Come* (Philadelphia: Society of Biblical Literature, 1952), 81.

Thus different definitions of this phenomenon have further confounded the division, as we shall see in the following chapter.

Nonetheless, the Rabbinic doctrine of Messiah, just as the Christian doctrine of Messiah, has its roots in the Hebrew Scriptures[47] and there is a general consensus that the term *meshiah Yahweh* or *Ha-melekh ha-mashiah* is not only the term used of the Israelite king, but is the source of the concept of Messiah. This is because it is from the sacral role of the king that the ideology, which surrounds the concept, is derived.[48] Thus the king (and, post-Exile, the high priest) was not just anointed, but was *the* Anointed.[49] Therefore, whilst the term *ha-mashiah* used in the Hebrew Scriptures refers for the most part to the king, it is the ideology which surrounds this title, inherent in the original role, that has given rise to the idealized future Messiah, and hence the use of this same term for this figure. My focus, therefore, will be on the person and role of the Anointed and the developments of that role, commencing with the pre-exilic period through to the Second Temple period. As a consequence of my understanding of the developing role of the Anointed during this long period, I will also be considering the figures of the "Servant" in Isaiah and the "Son of Man" in the Prophets and inter-testamental writings.

A New Approach

We have seen that the approach adopted by those involved in the Jewish reclamation of Jesus leads to a dead-end for dialogue, producing the same results as the de-mythologizing or spiritualizing of the messianic concept from the Christian side. Indeed, adopting the methodology of comparative religion which Neusner suggests is not only inappropriate in the case of Judaism and Christianity, but also totally ignores the source of their division—the central issue of Messiah.[50] The approach adopted

---

47. See Gabriele Boccaccini, *Roots of Rabbinic Judaism* (Grand Rapids: Eerdmans, 2002), and Walter C. Kaiser, *Messiah in the Old Testament* (Grand Rapids: Zondervan, 1995).

48. Helmer Ringgren, *The Messiah in the Old Testament* (London: SCM, 1956), 21; Mowinckel, *He That Cometh*, 5; Aage Bentzen, *King and Messiah* (Oxford: Blackwell, 1970); A. R. Johnson, *Sacral Kingship in Ancient Israel* (Cardiff: University of Wales Press, 1967); Idel, *Messianic Mystics*, 21.

49. Mowinckel, *He That Cometh*, 6; Roland de Vaux, *Ancient Israel: Its Life and Institutions* (trans. John McHugh; 2d ed.; London: Darton, Longman & Todd, 1968).

50. Novak has also acknowledged this: "Our historical entanglement from the very beginning makes our encounters far more than exercises in comparative religions." Novak, *Talking with Christians*, 30.

here will be to consider the role of historical enquiry, not into the person of Jesus and his ministry—that is, this study will not follow the route of the "New Quest" for the historical Jesus[51]—but into the origins of the concept of Messiah itself. If the concept of the unity of truth is accepted, and if, as they do, Judaism and Christianity consider themselves to be historical religions, in the sense that not only have they developed historically, but they claim to originate from a revelatory incident within history, then both religions should be open to submitting to historical enquiry.[52] Thus, what is true in history must, or at least should, be true for these historical religions. Furthermore, the use of historical enquiry as a methodology broadens the field of research because Israelite religion did not evolve in isolation but was influenced by the cultures surrounding it, and with which it had intimate acquaintance. This is not only acknowledged by a number of scholars,[53] but is also substantially supported by internal evidence; the very fact that the Prophetic books are replete with denunciations of, or warnings against, pagan practices suggests that they were widespread. Furthermore, syncretism is evident in a number of places in the Hebrew Scriptures.[54] Therefore, no matter how, or when, the strict monotheism which became the hallmark of Israelite religion arose, there is overwhelming evidence to suggest that it was not always so, and that Israel was exposed to the ideology, which all Israel's Near Eastern neighbours shared. Consequently, whilst the extent of that influence may be a subject for debate, the fact that Israel was influenced is widely acknowledged.[55] This is particularly interesting since one of the

---

51. See Wright, *Jesus*, 1–124, for a survey of the "New Quest."
52. This has been acknowledged by Wright: "Christianity does itself a radical disservice when it appeals away from history, when it says that what matters is not what happened but 'what it means to me.'" Ibid., 661.
53. See Ringgren, *The Messiah*, 21; Mowinckel, *He That Cometh*, 56–57, and more recently, Idel, *Messianic Mystics*, 22.
54. Smith, however, suggests this was not a case of syncretism: "Although the Biblical witness accurately represented the existence of Israelite worship of Baal and perhaps of Asherah as well, this worship was not so much a case of Israelite syncretism with the religious practices of its 'Canaanite' neighbours, as some biblical passages depict it, as it was an instance of old Israelite religion." Mark S. Smith, *The Origins of Biblical Monotheism* (New York: Oxford University Press, 2001), 7. In this respect he cites: 1 Kgs 15:9–13; 2 Kgs 18:4–5; 23:4–5.
55. See Mowinckel, *He That Cometh*, 22; W. O. E. Oesterley, "Early Hebrew Festival Rituals," in *Myth and Ritual* (ed. S. H. Hooke; London: Oxford University Press, 1933), 146; Ivan Engnell, *Studies in Divine Kingship in the Ancient Near East* (2d ed.; Oxford: Blackwell, 1967), 174–75; Bentzen, *King and Messiah*, 11. Idel, *Messianic Mystics*, 21; Day, "The Canaanite Inheritance of the Israelite Monarchy,"

charges brought against Christianity by the Jewish writers in dialogue is that it was Christianity that was open to syncretism, that it was Hellenized and adopted pagan ideas as a consequence of its increasingly Gentile membership. In contrast, Judaism is portrayed as strictly monotheistic, rational and unchanging.

Furthermore, it becomes apparent in any dialogue surrounding the concept of Messiah that the concept itself has undergone some transformation from its origins in history to the present time.[56] This is not only evident because of the divergent concepts held by Christianity and Judaism as they now stand, but also because of the diversity of concept within first-century Judaism which first led to the division. Although more recent scholarship has shown increasing awareness of this diversity,[57] this is not always acknowledged in works engaging in dialogue. This will become apparent in the following chapter. The difference did not apply solely to the two groups which emerged from first-century Judaism, but also to those groups which did not, such as the group at Qumran, whose messianism shows some variation from both the messianism of the New Testament and that proposed by the Rabbinic tradition.[58]

It should be apparent from the foregoing that while the concept of Messiah provides the focus for division in Jewish–Christian dialogue, in order to explore this further and to address the contentions it is first of all necessary to establish just what form these contentions take. Although the concept of Messiah provides the focus, it will become apparent that within this one concept are subsumed a number of other equally contentious issues. These issues concern the claims of Christianity surrounding the person of Jesus. This is because the rejection of Jesus as Messiah does not rest solely on the non-realization of the messianic era, although this does serve as a major contention, but also, as highlighted above, on

---

in Day, ed., *King and Messiah*, 72; Collins and Collins, *King and Messiah as Son of God*, xi, although, as mentioned above, the focuses is particularly on the Egyptian influence on the monarchy.

56. See Joseph Klausner, *The Messianic Idea in Israel: From Its Beginning to the Completion of the Mishnah* (trans. W. F. Stinespring from the 3d Hebrew ed.; London: Bradford & Dickens, 1956), 11.

57. Although not directly engaged in dialogue, Wright is one scholar who does consider this diversity. Wright, *Jesus*, 482.

58. See Jacob Neusner, William J. Green and Ernest Frerichs, eds., *Judaisms and Their Messiahs at the Turn of the Christian Era* (New York: Cambridge University Press, 1987). Note, however, that it may be argued that the messianism at Qumran shows close affinity with that of the New Testament. See James C. VanderKam, *The Dead Sea Scrolls Today* (Grand Rapids: Eerdmans, 1994), 177–80.

contingent claims of his divinity. This includes his place in the Trinitarian concept of God, considered unique to Christianity, as well as the suffering aspect of his mission, including his death and resurrection.[59] Therefore, the Jewish contentions concerning the messiahship of Jesus are focussed on three areas: (1) the person of the Messiah; (2) his role; and (3) the outcome of his messiahship, that is to say, the conditions expected in the messianic era. Even though, as noted above, there exists a traditional ambiguity within Judaism itself as to what constitutes the Messianic Age and what constitutes the Age to Come, most modern Jewish writers make no distinction between them.[60] Nonetheless, the expected changes or conditions which the Messiah is thought to bring about form one of the criteria by which New Testament messianism is judged.[61] Having outlined the Jewish contentions concerning the messiahship of Jesus, I will now look at them in detail through the work of four influential Jewish writers on the subject.

---

59. See Vermes, *Jesus the Jew*, 15.

60. W. D. Davies discusses this topic in his book cited above, the very title of which—*Torah in the Messianic Age/Age to Come*—indicates this ambiguity. Klausner is an exception. Klausner, *The Messianic Idea*, 411.

61. See Randall Falk, "Understanding Our Relationship to Jesus: A Jewish Outlook," in Harrelson and Falk, eds., *Jews and Christians*, 105.

Chapter 2

JEWISH WRITERS IN DIALOGUE

The Jewish Reclamation of Jesus

Since the Enlightenment and the emancipation of the Jewish people, a paradigm shift in dialogue has occurred. This has resulted, according to Sandmel, in the historical animosities being eased and replaced by "both knowledge and a disposition towards genuine understanding" in Jewish and Christian attitudes to each other.[1] This is particularly remarkable in view of the depth of the animosity and the appalling treatment of the Jewish people by the increasingly powerful Church in the preceding seventeen hundred years. As Hagner has noted, "The disheartening story of the treatment of the Jews by Christians throughout these long, dark centuries constitutes one of the saddest chapters in the history of the church."[2]

This mistreatment of the Jews by Christians precipitated a reaction within Judaism, one which saw the "consolidation of Rabbinic piety as normative Judaism" and "the careful definition of Jewish doctrine, especially in those areas relevant to the claims of Christianity."[3] It is against this backdrop that the work of the writers under examination here is to be read. The writers in question form part of the movement within Judaism that has been dubbed "the Jewish reclamation of Jesus."[4] Rather than consider a greater number of writers, I have focused on four main writers in order to look in detail at their objections to the Christian claim, as evidenced in the New Testament, that Jesus was the expected Messiah of Judaism.[5] The four writers in question are Joseph Klausner, Samuel

---

1. Sandmel, *We Jews*, 3.
2. Hagner, *The Jewish Reclamation*, 41.
3. Ibid., 53.
4. Ibid., 286. Hagner includes a detailed bibliography of the writers engaged in the Jewish reclamation of Jesus (pp. 305–11).
5. Hagner, who similarly considers dialogue to be at an impasse, also concentrates on the work of "certain important and influential Jewish scholars." Amongst these are three of those that I will be considering here: Samuel Sandmel, Joseph Klausner and Geza Vermes. See ibid., 28–30.

Sandmel, Geza Vermes and Hyam Maccoby. Klausner's work emanates from the early half of the twentieth century and demonstrates his Zionism and his orthodoxy. Maccoby also speaks from within the Orthodox position. Sandmel writes in the second half of the last century and represents Liberal Judaism. Geza Vermes writes as a historian whose work spans a number of years, right up to the present time. Notably, Vermes' position on the present topic has not moved significantly, meaning that it is acceptable for me to take as representative his 1993 volume, *The Religion of Jesus the Jew*, which sets forth his clearest position on Jesus. Whilst I engage with the work of more recent Jewish scholarship in Chapter 9, the writers considered here have been chosen because they specifically deal with the messiahship of Jesus. These writers are important and influential scholars whose work, I would argue, lies in the background of later Jewish–Christian dialogue.

When the work of the above-mentioned writers is considered, a distinct pattern emerges, one which focuses on the teaching rather than the person or the miracles of Jesus depicted by the New Testament writers. Hagner suggests that this is because Jesus' teaching is more "readily reclaimable" for Judaism, whereas Jesus' claims about his person are more problematic.[6] In his work on the subject, Hagner identifies two categories into which the Jewish writers divide the designations of Jesus: first those deemed "more acceptable" and second those deemed "less acceptable" to the Jewish reclamation of Jesus.[7] The former category includes those designations outlined in Chapter 1: "Pharisee," "Essene," "Zealot," "Hasid" or "Prophet"—none of which, with the exception of the latter, is actually to be found in the New Testament as a designation of Jesus, but all of which find resonance in modern Judaism, being recognizable as "legitimate" Jewish categories.[8] Those identified as "less acceptable" by Hagner include "Lord," "Son of God," "Son of Man" and "Messiah," that is, those epithets which the New Testament writers themselves apply to Jesus.[9] These designations concern the person of Jesus, that is, who the New Testament writers claim that Jesus is.

However, an examination of the work of the Jewish writers reveals that they also object to the *type* of Messiah that Jesus is portrayed as being in the New Testament and the "results," or in most cases, the lack of results, of that messiahship. In other words, there are three main topics on which discussion has centred, viz., the Messiah's person, his

6. Ibid., 227.
7. Ibid., 228.
8. Ibid., 228–42.
9. Ibid., 242–57.

role and the outcome of that role. It is the views of our four writers on these topics that I will consider thematically, whilst acknowledging, as Maccoby does, the difficulty in trying to separate the different aspects of the Messiah in order to examine them individually.[10] Subsequent analysis will be structured around the same three topics in order to facilitate a comparison and a contrast. It should be noted that the writers in question engage mainly with the Synoptic Gospels, a feature which again highlights the significance of the teaching of Jesus for the Jewish writers, rather than what is said about him. The avoidance of John's Gospel is based on the belief that it is more theologically developed than the others.[11]

The Person of the Messiah

Whilst each of the writers under examination denies that Jesus was the expected Messiah of Judaism, nonetheless they all, with the exception of Vermes, acknowledge that Jesus considered himself to be such. According to Maccoby, Jesus considered himself to be the Messiah "in the normal Jewish sense of the term," that is, as a purely human leader[12] albeit a charismatic one.[13] Klausner also concludes that Jesus considered himself to be the Messiah[14] and that Jesus' messiahship contained "a genuinely political element," even though he affirms that he was not a revolutionary.[15] Sandmel also believes that the messianic claims concerning Jesus actually arose during his lifetime, even if (in Sandmel's view) Jesus did not actively announce himself as Messiah.[16] Although Jesus does announce himself as Messiah in John 4:26, as noted above, John is considered to be too "theologically developed" to provide any concrete historical information.[17] Vermes not only believes that Jesus

    10. Maccoby, *The Mythmaker*, 15.
    11. Geza Vermes, *The Religion of Jesus the Jew* (London: SCM, 1993), 4.
    12. Maccoby, *The Mythmaker*, 15.
    13. Ibid., 1.
    14. Joseph Klausner, *From Jesus to Paul* (trans. William F. Stinespring; London: George Allen & Unwin), ix.
    15. Klausner, *From Jesus*, 437.
    16. Sandmel, *We Jews*, 48.
    17. According to Sandmel, the background to the Gospel is the second-century Greek world and this forms part of its weakness. Samuel Sandmel, *A Jewish Understanding of the New Testament* (Cincinnati: Alumni Association of the Hebrew Union College—Jewish Institute of Religion, 1956), 282. Smalley, on the other hand, proposed that John was shaped "in a Jewish–Christian environment at a fairly early date" and therefore concludes that is it no longer possible to distinguish

never asserted "directly or spontaneously that he was the Messiah,"[18] but that in fact Jesus actively denied that he was the Messiah.[19] Furthermore, whilst he recognizes the centrality of the question of Messiah for the Church (which, according to Vermes, reinterpreted the concept), and whilst he accepts that the early followers of Jesus did see in him the fulfilment of the expected Messiah of Judaism,[20] nonetheless he concludes "it is clearly not an exaggeration to suggest that messianism is not particularly prominent in the surviving teaching of Jesus."[21] He also believes that Jesus "deliberately withheld his approval of Peter's confession."[22] This leaves Vermes with the problem of reconciling this rejection with the later Church's adherence to the doctrine,[23] as, according to Vermes, the Church could only envisage Jesus *as* Messiah.[24] His own conclusion is that "the success of the messianic idea probably owed more to polemical convenience than to theological usefulness."[25]

With the exception of Vermes, therefore, each of the writers in question considers Jesus to have believed himself to be the expected Messiah. Notably, by this, as Sandmel points out, is meant "a purely human leader." Again, this poses a problem for the writers under examination: if Jesus considered himself to be a political Messiah and never claimed divinity, then the charge of blasphemy brought at his trial by the Jewish religious authorities fails to make sense. According to Maccoby, Jesus' claim to be the Messiah was not in any way blasphemous in the eyes of the Pharisees, or indeed, of any the Jews, for the title "Messiah" carried

---

between the Synoptics as history and John as theology. Stephen Smalley, *John—Evangelist and Interpreter* (rev. ed.; Carlisle: Paternoster, 1998), 40–41. However, Carson dates John's Gospel to ca. 80 C.E. D. A. Carson, *The Gospel According to John* (Grand Rapids: Eerdmans, 1991), 82.

18. Vermes, *Jesus the Jew*, 140.
19. Vermes considers Jesus' answers to both Peter and to the high priest a denial of his messiahship. Ibid.
20. Ibid., 129.
21. Ibid., 143.
22. Ibid., 149.
23. Ibid., 154.
24. It is interesting to speculate why Vermes considers "the Church" as unable to envisage Jesus in any other context than that of the awaited Messiah, in light of his claim that there is little messianic teaching or claim made throughout the New Testament. According to Vermes, if Jesus' mission was not understood as political, and if he never claimed to be Messiah himself, why did his followers not just accept him as a prophet, who like many of the prophets before him had been put to death?
25. Vermes, *Jesus the Jew*, 156. However, Vermes does not explain why a group which for the first 200 years of its existence formed a persecuted minority would choose a title for polemic reasons against the dominant group.

no connotation of deity or divinity.[26] Furthermore, according to Maccoby, Jesus never regarded himself as a divine being[27] and would have seen such an idea "as pagan and idolatrous, an infringement of the first of the Ten Commandments."[28] He therefore suggests two possible solutions: either the charge of blasphemy was a fabrication of later Christianity,[29] or, since the Synoptics portray the high priest rather than the Pharisees as levelling the charge of blasphemy, it was politically motivated.[30] Thus Maccoby wavers between reinterpretation of the event by Christianity and political expediency of the religious rulers as the solution to the problem. Maccoby argues, however, that the Gospels' attempts to portray Jesus as a rebel against the Jewish religion are all implausible and "therefore the only possible charge that led to his death that makes sense is that of political subversion."[31]

Sandmel also finds Jesus' trial particularly difficult to explain, but for him the difficulty lies in the title of "king," because it is here that Jesus is for the first time explicitly called "King of the Jews."[32] Sandmel therefore states: "in light of Mark's supposition that it was blasphemy not political revolt which occasioned the wish on the part of the Jews to have Jesus crucified we become puzzled by the titulus."[33] His own solution to the problem is that the titulus was such common knowledge and so strong within the tradition which Mark inherited "that even despite his inclination to represent Jesus as non-political, he was impelled to reproduce the words 'The King of the Jews'."[34] On the charge of blasphemy, Sandmel comments:

26. Maccoby, *The Mythmaker*, 37.
27. Hyam Maccoby, *Judaism in the First Christian Century* (London: Sheldon, 1989), 35.
28. Ibid., 15.
29. "[A]fter the death of Jesus the Greek translation of the Hebrew word Messiah (i.e. 'Christ') had come to mean a deity or divine being. Consequently, Christians reading this meaning back into Jesus' lifetime found it easy to believe that Jesus' claim to Messiahship would have shocked his fellow Jews and made him subject to a charge of blasphemy." Ibid., 38.
30. Maccoby conjectures that the high priest is a "Roman-appointed quisling whose interest therefore is political and not religious." He further suggests that there would be an element of self-interest, because it is the "High Priest and his entourage who could expect to see themselves swept away by the projected Messianic regime." Ibid., 39.
31. Ibid., 49.
32. "Nothing in the first fourteen chapters of Mark has prepared us for Jesus to be addressed or spoken of as king." Sandmel, *A Jewish Understanding*, 129.
33. Ibid.
34. Ibid., 130.

> The Gospels show me no persuasive basis on which Jews as Jews would have levelled an accusation against a fellow Jew, all that I read in the Gospels is a vague charge of "blasphemy," a charge unaccompanied by any broad effort to adduce relevant particulars.[35]

He continues: "The reason for Jesus' crucifixion, then, was simply that he was a rebel against Rome. He was not framed on a political charge by the Jews; rather it was the Jews who were framed by the Gospels."[36]

Also on the question of kingship, Vermes rejects the New Testament portrayal of Jesus' entry into Jerusalem as that of a king. He records the suggestion that some New Testament interpreters have made that the "so-called" triumphal entry into Jerusalem was arranged by the followers of Jesus as a royal procession to fulfil the prophecy of Zech 9:9.[37] Vermes' own "simple and more likely explanation" is that Jesus entered the capital on the back of a donkey "because he found this mode of transport more suitable and convenient than walking. It was only at a later stage that Jesus' ride was seen against a background of messianic prophecy."[38] Therefore, for Vermes, the title of king plays no part in the ministry of Jesus, and consequently he states, "The random use of the title 'Son of David' seems therefore to have no particular historical bearing."[39] He does concede, on the other hand, that the phrase may have acted as a useful support in the early Christian argument concerning the messiahship of Jesus.[40] Furthermore, because of this seeming lack of messianic or political reference in the Gospels, Vermes, in common with Sandmel, is perplexed by the sudden reference to Jesus at his trial as "King of the Jews." He asks, "In the absence of any substantial messianic preaching on the part of Jesus or debate concerning his messiahship, how is this action to be explained?"[41] His own suggestion is that a political charge was the simplest way of eliminating Jesus.[42] In common with Sandmel, Vermes does not offer an explanation as to why two of the Gospel writers record the original charge as blasphemy at Jesus' hearing before the chief priests and the elders.[43]

---

35. Sandmel, *We Jews*, 140.
36. Ibid.
37. Vermes, *Jesus the Jew*, 145.
38. Ibid.
39. Ibid., 157.
40. Ibid.
41. Ibid. 144.
42. Ibid.
43. Matt 26:65; Mark 14:64.

Whilst Klausner acknowledges the correlation of kingship and Messiah,[44] he suggests that Christianity transformed this concept under the influence of the ancient understanding of kingship within the surrounding cultures.[45] He believes that the "political" aspect of Jesus' messiahship was abandoned for two reasons: one was that the crucifixion had put an end to all political hopes, and the other was the danger that a political Messiah posed in that period:[46] "For Jesus had been crucified as a political Messiah, and hence as a rebel against the Roman Empire."[47] Accordingly the early Church emphasized the "other side" of Jesus' preaching, the ethical, and in so doing they transferred the "blame" for his death from the Romans to the Jews.[48] Despite the consensus that Jesus was killed as a political rebel against Rome, none of the writers attempt to explain Pilate's (and Herod's) reluctance to crucify Jesus, nor Pilate's releasing of Barabbas, who, we are told, was imprisoned "for an insurrection started in the city, and for murder."[49]

Having rejected the charge of blasphemy on the grounds that Jesus never claimed divinity, each of the Jewish writers (with the exception of Maccoby) also reject the titles of "Son of God" and "Lord" on the same grounds. Sandmel comments, "Jews become confused by the title 'Lord,' wondering if Christians view Jesus as God as Jews do not."[50] Whilst acknowledging that the messianic expectations "were a blend of both the divine and human facets," Sandmel nonetheless states that the Messiah himself "could have been only human, though sent by God."[51] He makes clear the Jewish position: "To us Jesus is never more than a man and as deeply as some of us Jews are able to sympathise with the tragedy of his life and death, we do not see in it any special working of the divine."[52] Sandmel does, however, note the distinction in Paul's writing between the use of the words *Kyrios* and *Theos*, which also reflect the different

44. Klausner, *From Jesus*, 438.
45. Ibid., 108.
46. Ibid., 438.
47. Ibid.
48. Ibid., 439.
49. Luke 23:19. However, Winter discusses the different presentations of this episode in the various Gospels and the different readings of this which suggest that Barabbas may not have been held for insurrection. Paul Winter, *On the Trial of Jesus* (rev. and ed. T. A. Burkill and Geza Vermes; 2d ed.; Berlin: de Gruyter, 1974), 134–35.
50. Samuel Sandmel, *Antisemitism in the New Testament* (Philadelphia: Fortress, 1978), 133.
51. Sandmel, *We Jews*, 32.
52. Ibid., 48.

Septuagint renderings of the Hebrew words *Adonai* (*Kyrios*) *and Elohim* (*Theos*).[53] Furthermore, he recognizes that, for Paul, Jesus was the "form of God" in which the God of Israel appeared preliminarily to Moses and the Prophets before revealing himself decisively in Jesus.[54]

Vermes reproduces the suggestion made by Bultmann and Hahn, of an evolution in the process by which Jesus became "Son of God" and that it was the Gentile Hellenistic Church which metamorphosed "not the office but the nature—by analogy to half-divine half-human offspring of deities of classical mythology."[55] He further states: "it is no exaggeration to contend that the identification of a contemporary historical figure with God would have been inconceivable to a first-century AD Palestinian Jew."[56] Vermes proposes, therefore, that it was only when the Gentiles began to preach "the Jewish gospel" that the "Son of God" became identified with God himself.[57] Concerning the title "Lord," Vermes comments that the majority of New Testament scholars assume that it was an invention of the "post-Easter" period and has nothing to do with Jesus himself.[58] He notes that the use of "Lord" in Mark and Matthew is predominantly in the miraculous settings[59] and that in Luke the term is used in the absolute "the Lord."[60] Vermes also records the suggestion made by scholars that it was the use of *Kyrios* in the Septuagint to translate the tetragrammaton that may have prompted the equation of Jesus and God.[61] He comments that, whilst it can have a variety of usages,[62] "the term is connected with God in Jewish texts before, during and after the time of Jesus."[63] Despite this, in this case, Vermes rejects any divine connotation and concludes that the term "primarily links Jesus to his dual role of charismatic Hasid and teacher."[64]

Klausner too compares the human aspect of the Jewish Messiah with the divinity of the Christian Messiah. He states: "The Jewish Messiah is truly human in origin, of flesh and blood like all mortals."[65] Like Vermes,

---

53. Sandmel, *A Jewish Understanding*, 54.
54. Ibid.
55. Vermes, *Jesus the Jew*, 193.
56. Ibid., 212.
57. Ibid., 213.
58. Ibid., 103.
59. Ibid., 123.
60. Ibid., 126.
61. Ibid., 105.
62. Ibid., 121–22.
63. Ibid., 113–14.
64. Ibid., 127.
65. Klausner, *The Messianic Idea*, 520.

he identifies an evolution in the process of the deification of Jesus until the point is reached where "the messiahship of Jesus became secondary to his deity."[66] According to Klausner, a number of factors came together to produce Jesus' title "Son of God," the first being Jesus' "over-emphasis" on God as his Father, coupled with the "foreign influences" in the environment of his disciples which caused them to "take his words too literally and to make him only a little less than God and finally—even to see in him the real Son of God."[67]

Klausner suggests that the foreign influences were also coupled with elements of Judaism to produce the deification of Jesus.[68] He discusses the mystery religions and states: "The idea that a god can die and return to life was, therefore, in existence centuries before the rise of Christianity and was widely current in the pagan world also in the very time of the rise of Christianity."[69] Although Klausner acknowledges that Jesus' story is not just a reflection of the fate of these gods, "on the other hand there can be no doubt that, had it not been for the general influence—however obscure and remote—of these pagan stories, a Jewish Messiah would never have become the Christian Son of God."[70] Whilst Klausner understands Paul to be the author of the "un-Jewish" designations of Jesus, under the influence of the Graeco-Roman environment in which Christianity flourished,[71] nonetheless he states: "To be sure, the beginning of the exaltation of Jesus to this high estate was made by the Twelve."[72]

One aspect of the difference for Klausner between the "Jewish" and "Christian" concept of Messiah is that "the Redeemer of Israel for Judaism is only ever God whereas in Christianity the Redeemer is Jesus only."[73] Further on, however, in this same passage, Klausner states that the Jewish Messiah *is* the redeemer of his people and the redeemer of humankind—"but he does not redeem them by his blood—instead he lends aid to their redemption by his great abilities and deeds."[74] Klausner goes on to state that it is humans who must redeem themselves through their good deeds and that they cannot "lean upon the Messiah or upon the

---

66. Ibid., 528.
67. Klausner, *From Jesus*, 5.
68. Ibid., 112.
69. Ibid., 105.
70. Ibid., 107.
71. Ibid., 112.
72. Ibid., 437.
73. Klausner, *The Messianic Idea*, 529.
74. Ibid., 530. Unfortunately he does not elaborate on what they are or how they achieve redemption.

Messiah's suffering and death,"[75] illustrating the point made earlier that whilst the Jewish writers are consistent in what they reject, they are less consistent in what they affirm.

These four writers, then, assert that the charge of blasphemy and the titles "Son of God" and "Lord" provide evidence for the divinity of Jesus, or that Jesus thought of himself as divine. Furthermore, whilst some of the writers acknowledge the supernatural aspects of the "Son of Man" title applied to Jesus (through allusion or directly by himself), they, for the most part, dismiss the idea that this was meant by the New Testament writers to indicate that Jesus was somehow God. Sandmel, however, does acknowledge that linking Jesus with this title has supernatural implications.[76] Furthermore, he states:

> …once the followers of Jesus were convinced that he was resurrected there was nothing inconsistent with their Judaism in conceiving of him as the heavenly Son of Man. On the other hand, those who did not believe that he was resurrected, denied that he was the Son of Man, not so much because they disbelieved in the *idea* but because they did not believe in this particular identification.[77]

However, despite acknowledging the use of the term as a synonym for Messiah in some extra-biblical books, Sandmel expresses surprise that Mark appears to use it in this same way.[78] Nonetheless, he accepts that in his lifetime "or shortly thereafter" Jesus came to be viewed as the supernatural "Son of Man" in the book of Daniel.[79] He further contends that the term in the New Testament was an assertion "that was expressed fully within the framework of a segment of Judaism and was in no way, in itself, a product of Gentile thinking."[80] Thus, for Sandmel, "Son of Man" was not only a "title" but carried with it a particular concept, one which was fully Judaic and not part of a later reinterpretation of Jesus.

Vermes, on the other hand, does not consider the term to be a title[81] and thus denies it holds any supernatural connotation. Although his survey of the "Son of Man" passages in *1 Enoch* confirms for Vermes "the messianic connotations of Dan 7 in post-biblical Jewish religious thought,"[82] he fails to identify any evidence of humiliation or suffering.[83]

75. Ibid.
76. Sandmel, *We Jews*, 34.
77. Ibid., 35.
78. Sandmel, *A Jewish Understanding*, 129–30.
79. Sandmel, *We Jews*, 34.
80. Ibid., 35.
81. Vermes, *Jesus the Jew*, 185.
82. Ibid., 175.

He states, "There is in addition no valid argument to prove any of the gospel passages directly or indirectly referring to Daniel 7.13 may be traced back to Jesus."[84] Instead, Vermes believes that these are Aramaic circumlocutions and that it is the disciples who eschatologized the term "by means of a midrash based on Daniel 7.13."[85]

Klausner appears ambivalent about the "Son of Man" figure: after considering the literature of the Second Temple period and in particular the book of Daniel, he concludes that although the "Son of Man" was equated with the Messiah, this was an entirely human and not a heavenly figure. However, he goes on to say:

> ...in a comparatively short time after the composition of the book of Daniel it was thought among the Jews that this "Son of Man" was the Messiah. This is not surprising: a "human being" that could approach the throne of God and that could be given "dominion, and glory and a kingdom" and whom all the peoples would serve and whose dominion would be an everlasting dominion could not possibly be other than the King-Messiah.[86]

This also, according to Klausner, is the understanding of the term within the earlier sections of the Ethiopic book of Enoch (chs. 37–71) and was also that of Jesus himself.[87] The connection between the "Son of Man" figure and the Messiah in *1 Enoch* and the similar connection between the "Son of Man" figure and the Messiah in the New Testament has led to the charge that in fact these passages have suffered from Christian interpolations. Klausner refutes this:

> To consider all these chapters as a Christian interpolation is not reasonable: a Christian interpolator would have found here ample opportunity to refer to the sufferings of the crucified Christ—but there is no mention of them. These are popular Jewish notions about the personality of the Messiah, as revealed also at a later time in the Midrashim—the popular collections of legends, stories and national hopes, both early and late.[88]

Maccoby also considers the term "Son of Man" in the *Similitudes of Enoch* and concludes that the "Son of Man" is equated there with "the Elect One" and "the Anointed One" and appears to be a "conflation of the "Son of Man" in Dan 8:15; 9:2 and 10:5, the "Suffering Servant" of

---

83. Ibid. Vermes does not clarify this comment but it may be supposed that he is referring to the use of the term in the Synoptics and its association there with Jesus' humiliation and suffering.
84. Ibid., 185–86.
85. Ibid., 186.
86. Klausner, *The Messianic Idea*, 230.
87. Ibid.
88. Klausner, *The Messianic Idea*, 292.

Isa 53 and the Davidic Messiah.[89] Despite uncovering this messianic connection, Maccoby still opts for the explanation, also shared by Vermes, that this term most usually represents an Aramaic circumlocution; in the episodes where it does not, he suggests it implies prophetic and not divine status, as in the book of Ezekiel.[90]

Sandmel is one of the few writers who considers, however briefly, the designation of high priest. His particular concern is that the identification of Christ as a priest in the order of Melchizedek (who was without parentage) in the Letter to the Hebrews conflicts with the genealogies of Matthew and Luke, which link Jesus with the line of David.[91] Vermes dismisses any allusion to Jesus as Priest Messiah because he claims that Jesus himself made no such allusion.[92]

The Role of the Messiah

According to Maccoby, the Messiah was expected to "restore the Jewish monarchy, drive out the Roman invaders, set up an independent Jewish state, and inaugurate an era of peace, justice and prosperity (known as 'the kingdom of God') for the whole world."[93] For Maccoby, Jesus was a charismatic Messiah: "He was not a militarist and did not build up an army to fight the Romans, since he believed that God would perform a great miracle to break the power of Rome."[94] (We must assume that this is Maccoby's latest position superseding his earlier portrayal of Jesus as a revolutionary.[95]) "The miracle would take place on the Mount of Olives, as prophesied in the book of Zechariah. When this miracle did not occur, his mission had failed."[96] Klausner, on the other hand, asserts that Jesus "was crucified as a political Messiah and hence as a rebel against the Roman Empire."[97] Nonetheless he acknowledges that within

---

89. Maccoby, *The Mythmaker*, 23.
90. Ibid., 43.
91. He asks: "Can this passage in Hebrews be any less than a rejection of the entire process of genealogical tracing?" Sandmel, *A Jewish Understanding*, 175.
92. Vermes, *Jesus the Jew*, 153.
93. Maccoby, *The Mythmaker*, 15.
94. Ibid.
95. Hyam Maccoby, *Revolution in Judea: Jesus and the Jewish Resistance* (London: Ocean, 1973), 133.
96. Maccoby, *The Mythmaker*, 15.
97. Klasuner, *From Jesus*, 438. This assumption leads Klausner to conclude that the later books of the New Testament, which include the Gospels, were redacted as a matter of political expediency, following the Jewish revolt of 66 C.E., placing the blame for Jesus' death with the Jews instead of the Romans.

the Jewish concept of Messiah, national/political and universal/spiritual elements have always existed side-by-side:

> In the Jewish Messianic conception throughout its history, the national and universal elements are so combined and fused together that they cannot be separated. There was to be sure a time, not long after that of Paul, the time following the downfall of Bar Cochba, when Jewish messianic speculation was forced to create for the purely politico-national Messiah who fights and falls in battle a special designation and to split the Messiah redeemer into two individuals—*Messiah ben David* and *Messiah ben Joseph*, the spiritual universalistic Messiah and the fighting politico-national Messiah.[98]

Although the Jewish writers hold in common the view that the suffering aspect of Jesus' messiahship is "un-Jewish," nonetheless they do acknowledge the provenance of a number of related New Testament themes as Jewish. Maccoby, for example, makes the connection between the scapegoat of the Day of Atonement and Jesus, and also notes that Paul likened the death of Jesus to the sacrifice of the Paschal Lamb.[99] He comments that in doing so, Paul was reverting to the "oldest most primitive stratum of Israelite religion in which the paschal lamb was regarded as a blood-victim warding off evil, rather than as a joyful means of gratitude to God for the deliverance of the Exodus."[100] Another suggestion for the influence on the Eucharist is the sacred meals of the mystery religions to which the Passover Seder was adapted and thereby "took on a new festive-mystical form."[101] Klausner also identifies the origins of the Eucharist as pagan, and suggests that in particular it was influenced by the *Taurobolium*. He states, "It is hard to doubt that these pagan practices of which perhaps only a faint and far away echo reached the first Christians from the pagans, influenced beliefs about the blood of Jesus."[102]

Although, in common with the other writers under review, Sandmel for the most part ignores John's Gospel, he does comment on the difference between the Synoptics and John in the dating of the crucifixion. Sandmel argues that the date was not a matter of historical fact but was "chosen" specifically for its significance.[103] Sandmel also rejects the idea

---

98. Ibid., 445.
99. Maccoby, *Judaism in the First Christian Century*, 93.
100. Ibid.
101. Klausner, *From Jesus*, 114.
102. Ibid., 115.
103. "The Passover or its eve was selected in order to equate Jesus with the sacrificial Passover lamb of the Bible." Sandmel, *A Jewish Understanding*, 131.

of Jesus' death as atonement, on the basis that it is "un-Jewish":[104] "We Jews do not accept the saving death of Jesus because of our special mood and disposition."[105] When speaking of the Passion, Sandmel also doubts its historicity, rather considering Ps 22 as the probable source for the mocking and the casting of lots.[106]

Sandmel attributes the identification of Jesus with the Paschal Lamb and the "interpretation" of his death as atonement to Paul,[107] and supplies two reasons for rejecting the Gospel version. One is that "the ceremonial with such a meaning fits in ill with Palestinian Judaism," and the other is that "it is so thoroughly Christian in its tone as to suggest the likelihood of its being still one more church item for which the authority of Jesus himself is sought."[108]

The charge is also made by Sandmel that what was originally Jewish concerning Jesus was reinterpreted for a Greek milieu,[109] and again it is Paul who is charged with bringing about this change: "Indeed, Paul views the Christ in ways so changed from the usual Jewish view that in most basic matters there is almost nothing in common but the word."[110] Although Maccoby is the only writer who contends that Paul was originally Gentile and thus a convert to Judaism, most of the other writers view Paul as a thoroughly Hellenized Jew; it is this Greek background which, for them, leads Paul to "borrow" from the surrounding mystery religions with which he would be familiar.[111] Sandmel states: "Pauline Christianity had an ancestry remotely oriental but it was born and nurtured in so completely Hellenised an atmosphere that it was a completely Grecian phenomenon."[112] However, he considers that it was the "genius" of Paul to amalgamate the new and exciting mystery religions with Judaism. The Church therefore sought to root its story of Jesus in the Hebrew Scriptures: "Since many of the claims of the Church rested neither on pure logic nor on ordinary historical attestation, the desire to prove them led to the search of the Old Testament for passages which

---

104. Sandmel, *We Jews*, 47.
105. Ibid., 48.
106. Sandmel, *A Jewish Understanding*, 131.
107. Ibid., 86.
108. Ibid., 133.
109. "Though the Christians retained the word Messiah (Greek Christ) the content and meaning of the term were significantly altered." Sandmel, *Antisemitism*, 131.
110. Ibid., 133.
111. Sandmel, *A Jewish Understanding*, 99.
112. Ibid., 104.

could be construed to support the Church's contentions."[113] Sandmel differs from the other writers, however, in that he recognizes that Jesus' death is a recurring theme throughout the New Testament and not, as the other writers propose, a hasty post-Easter reconstruction.[114] Consequently, Sandmel concludes Jesus' death was not a defeat, nor a surprise, but "a working out of preordained Divine providence."[115]

Vermes, on the other hand, views the "suffering Messiah" as a "specially fresh element in the Christology of Acts"; Jesus' death, rather than being an integral part of his mission and messiahship, for Vermes, was Jesus' tragedy:

> Had Jesus not caused an affray in the Temple by overturning the tables of the merchants and money-changers or had even chosen to do so at a time other than Passover—the moment when the hoped-for Messiah, the final liberator of the Jews was expected to reveal himself—he would most probably have escaped with his life.[116]

According to Vermes, the "incongruent" portrayal of the Messiah in the New Testament necessitated that the Church find a solution both for itself and its converts,[117] a solution which, however, according to Vermes, proved unpalatable to "first-century Palestinian Aramaic speaking Jews":

> Jews in Judea and Galilee must have found this new kind of Messiah alien, untraditional and unappealing and it can cause no surprise that apart from cosmopolitan Jerusalem, with its substantial immigrant population from the Diaspora, the New Testament is silent on any progress of the new movement in the Palestinian Homeland.[118]

According to Klausner, the solution which the Church found for the "failed mission" of Jesus was a reinterpretation of events; instead of his disciples accepting the crucifixion as the defeat of Jesus' messianic claims, they reinterpreted it in terms of the Suffering Servant of Isa 53:

---

113. Ibid., 109.
114. Sandmel, *Antisemitism*, 135.
115. Ibid.
116. Vermes, *The Religion of Jesus*, ix–x.
117. "The disappearance of the Master called for a radical rethinking and reorientation during the years and decades following Golgotha, when Jesus' disciples had to explain to themselves and then to their listeners, the significance of the cross and the 'resurrection'… [T]heir task was not easy…because of the absence of contemporary evidence of an expectation of a suffering and dying Messiah…" Ibid., 210.
118. Ibid., 211.

> As to the fact that the Messiah had suffered scourging and the agonies of crucifixion—behold, they quickly found justification and support for this in Isaiah 53, a chapter in which they saw a "suffering Messiah" and "vicarious atonement." Thus the primitive community was saved from disillusionment and Jesus as Messiah was saved from oblivion.[119]

Again Paul is credited with this reinterpretation.[120] Nonetheless Klausner acknowledges that vicarious suffering is known to Judaism "even if we do not interpret Isa 53 messianically."[121] Nonetheless, this passage *is* understood messianically in the *Targum*, albeit with a different interpretation than that of the Christian tradition.[122] And whilst Maccoby also considers Paul to be the initiator of the "new religion," he regards the Christian "deification" of Jesus, considered above, as the reason why links with "Judaism" were severed.[123]

Outcome of the Messiah's Role

The enigma for Maccoby, one which he holds in common with the other writers under consideration, is why, when Jesus' mission failed, a distinctive Christian sect appeared, when the followers of other failed Messiahs had simply given up. As Maccoby understands it, there was no distinctive teaching or doctrine to account for it: "Jesus and his immediate followers were Pharisees. Jesus had no intention of founding a new religion."[124] Maccoby's own solution to the enigma is the suggestion that it was the apostle Paul, "the mythmaker," who transformed the Jewish Jesus into the Christ of Christianity.[125] The result of Jesus' messianism, according to Maccoby, was, therefore, not an ensuing Messianic Age, but a new religion.[126] This "new religion" was derived from Hellenistic sources, particularly the mystery religions, which Paul then amalgamated with the Hebrew Scriptures and "elements derived from Judaism," thus providing "a sacred history for the new myth" and thereby presumably legitimizing it as an ancient source for an idea gave it greater kudos. But it was "Paul alone" who was the creator of this "amalgam."[127]

---

119. Klausner, *From Jesus*, 440.
120. Ibid.
121. Ibid., 525.
122. See Samson H. Levey, *The Messiah: An Aramaic Interpretation* (New York: Hebrew Union College–Jewish Institute of Religion, 1974), 63–66.
123. Maccoby, *The Mythmaker*, 37.
124. Ibid., 15.
125. Ibid., 16.
126. Ibid.
127. Ibid.

Klausner, who is also puzzled why Jesus was not forgotten like all the other slain Messiahs,[128] offers a different solution. He suggests that the answer lies in the "story" of Jesus' resurrection.[129] It is not that Klausner denies the resurrection, "since a faith that embraces millions of men and endures for thousands of years cannot be based on fabrication and conscious deception";[130] rather, for him, the resurrection appearance of Jesus was a "vision," not a real appearance.

Sandmel argues against the messiahship of Jesus on the basis of what *did not* occur as a result of his messiahship:

> Any claims made, during the lifetime of Jesus, that he was the Messiah whom the Jews had awaited, were rendered poorly defensible by his crucifixion and by the collapse of any political aspect of his movement, and by the sad actuality that Palestine was still not liberated from Roman domination.[131]

This represents one of the major contentions of the Jewish writers under consideration, in that whatever is made of the teaching or claims about divinity or other contentious issues, such as suffering and atonement either by Jesus himself or on his behalf, it is what *did not* transpire that most condemns the claim to his messiahship. A corollary of this is the suggestion that the failure of the messianic mission forced the nascent Church into a reinterpretation of the messiahship as a "two-stage" system.[132]

Conclusion

The contentions concerning Jesus' person centre on the claim to divinity. The Jewish writers all reject such a claim and contend that instead the Jewish Messiah was expected to be a human political leader and not a divine figure, who "would restore the Jewish monarchy, drive out the Roman invaders, set up an independent Jewish state, and inaugurate an era of peace, justice and prosperity for the whole world."[133] The Jewish writers therefore also reject the idea found in the New Testament of a

---

128. Klausner, *From Jesus*, 255.
129. Ibid., 256.
130. Ibid.
131. Sandmel, *A Jewish Understanding*, 33.
132. "Those Jews who had accepted Jesus as the Messiah, despite his death on the cross, made an initial significant alteration in the Messianic pattern, changing it, as it were, from one single event, ushering in the great climax, into two parts, preparation first, and after an interval, the climax." Sandmel, *We Jews*, 33.
133. Maccoby, *The Mythmaker*, 15.

suffering Messiah whose role is to effect atonement through his suffering death and resurrection. Their third contention concerns the expected outcome of the coming of the Messiah; that is, in their opinion Jesus did not inaugurate the Messianic Age.

Finally, before leaving the subject in hand, it should be noted that despite the fact that the writers examined make a serious attempt to engage with the differences between the two faiths, it should not be assumed that they believe this will in fact further dialogue. Klausner, although he engages with the New Testament, nonetheless states: "My deepest conviction is this: Judaism will never become reconciled with Christianity...nor will it be assimilated by Christianity; for Judaism and Christianity are not only two different religions but they are also *two different world-views*."[134] This is a view that Neusner was to echo some fifty years later: "Judaism and Christianity are completely different religions"; for him the two faiths "stand for different people talking about different things to different people."[135] He therefore asks:

> Is there no bridge from Christianity "back" to Judaism, and is there no connection that links Judaism to Christianity? My argument is that there is none, there should be none, and when we recognise that the two are utterly distinct and different families of religions, the work of attempting a dialogue can begin.[136]

---

134. Klausner, *From Jesus*, 609 (original emphasis).
135. Neusner, *Jews and Christians*, 1.
136. Ibid., 120.

Chapter 3

KINGSHIP IN THE ANCIENT NEAR EAST

Introduction

In Chapter 1 it was argued that the concept of messiah has its origins in the ideology of kingship in ancient Israel. Yet ancient Israel, as scholarship has come increasingly to recognize, participated in the culture of the ancient Near East,[1] and this applied especially to kingship. In this chapter, therefore, I will consider the ideology of sacral kingship in the nations surrounding Israel in order to facilitate our understanding of the idea of kingship in ancient Israel itself. It is necessary to supplement the evidence from the Hebrew Bible regarding the person, role and outcomes of the role of the king in ancient Israel for two reasons: first, because the biblical evidence is not only allusive but has arguably undergone Deuteronomic redaction[2] which has demythologized it and so obscured important features of the king's role;[3] secondly, because when the Israelites ask for a king over them, they ask for a king "like all the nations."[4] Whilst this latter point does not of necessity imply "similar to,"[5]

---

1. John H. Walton, *Ancient Israelite Literature in Its Cultural Context* (Grand Rapids: Zondervan, 1990), 13.
2. "It must not be forgotten that the Deuteronomistic historian was not only concerned to pour out his prejudices, he also intended to paint some kind of credible picture of events. He was attempting to write not just a stream of polemic, but a 'history' of sorts, whatever his motives and however polemical it might become." Carol Smith, "Queenship in Israel? The Cases of Bathsheba, Jezebel and Athaliah," in Day, ed., *King and Messiah*, 149.
3. See Gerald Eddie Gerbrandt, *Kingship According to the Deuteronomistic History* (Atlanta: Scholars Press, 1986), 98–99. Although he does not enter into discussion concerning the suggested demythologizing redaction by the Deuteronomists, Gerbrandt does set forth what he understands as the Deuteronomist's view of kingship.
4. "Since this [the monarchy] was new to Israel it was inevitably modelled on foreign precedent." Day, "The Canaanite Inheritance," 72.
5. Cooke's statement concerning the force of the Hebrew word *ke*, in which he contends that "likeness and identity are one," may be pertinent here. Cooke cited in Engnell, *Studies*, 29.

nonetheless it must have been their perception that within the ideology of kingship there was something more than that of the rule of the judges.[6]

Therefore, although the rise of kingship in ancient Israel is often explained as a natural historical development, necessitated by the growing power and threat of the Philistines,[7] it is possible that there was more involved in the desire for a "king like all the nations" than merely a unifying political head. As Frankfort states,

> ...if we refer to kingship as a political institution, we assume a point of view which would have been incomprehensible to the ancients. We imply that the human polity can be considered by itself. The ancients, however, experienced human life as part of a widely spreading network of connections which reached beyond the local and the national communities into the hidden depths of nature and the powers that rule nature. The purely secular—in so far as it could be granted to exist at all—was the purely trivial. Whatever was significant was imbedded in the life of the cosmos, and it was precisely the king's function to maintain the harmony of that integration. This doctrine is valid for the whole of the Ancient Near East and for many other regions.[8]

And so I will briefly examine the ideals of kingship in the surrounding cultures in order to ascertain what it was that the Israelites wanted and how this may have influenced their own concept of kingship and in turn the concept of Messiah.

The concept of sacral kingship was fundamental to the old cultures of the ancient Near East, and it was a concept transmitted from them to the younger cultures of the region, such as ancient Israel and even westwards to the Greeks and Romans. This was first suggested by those scholars who formed part of the "myth and ritual" school, most notably the Scandinavian scholars Engnell and Mowinckel, as well as British writers Hooke, Robinson and Oesterley. Whilst this theory to a large extent has fallen out of favour, nothing has arisen which has thoroughly disproved it. Nonetheless, there has been some criticism of their ideas; Frankfort, for example, whilst acknowledging the centrality of sacral kingship in the ancient Near East, suggests that although common features may be found in these cultures, they were in fact understood and applied differently in each culture.[9] Frankfort criticizes a number of scholars for their "neglect of the individual nature of distinct

---

6. See Mowinckel, *He That Cometh*, 21–22.
7. See Gerbrandt, *Kingship*, 192.
8. Henri Frankfort, *Kingship and the Gods* (London: University of Chicago Press, 1978), 3.
9. Ibid., 382 n. 5.

civilisations."[10] Brandon is also critical of a number of features of the theory, including the motivation of the Old Testament scholars involved,[11] and suggests that the Christian *mythos* has been read back into the ancient cultures, thereby, in effect, suggesting the pattern. In addition, he proposes that a cyclical view of existence presupposed by this pattern must, in the case of Israel, have been supplanted by the teleological view of the Hebrew Scriptures.[12]

Whilst I would take issue with a number of these objections, space prohibits a detailed analysis of them here, or of the alternative view of Brandon himself who acknowledges that the "myth and ritual" position has not only established the fundamental importance of kingship in the ancient Near East but has "succeeded in showing that kingship in Israel must be evaluated in this light."[13] Furthermore, the acknowledgment that sacral kingship and the myth and ritual accompanying it forms the background of Jewish messianism has more recently been affirmed by Moshe Idel,[14] who welcomes the contribution made by the "myth and ritual" school to the debate.[15] This is also Wyatt's view:

> Divine kingship is a theme that is perhaps somewhat out of fashion, with many treatments of Egyptian and West Semitic kingship stressing the human aspect of the institution, with a tendency to downplay, or represent as merely figurative, the divine aspect. In my estimation such modern pleading misrepresents the institutions of the ancient world and flies in the face of clear evidence to the contrary.[16]

The cultures to be examined are the Egyptian, Mesopotamian, Hittite and Ugaritic ones, each of which has left a wealth of textual data through which kingship can be investigated.[17] For ease of comparison I will

---

10. Frankfort, *Kingship*, 405 n. 1. However, Hooke brings a counter-criticism in Samuel Henry Hooke, *The Siege Perilous: Essays in Biblical Anthropology* (London: SCM, 1956), 173–82. For fuller expositions and defence of the theory, see Robert Ackerman, *The Myth and Ritual School: J. G. Frazer and the Cambridge Ritualists* (Cambridge: Routledge, 2002), 191–92; Robert A. Segal, ed., *The Myth and Ritual Theory: An Anthology* (Oxford: Blackwell, 1998).
11. S. G. F. Brandon, "The Myth and Ritual Position Critically Considered," in *Ritual and Myth: Robertson Smith, Frazer, Hooke, and Harrison* (ed. Robert A Segal; Theories of Myth 5; London: Garland, 1996), 16.
12. Ibid. 36–41.
13. Ibid., 42.
14. Idel, *Messianic Mystics*, 21.
15. Ibid.
16. N. Wyatt, "Epic in Ugaritic Literature," in *A Companion to Ancient Epic* (ed. John Miles Foley; Oxford: Blackwell, 2005), 253.
17. A selection of texts is reproduced in translation in *ANET*.

consider the material using the same three categories adopted in the previous chapter. This material does not constitute a survey of kingship in these cultures, but seeks only to identify the sacral role of the king, as it is this aspect of kingship which is believed to have influenced Israel's ideology of kingship from which developed the concept of Messiah.

The Person of the King

Egyptian Culture

Not only did the Egyptian concept of kingship develop and shift through time, but at any one time there was a variety of images within the sources.[18] Nonetheless, it is in Egypt that we find the closest indication of the divinity of the king. This is articulated in two different ways: either the king is considered to be divine from birth (or earlier),[19] or as crown prince he "becomes" divine at his coronation.[20] Frankfort disagrees with the latter suggestion: "His divinity was not proclaimed at a certain moment… His coronation was not an apotheosis but an epiphany."[21] Instead Frankfort contends:

> Pharaoh was not a mortal but a god. This was the fundamental concept of Egyptian kingship, that Pharaoh was of divine essence, a god incarnate; and this view can be traced back as far as texts and symbols take us.[22]

Although Frankfort's opinion still carries weight, later scholarship is more ambivalent about the extent to which Pharaoh was considered to be divine. Baines, for example, suggests that the Pharaoh's deity is to be understood metaphorically,[23] whereas O'Connor argues that the Egyptian attitude toward the Pharaoh depended upon the particular frame of reference and on the specific situation.[24] Oakley, on the other hand,

---

18. Lester L. Grabbe, *Priests, Prophets, Diviners, Sages* (Pennsylvania: Trinity Press International, 1995), 30.
19. In reference to Re, King Piankhi states: "I am he who was fashioned in the womb and created in the divine egg, the seed of the god being in me." Cited in Frankfort, *Kingship*, 42.
20. David P. Silverman, "The Nature of Egyptian Kingship," in *Ancient Egyptian Kingship* (ed. David O'Connor and David P. Silverman; Leiden: Brill, 1995), 67–71.
21. Frankfort, *Kingship*, 5.
22. Ibid.
23. John Baines, "Ancient Egyptian Kingship: Official Forms, Rhetoric, Context," in Day, ed., *King and Messiah*, 22.
24. David B. O'Connor, "Beloved of Maat, The Horizon of Re: The Royal Palace in New Kingdom Egypt," in O'Connor and Silverman, eds., *Ancient Egyptian Kingship*, 263.

contends that the Egyptian kingship was divine and dated back "to the very creation of the universe" and was "embedded in the cosmic order itself."[25]

Pharaoh is the "Good Shepherd"[26] and the "Good God,"[27] and whilst closely identified with Re the sun-god,[28] he is also understood to be the Sun god's "Chosen"[29] "Servant"[30] and "Son."[31] However, just as the king could be proclaimed the son of various gods, "so all goddesses could be addressed as his mother."[32] In his association with the creator god[33] the king maintains *ma'at*,[34] or right order of nature,[35] and is therefore the pivot of cosmos and state.[36] The king is also associated with a number of other gods;[37] he was the incarnation of Horus and after his death was assimilated to his father Osiris.[38] The king therefore is identified with both the father and the son.[39] As Osiris he is the bestower of fertility.[40]

---

25. Francis Oakley, *Kingship: The Politics of Enchantment* (Oxford: Blackwell, 2006), 39.
26. Jeffrey Jay Niehaus, *Ancient Near Eastern Themes in Biblical Theology* (Grand Rapids: Kregel, 2008), 39.
27. Baines, "Ancient Egyptian Kingship," 21.
28. Silverman, "The God-King on Earth," in O'Connor and Silverman, eds., *Ancient Egyptian Kingship*, 108.
29. The Sun-god as creator of the world and primordial king retains the absolute right to bestow or to remove kingship wherever he pleases. From this stems the notion of the selection of the king-to-be; see Donald B. Redford, "The Concept of Kingship during the Eighteenth Dynasty," in O'Connor and Silverman, eds., *Ancient Egyptian Kingship*, 170.
30. O'Connor, "Beloved of Maat," 265.
31. Baines, "Ancient Egyptian Kingship," 20.
32. Frankfort, *Kingship*, 42.
33. "A few literary texts, mainly of the Middle Kingdom, incorporate very strong eulogistic claims that give the king a role essentially like a creator god." Ibid., 29.
34. "Central to the Egyptians' views of kingship was the concept of *ma'at* which, whilst sometimes translatable as 'justice' or 'truth,' is a term whose meaning goes far beyond legal fairness or factual accuracy. It was used to refer to the ideal state of the universe and society..." Barry J. Kemp, "Old Kingdom, Middle Kingdom and Second Intermediate Period c. 2686–1552 BC," in *Ancient Egypt: A Social History* (ed. B. G. Trigger et al.; Cambridge: Cambridge University Press, 2001), 74.
35. "Without Pharaoh, the cosmos would be in disarray and the world would descend into chaos." Silverman, "The God-King on Earth," 108.
36. Baines, "Ancient Egyptian Kingship," 16.
37. Ibid., 22.
38. Day, "The Canaanite Inheritance," 81.
39. Baines, "Ancient Egyptian Kingship," 23.
40. Mowinckel, *He That Cometh*, 29.

The king was also "Horus-and-Seth,"[41] "the antagonists per se—the mythological symbols for all conflict."[42]

The king is the Ka or life for all his subjects,[43] and the king's own Ka, or vital force, is personified and worshipped as a God.[44] The king is "the breath of life,"[45] as well as being identified with the tree of life[46] and life-giving water in the guise of the Nile.[47] The Pharaoh is the recipient of divine wisdom[48] and was the "one" who uniquely mediates between humanity and the gods as well as the wider cosmos.[49] It was because of this unique status[50] that he officiated as high priest in the temple,[51] whilst at the same time, being "god," he was also the object of the cult.[52]

Mesopotamian Culture
Whilst it is difficult to classify the next area under consideration as a single culture since there is certainly significant variety detectable across a long chronological span and a large geographical area, accepting the evidence of "Mesopotamian culture" seems appropriate.[53] It is to be noted that Lambert identifies three main areas from whose documentation we are able to study the ideology of kingship: Sumer in the third millennium B.C.E., then Babylonia ca. 2000–39 B.C.E. (which embraced the former Sumer) and Assyria ca. 2000–612 B.C.E.[54] Whilst acknowledging the vicissitudes of these cultures, Lambert suggests: "In one respect all three of these cultures were unanimous. Rulers ruled by the express authority of the gods, and were expected to create a prosperous,

41. Frankfort, *Kingship*, 20.
42. "This embodiment of the two gods in the person of Pharaoh is another instance of the peculiar dualism that expresses a totality as equilibrium of opposites." Ibid., 22.
43. Ibid., 62.
44. Ibid., 69.
45. Baines, "Ancient Egyptian Kingship," 22.
46. "At Heliopolis the *Ished* tree of life arose when Re, the Sun-god, first appeared..." Edwin Oliver James, *The Tree of Life* (Leiden: Brill, 1966), 41.
47. P. G. P. Meyboom, *The Nile Mosaic of Palestrina* (Leiden: Brill, 1995), 74.
48. Silverman, "The Nature of Egyptian Kingship," 63.
49. Baines, "Ancient Egyptian Kingship," 28.
50. The king was the only route for access to the gods. According to Baines, "he was one and they [i.e. the gods] were many." Ibid.
51. O'Connor, "Beloved of Maat," 265.
52. Baines, "Ancient Egyptian Kingship," 39.
53. A general survey of the ancient Mesopotamian civilization is given in Wolfram von Soden, *The Ancient Orient* (Grand Rapids: Eerdmans, 1994).
54. W. G. Lambert, "Kingship in Ancient Mesopotamia," in Day, ed., *King and Messiah*, 55.

well-governed land."⁵⁵ Grabbe, on the hand, articulates the difficulty when trying to look at the ideology of kingship in this region; there was, Grabbe notes, a variety of ideas and views, depending on the particular period and the particular area (Sumer, Assyria, Babylonia).⁵⁶

For example, there appears to be greater evidence for the understanding of the king as divine in the Old Babylonian period (ca. 2000–1600) than in the Old Assyrian period (2000–1750).⁵⁷ Nevertheless, in the latter period the king was understood as the intermediary and chief priest between the gods and the people.⁵⁸ According to Grabbe,

> The original cult figures in the small Sumerian city-states were "priest-kings." As time went on, a separation was made between the *en* with the routine priestly function and the *ensi* who ruled. The king always remained the main cultic official, and some ceremonies (e.g. the New Year celebration) required his participation in a central role.⁵⁹

The king therefore also represents the people before the gods, and as such "he must expiate and atone for the people's sins, and must personally submit to the rites of atonement."⁶⁰ In Assyrian times the king was particularly held responsible for the actions of the people, either becoming the scapegoat "charged before the god with all the sins of the community," or being "manipulated" to avoid evil befalling the country.⁶¹ According to Baines, however, it was only in the earliest times—the Sumerian period—that the kings were deified, and in the later period they were regarded "rather as representatives of the god."⁶² Nonetheless, a few examples are to be found in the Kassite period.⁶³

The king can appear as the son of a number of gods and goddesses contemporaneously. Gudea calls himself the son of Ninsun, Nanshe or Baba, and to the goddess Gatumdug he states: "I have no mother, thou art my mother. I have no father; thou art my father."⁶⁴ The king is therefore son of the god/goddess.⁶⁵ On the other hand, Frankfort contends

---

55. Ibid.
56. Grabbe, *Priests, Prophets*, 31.
57. Ibid., 32.
58. Ibid.
59. Ibid., 54.
60. Mowinckel, *He That Cometh*, 38–39.
61. This could involve fasting, having his whole body shaved and penitential prayers. Frankfort, *Kingship*, 259.
62. Baines, "Ancient Egyptian Kingship," 2.
63. Grabbe, *Priests, Prophets*, 32.
64. Frankfort, *Kingship*, 300.
65. Again, this is found only in the early period. Grabbe, *Priests, Prophets*, 32.

that despite the numerous texts in which Mesopotamian kings are called the "sons" of gods or goddesses this does not imply that they are divine.[66] He does, however, acknowledge that the divine determinative was used by certain kings and that a few texts "established beyond doubt" that a fusion occasionally took place in certain kings of humanity and divinity, especially when a goddess had chosen a king to act as her bridegroom.[67]

The king is also said to be servant of the gods and "chosen by the gods"[68] and thought to be destined from the womb.[69] According to Mowinckel, "The king is the channel through whom the blessing flows down. In poetic language he may be called 'the sun.' He is 'like the tree of life.'"[70] The Assyrian king Esarhaddon was called "a precious branch of Baltil…an enduring shoot."[71] In the Amarna Letters he is "the breath of life" to his people.[72] "Shepherd imagery was also frequently used in the Old Babylonian royal inscriptions to describe the appointment of the king and the responsibility he had to care for the people."[73] In a Sumerian hymn to King Sulgi he is called "shepherd" and, again using the metaphor of a tree, he is identified as the source of abundance:

> On the day when he was elevated to the office of kingship,
> He was resplendent like a noble mes-tree watered by fresh water.
> Over the pure watercourse he spread (his) shining branches,
> (And) over his shining branches Utu decreed a fate for him:
> "Being a noble mes-tree he bears pure fruit,
> the noble shepherd, he will truly spread abundance in Sumer."[74]

Engnell's translation has Sulgi associated with life-giving water and the date palm.[75] In Babylonia and Assyria, the sacred tree, the date palm, was the source of life.[76]

---

66. Frankfort, *Kingship*, 301.
67. Ibid., 295.
68. Ibid., 299.
69. Mowinckel, *He That Cometh*, 35.
70. Ibid., 45.
71. Collins comments that "the image of a branch with reference to royalty must be regarded as a common near Eastern motif." John J. Collins, *The Scepter and the Star: The Messiahs of the Dead Sea Scrolls* (New York: Doubleday, 1995), 26.
72. Mowinckel, *He That Cometh*, 48.
73. Dale Launderville, *Piety and Politics* (Grand Rapids: Eerdmans, 2003), 292. The term "shepherd" is also found in the Ur III dynasty and the Late Babylonian dynasty (626–539 B.C.E.). See also Lambert, "Kingship in Ancient Mesopotamia," 60–63.
74. Andrew C. Cohen, *Death Rituals: Ideology and the Development of Early Mesopotamian Kingship* (Leiden: Brill, 2005), 123.
75. Engnell, *Studies*, 28.

Hittite Culture
The next culture to be examined is that of the Hittites, a culture which again spans a broad chronological and geographical range.[77] In Hittite culture there existed a relatively fixed pantheon of gods.[78] However, because of the widespread nature of the culture these gods appear under different names and guises at various locations and times throughout the duration of this empire. Nevertheless, the principal god appears to be the Storm God,[79] and it is he who features in the dragon-slaying myth related at the New Year festival.[80] Notably, the Sun-goddess of Arinna, "Queen of the Land of Hatti, Queen of Heaven and Earth," was also prominent.[81] The different features of the high god at times manifest themselves as distinct and separate gods.[82] However there is a close identification between the king and the Sun-god and they are often portrayed identically.[83] The king is understood to be the "shepherd of mankind."[84] Significantly, unlike the two cultures mentioned above, the divinity of the king from birth is not attested; rather, it was in death that the king "became a god,"[85] although this may have been meant euphemistically.[86] Despite the fact that the humanity of the king is not denied, nonetheless he is referred

76. James, *The Tree of Life*, 42.
77. "Speaking of Hittite mythology we have to keep in mind that the Hittite Empire, as it spread over all of Anatolia and parts of Syria and north Mesopotamia, included regions of different background culturally as well as ethnically and linguistically." Hans G. Güterbock, "Hittite Mythology," in *Mythologies of the Ancient World* (ed. Samuel Noah Kramer; New York: Doubleday, 1961), 141.
78. "The Hittite pantheon grew in complexity over time, owing to the contributions from various cultural traditions." David P. Wright, "Anatolia: Hittites," in *Religions of the Ancient World* (ed. Sarah Iles Johnston; Cambridge: The Belknap Press of Harvard University Press, 2004), 189.
79. "In the later years of the Hittite Empire the state religion is understood to have come under strong Hurrian influence and for example the Hurrian storm God *Teshub* is identified with the Weather-god of Hatti." O. R. Gurney, *The Hittites* (London: Book Club Associates, 1975), 141.
80. Ibid., 182.
81. Ibid., 139.
82. Cem Karasu, "Why Did the Hittites have a Thousand Deities?," in *Hittite Studies in Honour of Harry A. Hoffner, Jr.* (ed. Gary Beckman, Richard Beal and Gregory McMahon; Winona Lake: Eisenbrauns, 2003), 225.
83. Gurney, *The Hittites*, 66.
84. Trevor Bryce, *The Kingdom of the Hittites* (Oxford: Oxford University Press, 2005), 20.
85. Wright, "Anatolia Hittites," 195.
86. Nonetheless, there was a recognized cult of the spirits of former kings. Gurney, *The Hittites*, 65.

to in various sources as "son of the weather-god," and the king's mother is also known as "the mother of the god."[87] The king also functioned as the chief priest.[88]

Ugaritic/Canaanite Culture

The final culture to be examined is again problematic to define.[89] Whilst the Ugaritic texts have traditionally been taken to be of "Canaanite" origin, and thereby representative of the "Canaan" mentioned in the Hebrew Bible/Old Testament, serious doubts exist about whether such a label can appropriately be applied to Ugarit. Thus, for instance, Tasker uses Ugaritic material in his research on Canaan even though, by his own admission, "strictly speaking, Ugarit is not part of Canaan." He does so not only because of the lack of material from Canaan, but also because of the "close proximity and wealth of material" from Ugarit.[90] Therefore, despite the difficulty in defining the exact parameters of this culture, I have chosen to examine it because of its acknowledged influence on ancient Israel.[91]

In the Ugaritic pantheon, El is the high god and leader of the divine assembly (known as "the sons of El"),[92] and in the Ugaritic texts is said to dwell on a mountain at the source of the rivers.[93] El is the creator god, "possessed of wisdom";[94] he is also "the breath of life" (*sar balati*).[95] El

---

87. Mowinckel, *He That Cometh*, 51.
88. Gurney, *The Hittites*, 66.
89. Grabbe discusses this complexity and disagrees with Lemche's view that Canaan/ites is a biblical construct. Grabbe states, "Original sources from the second millennium B.C.E. and elsewhere indicate a geographical content to Canaan and Canaanite that is as specific and meaningful as many other such names in the texts." Lester L. Grabbe, *Ancient Israel: What Do We Know and How Do We Know It?* (London: T&T Clark International, 2007), 50. He concludes: "'Canaan/ite' had meaning in antiquity, but whether we have the precise usage pinned down might still be debated." Ibid., 51.
90. David R. Tasker, *Ancient Near Eastern Literature and the Hebrew Scriptures About the Fatherhood of God* (Studies in Biblical Literature 69; New York: Lang, 2004), 15.
91. "Ugaritic culture, more than any other single force in the ancient world, is now generally recognised as a vital component in the cultural matrix, in which Jewish, and after it, Christian thought first took shape." Nicolas Wyatt, *Religious Texts from Ugarit* (London: Continuum, 2006), 23.
92. John Day, *Yahweh and the Gods and Goddesses of Canaan* (London: Sheffield Academic, 2002), 25.
93. Ibid., 28.
94. Ibid., 15.
95. Engnell, *Studies*, 93.

is called "Father of Years"⁹⁶ and is sometimes described as an old man with white hair and beard. Baal, his son,⁹⁷ "the youthful, vigorous god"⁹⁸ who is sometimes referred to as "Rider on the Clouds," is the Storm-god "who sends rain and snow on the earth and causes the growth of vegetation."⁹⁹ He is "the Prince, Lord of Earth," "Victor (Aliyan)"¹⁰⁰ and dragon killer.

The king who is anointed¹⁰¹ is identified with both the high god and the vegetation god. Although not explicitly stated in the texts, there are indications of the divinity of the king¹⁰² and the suggestion that he is therefore born of divine parentage.¹⁰³ Baines comments:

> In the Canaanite world, which is the part of the ancient Near East most likely to have influenced the Israelites in matters of kingship, because of its geographical proximity, we do have some evidence of the king's both being a god and son of the god El. Thus in the Ugaritic king lists, each of the names of dead kings is preceded by the world *'il* "god" (*KTU* 1.113).

In addition, divinity may also be indirectly indicated through the king's participation in the Baal cycle. According to Wyatt, Baal and Athtar "represented in the celestial world of the gods apotheosized aspects of kingship and were believed to be present in some measure in the person of the reigning king, who resided in both the divine and human realms."¹⁰⁴ Wyatt, however, finds no clear evidence for this understanding outside the king's function in the cult.¹⁰⁵ Within the cult, the king not only represents the gods to the people but the people to the gods:

---

96. Day, *Yahweh and the Gods*, 19.
97. His mother is the goddess variously known as *Athirat* or *Asherah*. Wyatt, *Religious Texts*, 58.
98. Margaret S. Drower, "Canaanite Religion and Literature," in *CAH*, 2.2, 154.
99. Ibid., 153.
100. Ibid.
101. Day, "The Canaanite Inheritance," 81.
102. Baines, "Ancient Egyptian Kingship," 82.
103. Nicolas Wyatt, *"There's such Divinity doth Hedge a King": Selected Essays of Nicolas Wyatt on Royal Ideology in Ugaritic and Old Testament Literature* (SOTSMS; Aldershot: Ashgate, 2005), 202.
104. Nicolas Wyatt, "The Religious Role of the King in Ugarit," in *Ugarit at Seventy-Five* (ed. K. Lawson Younger Jr.; Winona Lake: Eisenbrauns, 2007), 48.
105. Instead, he understands the king to have been divinized periodically to bridge the ontological gap when he represented the nation before the gods in the cult. Ibid., 62.

> The king, then, is the one particularly qualified to approach the deity on behalf of the community. He is by his very nature priest. As representative or the embodiment of the society he maintains perpetual communion with the god of the community, a situation which is characterised by the description of the king as the son of God.[106]

According to Wyatt, a distinction could be made between the king as historical human individual and the king as "the persona of the nation" who therefore "somehow participated in the divine nature." The priestly status of the king and his sacramental communion with the deity also indicate that he had powers of healing and fertility.[107] This aspect of the king's[108] function is also suggested in the KRT text:

> Highly exalted be Krt
> Among the dispensers of fertility of the earth,
> In the assembly of the clan of Dtn.[109]

The Role of the King

Egyptian Culture

In the ancient Near East the king's role was to maintain order and to keep at bay or overcome the forces of chaos,[110] which not only concerned the forces of nature but anything outside of that nation which threatened its stability. This was maintained not only through political moves in the natural realm but also in the king's role in the rituals of the temple.[111] In Egypt, therefore, there were a number of festivals in which the king played a central role.[112] The main object of the cult and the festivals was to maintain right order (*ma'at*) and to renew life during periods of

---

106. John Gray, *The Legacy of Canaan: The Ras Shamra Texts and Their Relevance to the Old Testament* (Leiden: Brill, 1969), 153.
107. This idea was not only common in antiquity but also current in Britain until the time of Queen Anne. Ibid.
108. Scholars are divided about the person of Keret in the KRT texts, with some suggesting that this relates to a real king, and others suggesting that this is merely a heroic figure.
109. Gray, *The Legacy of Canaan*, 154.
110. Baines, "Ancient Egyptian Kingship," 27. "From the state perspective, the ideological alternative to kingship was not some other form of rule but chaos." Ibid., 17.
111. "The centrality of Egyptian kingship, its pivotal role in articulating the cosmos and creating order, and its religious, political and moral authority pervade the ancient record." Ibid., 50.
112. "In addition to major rituals such as those of accession and of renewal after many years (the Sed festival), the king's entire life was ritualised…" Ibid., 27.

3. *Kingship in the Ancient Near East*

transition, such as those which arose upon the death of a king[113] or at the transition of the seasons, when the powers of death or Chaos threatened to gain control.[114] The New Year was one such period and the accession of a king always took place at New Year.[115] The accession festival incorporated "The Mystery Play of Succession."[116] The burial of the dead king took place between the accession and the coronation and probably included a mock fight,[117] thereby enacting and so "realizing" the mythology of "the succession of Horus to the throne of the murdered Osiris."[118] The death[119] of Osiris is inevitable; and there must, therefore, be those who cause death. The protagonists in this death, however, remain anonymous, and are referred to only as "they."[120] There is some evidence of a processional march around the town during the Mystery Play.[121]

The Mystery Play was performed at several places throughout Egypt, with the king being repeatedly anointed and crowned; only with the final coronation of the king in Memphis, however, was the rite understood to be completed.[122] According to Frankfort,

> In the myth, Horus, born after Seth had killed Osiris, grew up to avenge his father and defeat Seth. Our play proclaims that at the coronation this change of fortune for the House of Osiris recurs. The king preparing to be crowned is Horus grown to maturity and ready to take charge of the kingdom…[123]

---

113. "The death of a king assumed, perforce, the character of a crisis with every chance of disaster. Chaos threatened…" Frankfort, *Kingship*, 101.

114. See Mowinckel, *He That Cometh*, 28.

115. "[T]he coronation could not take place at any time that might seem convenient. It had to wait for some new beginning in the progress of nature. For kingship, not being a merely political institution, had to conform with the cosmic events no less than with the vicissitudes of the community. Hence the coronation was made to coincide with one of the renewals of nature, in early summer and autumn." Frankfort, *Kingship*, 102.

116. A papyrus roll exists containing the script of such a play understood to have been performed at the accession of Senusert I. Ibid., 123.

117. Ibid., 113.

118. Ibid., 110.

119. According to Frankfort, being ill and being tired is to be understood as a euphemism for dying. Ibid., 126.

120. Ibid., 137.

121. Ibid., 127.

122. According to Frankfort, something changed in the world at each performance of the play and it was the cumulative effect of them that brought about "the restoration of the harmony between cosmos and society through the accession of a new king to the throne of Horus." Ibid., 124–25.

123. Ibid., 126.

The account of the creation of the world by *Ptah* is narrated at the end of the play. The raising of the *Djed* pillar is then understood to relate to the resurrection of Osiris in the afterlife, though it could also be understood to represent the resurrection of the dead king as Horus the new king.[124]

The *Sed* festival is another important festival. Although celebrated at the same time as the accession of a king (on the first of *Tybi*, one of the seasonal New Year's days), it was not itself an accession ceremony.[125] Nonetheless, it is understood as a renewal of the king's potency and the "renewal of all those beneficial relations between heaven and earth which the throne controls."[126] The festival was understood to contribute to the fertility of the land as well as the country's welfare.[127] The king played a prominent role in the ceremony, taking part in a great procession which included the statues of the gods[128] and concluded with the king performing a "dance" across a field (which is understood to symbolize Egypt).[129] Near the end of the ceremony the king shoots an arrow to the four points of the compass and is crowned and enthroned four times (one for each direction).[130] A new temple was often founded and dedicated at the *Sed* Festival[131] by the king[132]—though the dual shrines used in the *Sed* and *Min* festivals were themselves only temporary structures made of reeds.[133] The temples were identified with the primeval Hill, created out of the primeval waters, and considered by the Egyptians as the centre of the earth;[134] thus temples and creation are closely linked.[135]

---

124. Ibid., 128. "Osiris was the son of *Geb* and *Nut*, his life could not end; his death was transfiguration. His power was recognised in that life which breaks forth periodically from the earth, everlastingly renewed. Hence Osiris was the god of resurrection." Ibid., 184–85.

125. The event is thought to be a Jubilee festival, although the evidence suggests that some kings celebrated it on several occasions and at various intervals. Ibid., 79. Kuhrt comments: "The details of the ancient *Sed* festival can only be reconstructed in part and many uncertainties remain, although its function as a ritual re-enactment of the coronation seems plain." Amélie Kuhrt, *The Ancient Near East c. 3000–330 BC* (London: Routledge, 2003), 1:215.

126. Frankfort, *Kingship*, 79.
127. Ibid., 82.
128. Ibid.
129. Ibid., 87.
130. Ibid., 88.
131. Ibid., 79.
132. O'Connor, "Beloved of Maat," 265.
133. Frankfort, *Kingship*, 95.
134. Ibid., 151.
135. "This thought is applied even to temples built quite late in the history of Egypt. The Ptolemaic temple of Philae is inscribed: 'This (the temple) came into

During the festival of *Min*,[136] a harvest festival, a procession took place in which the king pretended to reap a sheaf of spelt with a sickle. According to Blackman, "the accompanying legend states that the king is 'reaping spelt for his father.'"[137] There is also evidence of a sacred marriage.[138]

Mesopotamian Culture

The New Year festival could be held in both spring and autumn since in Mesopotamia both periods were understood as "new beginnings" within the solar year. It was during these periods that the rains were important.[139] The New Year festival is also connected with the king's coronation in that the first year of his reign is officially reckoned from the New Year festival following the death of the previous king.[140] The greatest evidence of a New Year festival in this region is that of the Babylonian *Akitu* festival, in which the Babylonian king takes a central role.[141] However, it is unknown how extensively this festival was celebrated in earlier centuries or in other cities in this region. Be that as it may, the king's place in the cult is "well established."[142] The New Year festival opened with rites of atonement and finished with "a determination of destiny" by the gods.[143] According to Mowinckel,

> In Babylonia, as elsewhere in the East, the chief annual festival was regarded as an actual re-creation of the world, a deliverance from the domination of the powers of chaos, which had again brought about the withering of nature and death of the god of fertility, which had held Marduk "prisoner," and now threatened all life and order with destruction.

---

being when nothing at all had yet come into being and the earth was still lying in darkness and obscurity.'" Ibid., 152.

136. Min is the god who personified "the generative force in nature" as well as a rain god. Ibid., 188.

137. Aylward Manley Blackman, "Myth and Ritual in Ancient Egypt," in Hooke, ed., *Myth and Ritual*, 28.

138. In one text it is said that *Amon* takes the form of Tuthmosis I and has intercourse with the queen to beget a successor. Frankfort, *Kingship*, 44.

139. In Babylon the *Akitu* festival was celebrated in spring; in Ur and Erech it was celebrated in both autumn and spring. Ibid., 314.

140. Ibid., 40.

141. "The important place of the Babylonian king in the New Year festival is attested in texts copied out in the Hellenistic period (*ANET*, 331–34)." Grabbe, *Priests and Prophets*, 32.

142. Ibid. Nonetheless, whilst Frankfort acknowledges the necessity for the king to be present, he suggests that the king "moved on a lower plane" in the festivals than did the king of Egypt. Frankfort, *Kingship*, 313. Cf. also Oakley, *Kingship*, 42.

143. Frankfort, *Kingship*, 277.

> The god's advent, victory and resurrection or deliverance, which are brought about through effectual rites, signify therefore that the world is created anew.[144]

The suffering which the king underwent in the *Akitu* rites was understood to represent the king's atonement for the sins of the people.[145] The suffering God is understood to enter the Netherworld and revive the vegetation. Mowinckel comments, "'The suffering god' is an essential aspect of Mesopotamian gods, not only of Tammuz the god of fertility, but also of all the other gods of the power of life…"[146] According to Frankfort, the suffering god has a counterpart in the mourning goddess who not only mourns for him (as mother and bride) but also searches for and liberates him.[147]

Although the New Year festival comprised a number of rites, not all were present at each festival. At the New Year festivals of Babylon and Assur, for example, several rites are recorded which took place over a period beginning on Nisan 1 and culminating on Nisan 12.[148] These included: the preparation and purification of the king, the Day of Atonement,[149] the arrival of gods by barge, the releasing of Marduk from the Netherworld by Nabu, his son and avenger.[150] A further ritual took the form of a foot-race between Zu and Ninurat, in which Zu is defeated and afterwards, apparently, slain. In the myth, the counterpart of the ritual is the story of the struggle between Marduk and Tiamat. This is then followed by the First Determination of Destiny, a triumphal procession to the *Bit Akitu* under the king's guidance. There then follows the celebration of Marduk's victory at a banquet and the sacred marriage, a Second Determination of Destiny and the return of the gods to their temple.[151]

---

144. Mowinckel, *He That Cometh*, 40.
145. "Lors même que le roi n'est pas personellement coupable du péché, comme il est l'incarnation de son peuple, c'est encore lui qui, au regard des dieux, porte la responsabilité d'une faute anonyme ou d'un péché collectif." Labat cited in Engnell, *Studies*, 35.
146. Mowinckel, *He That Cometh*, 40.
147. Ibid., 283.
148. "Each day would stand for one month, the whole symbolising the mythic notion of twelve months of fertility and prosperity." Julye Bidmead, *The Akitu Festival: Religious Continuity and Royal Legitimation in Mesopotamia* (New Jersey: Gorgias, 2002), 110.
149. The king was the main actor in this ritual. Frankfort, *Kingship*, 319.
150. In later stages of the festival, Marduk's battle with Chaos was actually represented in the ritual. Ibid.
151. Ibid., 317–18.

The king represents both Tammuz/Marduk and human society "which, through him and his divinization in the cult, shares in the renewed vital force which belongs to Tammuz."[152] According to Stannard, the return of the procession from Esagil to the *Akitu* building in the New Year ceremony, led by Marduk and the king, meant that "Marduk's sojourn in the underworld lasted the classical period of three days."[153] The festival involved crossing water,[154] which compares with Marduk's crossing of the river in the creation epic. In the myth, the action constitutes Marduk's victorious contest; mythologically, the *Akitu* is at the centre of the cosmic waters, which is the place of combat.[155]

Lambert cites a text from the Late Babylonian period which also deals with the New Year ritual in Esagil on the fourth of Nisan. According to Lambert, this text portrays a "remarkable annual humiliation of the king of Babylon before the patron god of the town."[156] In this ritual the high priest takes the king's insignia and crown and places them before Bel. He then goes out and slaps the king's cheek, drags him by his ears and makes him kneel down to recite a negative confession beginning "I have [not] sinned, lord of the lands, I have not been negligent of your godhead, I have not destroyed Babylon…"[157] According to Bidmead,

> The stripping of the king's royal insignia and his negative confession are examples of a rite of reversal, when "normal" situations are inverted. The king, usually invested with divinely sanctioned authority, is now subject to the mercy of the priest and the god. A liminal period exists during this rite of reversal. Orderly and normal patterns disappear, resulting in a chaotic state. These patterns must be restored by a ritual action (hence, reversed again) before order can be re-established.[158]

Thus the high priest restores the king's insignia and assures him of the mercy of the god, victory over his enemies, a prosperous reign and a long life.[159] "In the enthronement ritual the king receives a twig from the 'tree

---

152. Mowinckel, *He That Cometh*, 43; Frankfort, *Kingship*, 285.
153. Brendan Stannard, *The Cosmic Contest* (Southport: CARIB, 1992), 49.
154. "In Mesopotamian mythology, as in archaic mythology in general, access to the underworld could involve crossing water." Ibid., 50.
155. Ibid. Stannard suggests that the *Akitu* is the cultic equivalent of the mythological *Apsu*. Ibid., 51.
156. Lambert, "Kingship in Ancient Mesopotamia," 65.
157. Amelie Kuhrt, "Usurpation, Conquest and Ceremonial: From Babylon to Persia," in *Rituals of Royalty: Power and Ceremonial in Traditional Societies* (ed. David Cannadine and Simon Price; New York: Past & Present, 1987), 33.
158. Bidmead, *The Akitu Festival*, 13.
159. Lambert, "Kingship in Ancient Mesopotamia," 65.

of life' as his sceptre; he is anointed with oil from the tree of life and baptised in the water of life."[160]

During the enthronement ceremony a reed hut symbolizing the cosmos was constructed.[161] This suggests that the enthronement festival is understood as a recapitulation of, or at least closely connected to, the original act of creation. This is also confirmed by the recitation during the festival of the *Enuma Elish*.[162] According to Engnell, this also explains the frequently encountered lament over the absence of god and the temple lying in ruins before the re-establishment of the "temple/cosmos" after the victory over Chaos.[163] As Oakley states,

> The festival evoked, therefore, the analogy between the renewal or "recreation" which each new Year involved, and solemnly "reactualised" the cosmogonic struggle between cosmic order and primordial chaos—rendered as the great victory of the valiant king-god Marduk over "raging Tiamat," the terrifying sea-monster who represented the watery chaos.[164]

Some scholars believe that the enemies in the battles represent real historical enemies (this relates to all cultures under examination); others believe that in fact the enemies are the original "enemies" of the god at creation, that is Chaos, often personified as some great creature such as the Dragon of *Apophis*, or *Tiamat* or, in the Israelite Psalms, Leviathan.[165]

Although unconnected with the New Year festival, a further practice surrounding the king which illustrates the connection of the king and the well-being of the country was that performed when an eclipse was foretold. In this a *sar puhi*, or substitute king, would be installed (for no longer than 100 days) to avert the danger to the real king and thus to the country.[166] When the time came to terminate the ritual, both the substitute king and his queen were put to death.[167]

160. Widengren, cited in Engnell, *Studies*, 29.
161. Ibid., 32.
162. This is recited on the fourth day of the festival: "for each New Year shares something essential with the first day when the world was created and the cycle of the seasons started." Frankfort, *Kingship*, 319.
163. Engnell, *Studies*, 33 and 49.
164. Oakley, *Kingship*, 42.
165. Engnell, *Studies*, 36.
166. Simo Parpola, *Letters from Assyrian Scholars to the Kings Esarhaddon and Assurbanipal*. Part 2, *Commentary and Appendices* (Winona Lake: Eisenbrauns, 2007), xxvi.
167. For fuller discussion of *sar puhi* ritual, see Jean Bottéro, *Mesopotamia: Writing, Reasoning and the Gods* (trans. Zainab Bahrani and Marc Van de Mieroop; Chicago: University of Chicago Press, 1995), 138–55.

Hittite Culture

For the Hittite culture, the large number of festivals and the importance of celebrating them in their right season is reflected in a tablet of instructions.[168] According to Bryce,

> The crucial times of the agricultural year were spring, between September and November, and autumn, between mid-March and mid-June, the times respectively of the sowing and reaping. Not surprisingly these were the periods when a number of the major festivals were celebrated. So much depended on the benevolence of those in whose honour they were held—the fertility of the soil, the abundance of rain, the fruitfulness of the harvest, the increase in flocks and herds and game for hunting.[169]

There were, however, four major festivals, two of which, the *Purulli* in spring and the *Nuntarias* in the autumn, are well documented.[170] There were two myths associated with the *Purulli* festival, both of which contain the themes of new life following on from death.[171] The myths in question are those of the vegetation god Telipinu[172] and of the dragon Illuyanka. "In all likelihood both myths were performed during the course of the festival, as a ritualistic re-enactment of the process of regeneration of life at the year's beginning."[173] The ritual combat, which took place during the course of the festival, was a combat "between a divine hero and an opponent which represents the forces of evil,"[174] and symbolized "the triumph of life over death or good over evil."[175] There are two versions of the myth, in one of which the son of the weather god is also killed by his father at his own request alongside the dragon.[176] The king's presence at the festival was essential; he was answerable to the gods not only for his own offences, but also for those of his subjects. The rites of the festival were understood to go some way towards the expiation of that guilt.[177]

---

168. Gurney, *The Hittites*, 151.
169. Trevor Bryce, *Life and Society in the Hittite World* (Oxford: Oxford University Press, 2002), 188–89.
170. Ibid., 194.
171. Ibid., 195.
172. "The Myth of the Missing God describes the paralysis of all life on earth caused by the disappearance of the god of fertility, the search for the god, and finally the re-invigoration of the earth when he is discovered and brought home." Gurney, *The Hittites*, 183–84.
173. Bryce, *Life and Society*, 195.
174. Gurney, *The Hittites*, 181.
175. Ibid., 152.
176. Ibid., 182.
177. Bryce, *Life and Society*, 206.

Therefore, whilst the king carried out all the duties associated with a head of state, he also had an important function in the cult. His role as chief priest superseded even that of commander of the army.[178] As chief priest the king officiated at each of the main cult centres and is depicted wearing the special costume of the sun god.[179] In the words of Wright,

> Functionally and conceptually, the high priestly figure was the king, who presided at the main festivals and was responsible otherwise for maintaining good relations with the gods and securing their favour for the people and land at large.[180]

As deputy of the Sun-god the king was also "the supreme earthly judge of his people."[181] Another possible feature of the *Purulli* festival was the "fixing of fates" by the gods.[182]

In the *Nuntarias* festival, the rituals involve the purification of the king and his ceremonial procession to the temple, whereupon he would ascend his throne.[183] There is also a suggestion of a royal marriage carried out as part of the enthronement ceremony. According to Bryce, there was also a festival of enthronement in which the king was anointed, given a throne name and enthroned, as a result of which he was "elevated to a higher plane."[184] Because of his sacrosanct nature, the king was guarded by an elite comprised of twelve guards.[185] At one of the festivals he was known to have drunk wine from a cup shaped like a bull or stag, an act understood as "drink[ing] the god": "This is a sacramental act. By it the king comes into mystical union with his god, for the cup symbolises the god himself."[186]

Ugaritic/Canaanite Culture

Included in the discoveries made at Ras Shamra from 1929 onwards were numerous texts written in a previously unknown script. Many of these texts, in a language that has come to be known as Ugaritic,[187] have

---

178. On occasions the king left important campaigns to come back to the capital to celebrate festivals in person. This was done in order to avert the wrath of the gods upon the nation. Gurney, *The Hittites*, 65.
179. Ibid., 66.
180. Wright, "Anatolia Hittites," 194.
181. Bryce, *The Kingdom of the Hittites*, 29.
182. Gurney, *The Hittites*, 152.
183. Engnell, *Studies*, 64.
184. Bryce, *Life and Society*, 19.
185. Ibid., 22.
186. Ibid., 190.
187. Translated texts appear in *ANET*; M. D. Coogan, *Stories from Ancient Canaan* (Philadelphia: Westminster, 1978); Wyatt, *Religious Texts from Ugarit*.

been identified as ritual texts, with others recording myths and legends. Three of the longest compositions are the legends of Keret and Aqhat, as well as the so-called Baal Cycle. The first two purport to be legends concerning actual former kings, although this remains a matter of dispute amongst scholars.[188] Wyatt discusses the views of various scholars, including the possibility that both the story of King Keret and the Baal texts were written to legitimatize the "rather shaky claims to the throne of Niqmad II," but draws no firm conclusion himself.[189] In the Keret and Aqhat texts the kings Dn'l and Aqhat are identified as having priestly functions.[190] Commenting on the Keret texts, Wyatt states, "the story has about it the power of words of institution or performative utterance, and the ritual described is a performative act. The enthronement of the king is thus his apotheosis."[191]

Engnell also discusses the opinions of a number of scholars concerning the Ras Shamra texts[192] and states that, in his own view, sections of them formed part of a liturgy for the enthronement ceremony. Gaster argues that the Baal cycle is "a seasonal myth based on the traditional ritual drama of the autumn festival."[193] This opinion is also shared by Gray[194] and Wright.[195] Stannard states, "By and large, those who have favoured a cultic dimension have emphasised that behind the text was a New Year, probably autumnal and agrarian, festival."[196]

Mowinckel gives a brief outline of the main points of the Baal cycle:

> The myth and the cultic drama describe how Baal dies in the conflict with Mot, the power of death, and how his beloved, "the virgin Anath," searches for him, how she defeats Mot, how Baal rises again or is born again in the son he begets by Anath, and, further, how he defeats the hostile powers of chaos, is enthroned on the divine mountain in the north as king of gods

---

188. See Wyatt, *Religious Texts from Ugarit*, 176–78, who gives a brief overview and selected bibliography on this subject. Tasker assumes Keret is a human king. Tasker, *Ancient Near Eastern Literature*, 58.
189. Wyatt, *Religious Texts from Ugarit*, 177.
190. Gray, *The Legacy of Canaan*, 152.
191. Wyatt, *"There's such Divinity,"* 196.
192. Engnell, *Studies*, 97–104.
193. T. H. Gaster, *Thespis: Ritual, Myth and Drama in the Ancient Near East* (New York: Norton, 1977), 129. Quoting the same words (seemingly positively), Wright follows the Gaster citation with "if not an accompaniment to that festival." David Pearson Wright, *Ritual in Narrative* (Winona Lake: Eisenbrauns, 2001), 4.
194. Gray, *The Legacy of Canaan*, 9–10.
195. Wright, *Ritual in Narrative*, 4.
196. Stannard discusses recent views on the ritual nature of the Baal cycle. Stannard, *The Cosmic Contest*, 227–29.

and men, how he is united with Anath, the mother goddess and goddess of fertility, how he recreates the universe, symbolized by the restoration of his temple.[197]

Stannard comments: "Although hierogamies lie very much in the background in the Baal epic, they occupy a central role in other Ugaritic texts."[198] One such text is *KTU* 1.23, which according to de Moor saw the parts of El and Asherah/Anat[199] taken by the king of Ugarit and the queen or princess.[200] Wyatt suggests that the sacred marriage of Baal and Pidray would have been impersonated by the king and queen. He comments, "Such impersonations were by no means pale echoes of divine patterns, but rather the effective reactualisations of the mythic paradigm."[201] Whilst Mowinckel disagrees with Engnell's suggestion that the king took the part of Baal in the ritual, he does concede that the god may be represented by the king in the cultic marriage.[202] Stannard, however, is of the opinion that the king was assigned the chief role in the drama.[203] According to Engnell, following his enthronement, the king is spoken of as seated at the right side of God.[204] He also identifies the release of prisoners as a further feature of the ritual.[205]

The mention of six months' provisions in the text is cited as indicating that the festival was possibly celebrated twice a year.[206] Stannard comments:

> Given that scholars have recognised that the epic embraces the two seasons of the Syro-Palestinian year, the wet and the dry, it is surprising that no consideration has been given to the possibility that the Baal epic embraces two New Year Festivals—Autumn and Spring.[207]

In this respect Gaster also discerns two major episodes present in the Baal epic:

---

197. Mowinckel, *He That Cometh*, 53. Day gives a similar outline. Day, *Yahweh and the Gods*, 117.
198. Examples are to be found in *KTU* 1.10, 1.12 and 1.23.
199. Asherah, Anat Astarte are all identified with one another in Egyptian texts of the same period. Stannard, *The Cosmic Contest*, 242.
200. De Moor quoted in ibid., 240.
201. Wyatt, *There's Such Divinity*, 196.
202. Mowinckel, *He That Cometh*, 456.
203. Stannard, *The Cosmic Contest*.
204. Engnell, *Studies*, 79.
205. Ibid., 77.
206. Ibid., 155 n. 1.
207. Stannard, *The Cosmic Contest*, 227.

In the wet season, from late September until early May, Baal rules after subduing Yam, Sea, who threatens to overwhelm the earth with floods. In the dry season, from early May to late September, the god of the underworld, death and aridity, Mot, rules after overwhelming Ba'al.[208]

Wyatt maintains that the king is made into a god by his royal ascent and suggests that the anointing of the king has an important role in the process of transformation. The king is divine for the duration of the rites but even though he resumes his normal status this is "transformed in some sense, since he is henceforth a sacral figure."[209] He further suggests that this deification was not a "once-for-all" event at the king's enthronement but was repeated in the cult: "Every time the king entered the cella, carrying with him the burden of his people's sins, their repentance, their pleas or their thanksgiving, it was by virtue of a repeated deification that the rituals were rendered effective."[210] This repetition in the cult of his ascent and descent also recapitulates the benefits wrought by his initial enthronement.[211] According to Wyatt,

> The king stood at the apex of society, on the borderline of the divine dimension. His involvement in the royal cultus took him across this divide, so that he became divine in order to represent his people and to acquire benefits on their behalf most effectively. He became a man again to bring these benefits down to earth. This capacity for transformation was probably understood to be initiated by the rite of unction which took place only once, at or in relation to his installation.[212]

Outcome of the King's Role

Egyptian Culture

In Egypt the king is the perfect ruler and as such administers justice. In his identification with Re, the king is judge, not just in the sense of administering justice. In Egyptian, as in other ancient Near Eastern thought, the sun maintains justice; that is, justice is part of the established order created by the Sun-god.[213] The gods give "life" to the king and in

---

208. Ibid.
209. Ibid., 198.
210. Ibid.
211. Ibid.
212. Wyatt, *"There's such Divinity,"* 202.
213. Frankfort, *Kingship*, 157. This thinking is still evident in the words spoken at the enthronement of the king or queen of England. The presiding archbishop prays that God may establish his/her throne in righteousness, that "it may stand fast for evermore, like as the sun before him/her, and as the faithful witness in heaven." Ibid., 39.

turn he gives life to his people. As such, he is "the breath of life"[214] and is depicted holding the hieroglyph for life.[215] According to Baines,

> In elaborate eulogies this concept is made more encompassing, and the king is responsible, like a creator god, for the destiny and nourishment of all, so that progeny increases during his reign.[216]

An example comes from the following Egyptian texts:

> Well tended are men, the cattle of god.
> He made heaven and earth according to their desire,
> And repelled the demon of the waters.
> He made the breath of life for their nostrils.[217]

Following his coronation, the king distributes bread, "the symbol of all sustenance," as a token of the abundance which his reign will effect.[218] The king's reign also has an impact on morality, but even so this is linked with the provision of water, the need for which connects each of these cultures:

> Truth has repressed falsehood
> The sinners are fallen on their faces
> All that are covetous are turned back.
>
> The water standeth and faileth not,
> The Nile carrieth a high flood,
> The days are long, the nights have hours, the months come aright.[219]

As a result of the reign of Rameses IV,

> They that hungered are satisfied and happy,
> they that thirsted are drunken,
> They that were naked are clad in fine linen
> and they that were tattered (?) have fine garments.
> They that were in prison are set free,
> and he that was in bonds is filled with joy.
> As for the "widows," their houses stand open and they suffer travellers to enter.
> Maidens rejoice and sing their songs of gladness.[220]

---

214. Baines, "Ancient Egyptian Kingship," 22–23.
215. Ibid.
215. Ibid.
216. Ibid., 23.
217. From the Instruction to Merikara, cited in Kemp, "Old Kingdom, Middle Kingdom," 74.
218. Frankfort, *Kingship*, 130.
219. Quoted from a hymn composed for the accession of Meneptah. Ibid., 58.

The king cares for the poor and meek and defeats his enemies,[221] who are understood to be an integral part of the "domain of disorder" or chaos outside Egypt which had to be mastered.[222] In a pyramid text it is said, "O Osiris, Horus has put thy enemy under thy feet."[223] That the enemies are not just physical but cosmological is suggested by the following line recited at the New Year festival: "They will be like the serpent Apophis on new Year's morn."[224] Frankfort comments, "The qualification 'on New year's morn' can only be explained as an intensification: the snake is defeated at every sunrise, but the New Year celebrates creation and daily renewal as well as the opening of the new annual cycle."[225]

Mesopotamian Culture
In the cultures grouped under Mesopotamia, similar outcomes are expected as a consequence of the king's reign and the renewal of his reign at the New Year festival. As a result of the New Year festival, "Nature revived; the vegetation re-emerged; the god was found, liberated, resurrected. But, also, nature promised to bear fruit again; the goddess had wed the god, and there would be issue."[226]

In one of the hymns to Sulgi we read:

> Le pays s'y repose
> Le pays s'y développe
> Les nations en paix
> Habitent côte à côte
> Du peuple la prospérité
> Brille comme le jour...[227]

Earlier in this hymn we learn that the goddess Ninsum bore Sulgi for three purposes: to bring prosperity to the realm, to bring the first fruits to the Temple in Nippur and to dispense justice.[228] At the end of one of the Tammuz hymns we find:

> Where there was no more grass, they graze;
> Where there was no more water, they drink;
> Where there were no more stables, a stable is set up;

220. Engnell, *Studies*, 14.
221. Baines, "Ancient Egyptian Kingship," 35.
222. Ibid., 24.
223. Frankfort, *Kingship*, 135.
224. Ibid., 150.
225. Ibid.
226. Ibid., 285.
227. Engnell, *Studies*, 39.
228. Cohen, *Death Rituals*, 123.

> Where there were no more hurdles for the flocks, they are plaited;
> Where there was no more reed shelter, they rest in its lee.[229]

A letter to Ashurbanipal states:

> there is a fine reign; days of security, years of justice, very heavy rains, massive floods, low prices... Old men dance, young men sing. Women and girls are happy and rejoice. Women are married and provided with (ear-)rings. Sons and daughters are born, procreation flourishes. The king my lord pardons him whose crimes condemned to death. You have released the prisoner sentenced to many years. Those who have been ill for many days have recovered. The hungry have been satisfied, parched ones have been anointed with oil, the naked have been clothed with garments.[230]

Lambert comments: "the description of an ideal reign correctly gives a picture of what the good Mesopotamian king was expected to bring about: messianic bliss."[231]

A heightened morality is also expected here as in Egypt as a result of the re-affirmation of the king's reign at the New Year festival. Hammurapi is entreated by the Gods Anu and Enlil:

> to cause justice to shine in the land,
> to destroy the wicked and the evil,
> that the strong oppress not the weak,
> to conduct the people, make the land enjoy righteousness,
> rightly to conduct orphan and widow,
> rightly to conduct the oppressed.[232]

It was also on New Year's Day that the gods determined the destiny of the country, as the last act of the festival.[233] Temple-building and the provision of water are also linked here.

The god Ningursu tells King Gudea to build the temple and in return promises "the return of the intercepted flood waters of the Tigris."[234]

Hittite Culture
In the Hittite culture the outcome of the king's function is the well-being of his people.[235] His tasks are elucidated in prayers and liturgies and include:

229. Frankfort, *Kingship*, 316.
230. Lambert, "Kingship in Ancient Mesopotamia," 69–70.
231. Ibid., 70.
232. Engnell, *Studies*, 41.
233. Frankfort, *Kingship*, 333.
234. Ibid., 257–58.
235. Engnell, *Studies*, 62.

giving bread to the hungry, clothes to the poor, oil (for purifications) to the wretched, coolness and warmth at need, maintaining justice in the country, carrying out holy wars, securing victory, giving and answering for "wholeness" and fertility.[236]

The outcome of the Spring New Year festival was to "re-invigorate the earth after the stagnation of winter, the ritual combat symbolising the triumph of life over death or good over evil."[237]

As in the other cultures, the provision of water is central, the Storm-god is entreated to: "Let soft rain come down from heaven. Let mankind be well, for mankind make health… Come Storm-god of Nerik. Come down with soft rain to the lands of Hatti…"[238] According to Bryce,

> The spring festival, which reached its climax in Nerik, celebrated the regeneration of the powers of nature. It was a time of renewals, of reconfirmation of the gods' endorsement of the king's authority, of regeneration of the life and health and vigour of the king and his consort. There was a direct connection between the king's well being and the rhythm of nature which was essential to the growth process.[239]

In the Telipinu myth, which is considered to have been enacted at the Spring festival, the god Telipinu departs the land, as a consequence of which crops wither and die, sheep and cattle reject their young and become barren, men and gods starve. On his eventual return, the land once again becomes fruitful.[240]

The earlier version of the Illuyanka myth begins: "this is the text of the Purulli Festival… When they speak thus: 'Let the land prosper and thrive, and let the land be protected'—and when it prospers and thrives, they perform the *Purulli* Festival." Again the ritual enactment of the myth is connected with the fertility and well-being of the land.[241] The fixing of destinies by the gods is also considered to have been a feature of the *Purulli* festival.[242]

Ugaritic/Canaanite Culture
In the Ugaritic texts, the expected outcome of the Baal cycle was fertility and, as a corollary, rain and dew. "All of the myths…lead up to the theme

---

236. Ibid., 68.
237. Gurney, *The Hittites*, 152.
238. Alberto Ravinell Whitney Green, *The Storm God in the Ancient Near East* (Biblical and Judaic Studies 8; Winona Lake: Eisenbrauns, 2003), 141.
239. Bryce, *Life and Society*, 195.
240. Ibid., 211.
241. Ibid., 215.
242. Gurney, *The Hittites*, 152.

of nature functioning with regularity and benevolence to bless mankind with fertility."[243] The acts of Anat bring on the corresponding functions of nature:

> Dew that the heavens pour
> Rain that the stars pour.[244]

Furthermore the manner in which Anat deals with Mot follows step-by-step the agrarian cycle:

> With a sword she sliced him;
> With a sieve she winnowed him;
> With a fire she burnt him
> With millstones she ground him;
> In the field she scattered him.[245]

Cross comments: "The imitative magic of Canaanite fertility rites could not be more obvious than here. With the victory of 'Anat, the dead god is strewn to fertilise the field."[246] In the next episode the god El sees in a prophetic vision the outcome of Anat's (and hence Baal's) victory over Death:

> Behold, Mighty Ba'al lives;
> Behold, the Prince, lord of earth exists.
> The heavens rain oil,
> The wadis flow with mead.[247]

In the KRT text King Keret is upbraided because he did not achieve the expected outcomes when he was ill:

> While bandits raid you turn (your) back,
> And you entertain feuding rivals.
> You have been brought down by your failing power.
> You do not judge the cause of the widow.
> You do not try the case of the importunate
> You do not banish the extortioners of the poor
> You do not feed the orphan before your face
> (nor) the widow behind your back.[248]

---

243. Cyrus H. Gordon, "Canaanite Mythology," in Kramer, ed., *Mythologies of the Ancient World*, 199.
244. Ibid., 203.
245. Frank Moore Cross, *Canaanite Myth and Hebrew Epic* (Cambridge, Mass.: Harvard University Press, 1997), 118.
246. Ibid.
247. Ibid.
248. Day, "The Canaanite Inheritance," 87.

Conclusion

In these texts it becomes apparent that the king has the unique role of representing the people corporately before the god(s), atoning for their sins. Simultaneously, he represents the god(s) to the people and it is through him that the blessings of the deities flow to the land and the people. It is through the king's participation in the ritual of the cult that the forces of chaos are overcome and cosmic harmony restored. The climax of this rationale occurs at the ceremonies performed at the New Year festival, a form of which is apparent in each of the cultures examined. This occurs either annually or bi-annually at the equinoxes to coincide with the periods of the agricultural year which cause the greatest anxiety—the hoped-for arrival of the rains.[249] This ceremony is understood to recapitulate the original creation, thus harnessing the creative powers of the creator/fertility god to "ensure" re-creation. The myth and ritual, which forms the ceremony, is understood actually to bring this about, with the king, in a number of the cultures, at the centre incarnating the god(s).[250] A number of features are present in the New Year festivals of each of the cultures, including the humiliation, death, resurrection and enthronement of the king/god. There is usually also some form of ritual battle with the enemies of the king/god (identified as actual enemies and/or the forces of Chaos) and a hierogamy. In a number of cultures, the releasing of a prisoner or prisoners may also feature.

Having established some of the features of the kingship ideology of the surrounding cultures I will proceed in the following two chapters to attempt to identify whether similar features are apparent in the Hebrew Scriptures, thereby confirming the suggestion that Israel's ideology of kingship and, consequently, the concept of messiah, was in fact influenced by the surrounding cultures.

---

249. Or, in the case of Egypt, the inundation and recession of the Nile.
250. See Herbert Weisinger, *Tragedy and the Paradox of the Fortunate Fall* (London: Routledge & Kegan Paul, 1953), 72.

Chapter 4

KINGSHIP IN THE HEBREW SCRIPTURES: THE PSALMS

Introduction

In the previous chapter I examined the role of the king in those cultures that surrounded Israel and are understood to have had some influence on Israelite theology. In these next two chapters I will examine the king's role in the Hebrew Scriptures, commencing in the present chapter with the book of Psalms. In the next chapter I will examine the books of the Prophets. Whilst space prohibits the examination of the rest of the Hebrew Scriptures, occasional reference will be made to relevant texts which relate to the ideology of kingship. Occasionally reference will be made to the Mishnah with regard to the accepted usage of Psalms. Indeed, although the Mishnah was compiled some 120 years after the destruction of the Second Temple, its authority on Temple practice is widely accepted. Before proceeding with an examination of the person and role of the king in this and the following chapter, it may be helpful to bear in mind the following comment by Grabbe:

> There is very little direct evidence about the religious function of the king, but there are many hints that the king was very important, and some historical reconstructions make him central... Much is said about the kings and their activities, but the impression left from clues in the text is that some important data have been suppressed at a time when the monarchy was no longer a reality.[1]

Grabbe suggests therefore that "a more indirect approach is needed, with more careful attention paid to inconsistencies, out of character statements and other small pointers within the text."[2]

---

1. Grabbe, *Priests, Prophets*, 20.
2. Ibid., 20.

The Person of the King

In the Psalms, the king is the LORD's (i.e. Yahweh's) Anointed;[3] he is also Yahweh's Servant, a title which in turn is linked to anointing. In Ps 89:20 Yahweh says that he will anoint with oil "David, my servant"[4] and Ps 23:5 also states that David was anointed with oil by Yahweh. Anointing is also associated with the giving of Yahweh's spirit. Following his anointing as king, Saul was told that the spirit of Yahweh would possess him and he would be "turned into a different person" (1 Sam 10:6). Similarly, when David was anointed as king "the spirit of Yahweh came mightily upon [him] from that day forward" (1 Sam 16:13).

King David has a particular connection with the Psalms,[5] for in them Yahweh promises that David's line will continue (Pss 89:3–4; 132:11–12) and from it will spring the future Anointed (Pss 89:24; 132:11).[6]

In Ps 2:6–7, classified as a coronation psalm,[7] the king is referred to as "son of God," seated on God's holy mountain:

> I have set my king
> on Zion, my holy hill
> I will tell of the decree of the LORD:
> He said to me, "You are my son,
> Today I have begotten you."[8]

---

3. In Pss 2:2; 18:50; 20:6; 28:8; 89:39, 51 and 132:10 the king is spoken of as "his" (i.e. the LORD's/Yahweh's) anointed.

4. King David is designated the LORD's servant 28 times in the Hebrew Scriptures, including Ps 89:20, 38, 50; 132:10, 17.

5. This is discussed in John Eaton, *The Psalms* (London: Continuum, 2005), 5–7.

6. This same promise is made to Solomon in 1 Chr 17:14. Knoppers states: "The reference to a connection between the Davidic–Solomonic Kingdom and Yhwh's kingdom is not accidental." He points out that on three other occasions David's kingdom is associated with God's kingdom (1 Chr 28:5; 29:11; 2 Chr 13:8) and the throne of Yahweh is also associated with the throne of David and Solomon (1 Chr 28:5; 29:23; 2 Chr 9:8). Knoppers, "David's Relation to Moses: The Contexts, Content and Conditions of the Davidic Promises," in Day, ed., *King and Messiah*, 102.

7. Goldingay suggests that this psalm may have formed part of the worship at the king's accession or at the annual celebration of the accession. John Goldingay, *Psalms*. Vol. 1, *Pss 1–41* (ed. Tremper Longman III; BCOTWP; Grand Rapids: Baker Academic, 2006), 96.

8. Following his discussion of this psalm, Collins concludes: "…it seems very likely that the Jerusalemite enthronement ritual was influenced, even if only indirectly, by Egyptian ideas of kingship. At least as a matter of court rhetoric, the king was declared to be the son of God, and could be called an *elohim*, a god." Collins and Collins, *King and Messiah as Son of God*, 15. Day is representative of a number of other scholars who take an adoptionist stance; see Day, "The Canaanite Inheritance," 82.

The father–son relationship identified in the surrounding cultures between the god and the king is also found in Ps 89:26–27.[9]

Other instances show a close identification between the king and Yahweh, notably Pss 98:6 and 110:1.[10] In Ps 45 the subject of the psalm, a royal bridegroom, is addressed as *"elohim"*:

> Your throne, O God (*elohim*), endures for ever and ever.
> Your royal sceptre of equity;
> You love righteousness and hate wickedness.
> Therefore God, your God, has anointed you
> With the oil of gladness beyond your companions. (Ps 45:6–7)

Day discusses these verses and the alternative renderings by those scholars who argue against a king–deity association. Day concludes that the king *is* addressed as *elohim* in v. 6 and cites Isa 9:6 as a further example of this phenomenon.[11] Collins also discusses v. 6 and draws a similar conclusion, citing the following verse, v. 7, "therefore God, your God, has anointed you," as further proof. For Collins, "the king is still subject to the Most High, but he is an *elohim*, not just a man."[12] Nonetheless, Collins contends that this does not mean parity with the Most High, only a special relationship.[13] Psalm 71:6 declares that the king was taken by Yahweh "from his mother's womb," again a possible allusion to divinity.

Psalm 72:5 may also suggest pre-existence of the king:

> May he live while the sun endures,
> And as long as he moon throughout all generations.[14]

---

9. Cf. also 2 Sam 7:12–16. Knoppers considers the employment of the adoption formula here as remarkable "because it expresses a high royal theology." Knoppers, "David's Relation to Moses," 108.

10. Cf. also 2 Sam 14:17 and Prov 24:21–22. Dell comments on the latter: "Here there is a striking parallel use of God and king in which the two terms virtually perform the same role." Katherine J. Dell, "The King in the Wisdom Literature," in Day, ed., *King and Messiah*, 178. Similar parallels are found in Prov 16 and 22.

11. Day, "Canaanite Inheritance," 84.

12. Collins and Collins, *King and Messiah as Son of God*, 15.

13. Ibid., 22. This special relationship is also evident in 1 Chr 28:5, where David says that Solomon has been Chosen "to sit upon the throne of the kingdom of the LORD over Israel" and that Yahweh will be his father, and Solomon will be his son (1 Chr 28:6). In 1 Chr 29:20 it is said the whole assembly "bowed their heads and prostrated themselves before the LORD and the king" and Solomon was anointed and sat "on the throne of the LORD" (1 Chr 29:23).

14. According to Gillingham, the second line of the Greek version of Ps 72:17 translates "before the sun was created, his name will remain," which is very close to *1 En*. 48:2–3: "Before the sun was created, His name was named before the Lord of Spirits." The latter text refers to a pre-existent Messianic figure. S. E. Gillingham,

Psalm 21:4 has also been thought to allude to the immortality of the king:

> He asked you for life; you gave it to him
> Length of days for ever and ever.

Whilst Day disputes this reading,[15] Collins states: "The psalm seems to hold out the possibility that a king might be granted life to fuller and greater extent than an ordinary human being."[16]

Although none of these examples necessarily speak of the king as divine, they do underline the special relationship between the king and Yahweh.[17]

And yet, the king not only represents Yahweh to the people,[18] but also represents the people before Yahweh: "As Yahweh's adopted son,[19] the monarch was effectively the deity's delegated surrogate on earth…and as such it was only natural that he should be answerable to Yahweh for the nation and should fulfil the function of national mediator between people and deity (Pss 20:7–10; 84:9–10)."[20]

There is a parallelism within the Psalms between *El Elyon* (translated "the Most High") and Yahweh (translated "LORD"),[21] a phenomenon which suggests a possible identification between the two. Whilst it is widely accepted that Yahweh eventually took over attributes of *El* the Canaanite god, nonetheless it is acknowledged that this was a gradual process.[22] In Deut 32:8 *El Elyon* appears as the high god with Yahweh as his foremost son having charge over Israel, with the other *elohim* (sons

---

"The Messiah in the Psalms: A Question of Reception History and the Psalter," in Day, ed., *King and Messiah*, 230–31.

15. Day, "The Canaanite Inheritance," 85.

16. Collins and Collins, *King and Messiah as Son of God*, 23.

17. Knohl discusses the differing status of the king in the Hebrew Scriptures, and suggests that the Psalms do hint at the deification of the king. Israel Knohl, *The Divine Symphony: The Bible's Many Voices* (Philadelphia: The Jewish Publication Society of America, 2003), 87–97.

18. "In Israel the king…passes on to the people the blessing which he has received from *Yahweh* through his anointing, and which is renewed for him and the body of the people through the coming of *Yahweh* in the cult." Sigmund Mowinckel, *The Psalms in Israel's Worship* (Grand Rapids: Eerdmans, 2004; first published Oxford: Blackwell, 1962), 138.

19. This is also Day's position; see Day, "The Canaanite Inheritance," 82.

20. Deborah W. Rooke, "Kingship as Priesthood: The Relationship between the High Priesthood and the Monarchy," in Day, ed., *King and Messiah*, 193.

21. Pss 7:17; 9:1–2; 21:7; 77:10–11; 83:18; 92:1–4.

22. For a discussion on the dating of this process, cf. John Emerton, *Studies in the Pentateuch* (Leiden: Brill, 1990), 99–100.

of god/angels)[23] having charge over the *goyim* (nations). Rather than simply representing two terms for the same God, I would suggest that this in fact represents the same complex idea found in the surrounding cultures, namely that, whilst *El Elyon* represents the high god and Yahweh the fertility or national god, nonetheless, as the parallelism shows, these figures in fact, at points, merge into one. Thus Yahweh represents an aspect of the high god, *El Elyon*, whilst, nonetheless, sharing overall the same features. Again, in the surrounding cultures we saw that the high god was often "split off" into other gods who represented his different aspects and that in the Rabbinic tradition the names Yahweh and *Elohim*[24] (another name frequently interchanged with Yahweh) were understood to represent two different aspects of God.[25]

This may be further evidenced in Ps 82, which is set in the divine council with God (*Elohim*) presiding over it.[26] The other gods (*Elohim*), "Sons of the Most High," are said to practise an unjust rule and their destruction is foretold. Here the language is couched in the same terminology as used that of the kings in the surrounding cultures. They are called upon to:

> Give justice to the weak and the orphan;
> Maintain the right of the lowly and the destitute
> Rescue the weak and the needy;
> deliver them from the hand of the wicked. (Ps 82:3–4)[27]

Although *Elohim* is used in both instances here, Goldingay submits that the first usage is governed by a singular verb and therefore refers to God, whereas the second instance is plural.[28] He further suggests that outside of the Elohistic Psalter the Divine Name would have been

---

23. The Masoretic Hebrew text reads "sons of Israel." I have preferred the Septuagint rendering here since I find it the more logical reading. In addition, this reading coheres with the theology found elsewhere, and is also supported by a manuscript from Qumran according to Collins, *Scepter and Star*, 161.

24. This thinking is evident in *Gen. Rab.* 12:15. The footnote to the Midrash states that the Rabbis held that the *Tetragrammaton* represents God under the aspect of Mercy whilst *elohim* describes him as God of Judgment. *Midrash Rabbah* (trans. Rabbi Dr. H. Freedman; London: Soncino, 1939).

25. In Chapter 6 I discuss the suggestion that this is in fact what is represented by the ritual surrounding the identical goats of the Day of Atonement.

26. Cf. also 1 Kgs 22:19 and Job 1:6.

27. "Nowhere does the universality of God's domain of *mišpāṭ* come to clearer expression than in Psalm 82." P. D. Hanson, *Isaiah 40–66* (Louisville, Ky.: John Knox, 1995), 43.

28. John Goldingay, *Psalms*. Vol. 2, *Psalms 42–89* (ed. Tremper Longman III; BCOTWP; Grand Rapids: Baker Academic, 2006), 561.

Yahweh.[29] This may therefore represent a further example of the theology found in Deut 32:8 and Dan 10 in which Israel is ruled through Yahweh, whereas the nations are ruled through lesser or fallen heavenly beings who therefore represent not just Israel's (and therefore Yahweh's) earthly, physical enemies, but also Israel's cosmic enemies, as well as evidencing the dualism between Yahweh/Elohim noted above.[30] Hanson also notes the correspondence here with Deut 32:8. He comments:

> Because the patron gods of the nations have failed to uphold justice and thereby threaten the universe with the spectre of a return to primordial chaos ("all the foundations of the earth are shaken," Ps 82:5), God asserts his powers as defender of *mišpāṭ*, condemns the unjust gods, and assumes universal rule.[31]

In conjunction with the renunciation of other gods in passages such as 1 Kgs 15:9–13; 2 Kgs 18:4–5; 23:4–5, as well as numerous places in the books of the Prophets, this would suggest that the strict monotheism claimed by the Jewish writers in Chapter 2 was a later conscious development within Judaism.[32]

A Sun-god/high god correlation was also identified in the surrounding cultures, and Pss 4:6; 31:16; 67:1; 80;[33] 97:1–5; 99:1; and 104:1–4 lend themselves to the interpretation that their original subject was a Sun-god.[34]

In the surrounding cultures, the king was often portrayed as a shepherd, an idea also found in the Psalms. There, the image is applied to Yahweh, as king (Pss 23:1–4; 28:9; 80:1; 95:7; 100:3), and to (the earthly king)

---

29. Ibid.
30. "The parallel of the cosmic and earthly levels in the royal worldview then consists of the divine and human kings centred at Zion against the divine and human enemies in the world. Yahweh the divine warrior-king parallels the human king ruling in Jerusalem and the cosmic enemies hostile to Yahweh parallel the human enemies opposed to the Judean monarch. This fundamental paradigm of cosmic and human royal power drew on a wider fund of West Semitic myth tradition represented in Ugaritic texts." Smith, *The Origins of Biblical Monotheism*, 157.
31. Hanson, *Isaiah 40–66*, 43.
32. "As a result of the editing of later monotheists, only scattered references to a number of other deities who belong to the middle levels of the pantheon have survived. Indeed, the Bible hardly provides an objective or complete picture of Israel's religion, because of significant editorial selection." Ibid., 153–55.
33. This has the refrain "Restore us, O God" (v. 3), "O God of hosts" (v. 7), "O LORD God of hosts" (v. 19), "let your face shine, that we may be saved!"
34. As does the priestly blessing in Num 6:24–27. This idea may also lay behind Prov 16:15, which is spoken of the king and also links him with the gift of rain: "In the light of a king's face there is life, and his favour is like the clouds that bring the spring rain."

David (Ps 78:70–71). *Yahweh* is also the source of life-giving water[35] and the "breath of life" to his creation (Pss 33:6; 104:30). Yahweh's name in the Psalms is connected with protection/salvation (Pss 44:5; 54:1; 89:24; 91:14; 105:1) and in Ps 118:21–22 the king is called "the chief cornerstone, the stone that the builders rejected."

In Ps 110:1, also considered to be a coronation psalm,[36] Yahweh says to the king, "Sit at my right hand until I make your enemies your footstool." Collins comments, "This position is not only one of honour, but bespeaks the very close association of the king and the deity."[37] The influence of the surrounding cultures on this psalm is widely acknowledged.[38] However, it is v. 3 which has traditionally presented difficulty. Goldingay translates this verse as "on the holy mountains from the womb of dawn, the dew of your youth is yours," and understands this to refer to "young warriors who comprise the army."[39] Otzen cites Widengren's translation, "From the womb of the dawn, as dew I have begotten you," and suggests that this refers to the birth of the Jerusalem king from Sahar (identified with dawn) and Salem (identified with sunset) in the Ugaritic pantheon: "thus the Jerusalem king was thought of as the child of these divine figures and himself identified with the dew."[40] Otzen compares this phenomenon to analogous ideas in the religion of Ugarit[41] and discusses the mythological understanding of Tal (dew);[42] he comments: "Behind nearly all the mentions of dew in the Old Testament (some 30 in all) stands the conviction that the dew is a gift of Yahweh, just as in the religion of Ugarit it is a gift of Baal. Yahweh is the giver of fertility, and without dew there is no fertility."[43] Collins also considers the variant translations and the Ugaritic analogies but suggests that an Egyptian background is more likely: "Like Psalm 2, it should be viewed as reflecting a Jerusalemite enthronement ceremony, which was influenced,

---

35. He is the "fountain of life" (Ps 36:9).
36. Day, "The Canaanite Inheritance," 73; see also Eaton, *The Psalms*, 384–85.
37. Collins and Collins, *King and Messiah as Son of God*, 16.
38. John Collins cites Assyrian parallels and parallels with Egyptian iconography, as well as the more obvious Canaanite influence. Ibid., 15–16. Goldingay notes the similarity to Akkadian prophecies to the king. John Goldingay, *The Psalms*. Vol. 3, *Pss 90–150* (ed. Tremper Longman III; BCOTWP; Grand Rapids: Baker Academic, 2006), 291.
39. Ibid., 290.
40. B. Otzken, "Tal," *TDOT* 5:329. Day also connects these Ugaritic deities with this verse. Day, "The Canaanite Inheritance," 83.
41. Otzken, *TDOT* 5:327.
42. Ibid., 5:323–29.
43. Ibid., 5:324.

if only indirectly, by Egyptian mythology about the divine birth of the king."[44]

In Ps 110:4–5 the king is designated high priest not in the line of Aaron but of Melchizedek, king of *Salem* (Jerusalem) and priest of *El Elyon* (Gen 14:18), the Jebusite cult which David is thought to have conquered and taken over.[45] Like the kingship, this is promised "for ever," further highlighting the correlation of the roles of king and high priest.[46] Rooke comments: "The idea of the Israelite monarchy as an example of sacral kingship has become an accepted piece of received scholarly wisdom; and of course one of the characteristics of sacral kingship is that it bestows upon its office-holders a priestly role."[47]

Throughout the Psalms, therefore, kingship is prominent—both the kingship of Yahweh[48] and David's kingship as Yahweh's "son" and representative.

The Role of the King

Although Gunkel was the first to suggest a cultic setting,[49] others have followed his lead and a number of psalms have been identified as royal or enthronement psalms,[50] that is to say, psalms thought to have been devised for use in a New Year ceremony similar to those celebrated by

---

44. Collins and Collins, *King and Messiah as Son of God*, 15–19.
45. According to Day, this is conclusive evidence that the Israelite kings functioned as priests. Day, "Canaanite Inheritance," 75.
46. According to Rooke, the priestly function of the king is specifically a mediatory role "within ritual and specifically sanctuary contexts," and stems from his unique position before Yahweh, arising from the sacral nature of his kingship. Rooke, "Kingship as Priesthood," 193.
47. Ibid., 187.
48. Not only is Yahweh called king in numerous psalms (Pss 5:2; 10:16; 24:7–10; 29:10; 44:4; 47:7; 68:24; 74:12; 84:3; 89:18; 93:1; 96:10; 97:1; 98:6; 99:1), the phrase "the LORD reigns" occurs repeatedly (Pss 47:8; 93:1; 97:1; 99:1; 146:10), as do allusions to his throne/being enthroned (Pss 9:7; 11:4; 29:10; 47:8; 80:1; 93:2; 99:1; 123:1).
49. Day comments: "The Psalms are littered with cultic allusions, which only make sense if they were used in public worship in the temple in Jerusalem." As further proof he cites the cultic interpretation of the psalms in the Mishnah and other rabbinic sources, "which stipulate various cultic occasions for the use of the psalms." John Day, *Psalms* (T&T Clark Study Guides; London: T&T Clark International, 2003), 15.
50. "Since the time of Gunkel, it has been agreed that the royal psalms include at least the following: 2, 18, 20, 21, 45, 72, 89, 101, 110, 132, 144:1–11." Grabbe, *Priests, Prophets*, 27.

the surrounding cultures (and discussed in the previous chapter),[51] ceremonies involving a dramatic ritual culminating in the enthronement of the king/god/God.[52] This interpretation found its fullest expression in Mowinckel's work on the Psalms,[53] although it should be noted that Mowinckel made clear the fact that he did not posit a separate festival but understood the enthronement festival to be part of the autumnal festival.[54] Notably, whilst the theory of an annual enthronement ceremony has subsequently been widely criticised,[55] in the past decade there has been a resurgence of interest and some appreciation for the fundamentals of this concept,[56] if not the full-blown theory posited by the "myth and ritual" school.[57] In this respect, Clines comments:

> It has at least become clear in recent years that a cavalier rejection of Mowinckel's theory is not sufficient, especially in the light of the modifications introduced by Mowinckel himself and others to the meaning of an enthronement festival. There are, indeed, certain *a priori* objections to postulating a full-scale "patternist" new year festival in Israel, but none at all, it seems to me, to a festival of Yahweh's enthronement, if all that is meant by that is a festival (the well-attested autumn festival) at which the accession of Yahweh to kingship at some point in the past is reactualized in the cult, perhaps with ritual accompaniment.[58]

Other contemporary scholars are in agreement that an enthronement ceremony is the most likely setting for a number of psalms.[59] Eaton, for

---

51. "It is probable that the autumn festival was also the setting for an important group of royal psalms." Eaton, *The Psalms*, 24.
52. For a brief outline of the various theories concerning the psalms of lament, including a bibliography, see Day, *Psalms*, 19–37.
53. Mowinckel identifies Pss 47, 93, 95–99 as enthronement psalms. Mowinckel, *The Psalms*, 106.
54. Ibid., 230.
55. For a discussion of Mowinckel's thesis and its critics, see D. J. A. Clines, *On the Way to the Postmodern* (Sheffield: Sheffield Academic, 1998), 639–40. Clines also offers a brief criticism of the myth and ritual school's understanding of divine kingship. Ibid., 690–93. See also Gillingham, "The Messiah in the Psalms," 209.
56. K. van der Toorn, "The Babylonian New Year Festival: New Insights from the Cuneiform Texts and Their Bearing on Old Testament Study," in *Congress Volume: Leuven 1989* (ed. J. A. Emerton; Leiden: Brill, 1991), 331.
57. Hooke, writing twenty years after his original publication, states: "So far as I know, no-one has satisfactorily rebutted the detailed demonstration of the sacrificial and central character of the king in the Jerusalem cultus" (*The Siege Perilous*, 180), which is further suggested by Eaton's acceptance of Mowinckel's interpretation of the setting of the psalms some fifty years later.
58. Clines, *On the Way to the Postmodern*, 653.
59. These are Pss 2; 21; 72 and 110, as well as Pss 18; 89; 101; 118 and 144, according to Eaton, *The Psalms*, 24; Pss 2; 72; 101; 110 and 132, according to

example, whilst discussing other theories for the *Sitz im Leben*[60] of these royal psalms,[61] also accepts this cultic view.[62] For him, "It is notable that such royal interpretation of these Psalms often reveals a powerful coherence in the psalm lost in other approaches."[63] The connection with these psalms and a New Year festival is further strengthened as a number of them are traditionally connected with the festivals of Passover and Sukkot,[64] both of which are understood by some scholars to have originally been New Year[65] as well as harvest festivals. Both festivals are held at the vernal and autumnal equinoxes respectively and it has been proposed that both these periods may have been regarded as "new years."[66]

At the same time, the lack of evidence for a ritual combat within the Psalms is cited as proof that such an enthronement ceremony/New Year festival did not take place within Israel. Van der Toorn states: "The biblical data bear witness to cult processions but they mention no cultic battle. The ritual battle is an article of faith rather than the result of textual study."[67] In addition, even though Oesterley, a proponent of the "myth and ritual" theory, argues for the existence of a ritual combat, he could find it "nowhere mentioned in our records as having taken

---

Gillingham, "The Messiah in the Psalms," 209–37; Pss 2 and 110, according to Collins and Collins, *King and Messiah as Son of God*, 12, 19.

60. Including the suggestions that these psalms represent the pleas of persons on trial at the Temple, general situations of individual distress, as well as the pleas of fugitives who have sought sanctuary in the Temple; yet others are thought to express the sickness of an individual. Eaton, *The Psalms*, 25. Gillingham examines Pss 18, 20; 21 and 89, and considers them to be battle psalms. She suggests that this concerns a time of national crisis although she is unable to pinpoint the exact crisis. Gillingham, "The Messiah in the Psalms," 212–15.

61. Pss 47; 93; 95–100 according to Eaton, *The Psalms*, 23.

62. Ibid., 25.

63. Ibid.

64. The Egyptian Hallel (Ps 113–118) is said to have been recited at both Passover (*m. Pes.* 5:7) and Sukkoth (*m. Suk.* 4:7).

65. Segal discusses this and concludes that both Passover and Sukkot (Tabernacles) were New Year festivals. J. B. Segal, *The Hebrew Passover* (London: Oxford University Press, 1963), 117.

66. Cf. Clines for a discussion of the dating of the new year in pre-exilic Israel. Clines concludes: "while there are no data that categorically exclude autumnal reckoning of the calendar year prior to c. 605 BCE, there are no data to support it, not even cumulatively." As to the spring dating of the new year, he states: "there is one piece of evidence…that may suggest a spring new year reckoning, but that admittedly does not amount to a strong argument in favour of such reckoning." Clines, *On the Way to the Postmodern*, 394.

67. Van der Toorn, "The Babylonian New Year Festival," 343.

place."⁶⁸ Eaton, however, identifies a number of psalms (Pss 18; 89; 101; 118; 144) "which in various ways envisage humiliation and deliverance" and suggests that these "may reflect a dramatic character in the presentation and consecration of the royal office."⁶⁹ Eaton also envisages Egyptian influence in Pss 2, 104 and 110, as well as the Babylonian ritual involving Marduk, and suggests that these Psalms may well in turn have influenced Isa 52–53, "a drama of atonement won for many by the suffering of a royal figure."⁷⁰ He concludes, "All in all the interpretation of these royal Psalms in terms of liturgical drama is not in itself far-fetched."⁷¹

From my own study of the Psalms I would suggest that there is in fact a great deal of evidence to suggest that the king underwent some sort of ritual trial.⁷² In a number of psalms the king speaks of "the day of my trouble" (Ps 86:7) and "the day of my distress" (Ps 102:2); he says "my soul is full of troubles, and my life draws near to Sheol" (Ps 88:3). Other occurrences are found in Ps 20:1; 59:16; 70:1–2; 71:2, 4; 77:2, with many more in which the king calls out in distress because of his enemies.⁷³

Furthermore, when examined, a significant underlying theme emerges whereby the suffering is spoken of in terms of the king being engulfed by water:

> Save me, O god!
> For the waters have come up to my neck.
> I sink in deep mire
> Where there is no foothold;
> I have come into deep waters,
> Where the flood sweeps over me. (Ps 69:1–2)

Further on in the psalm the king's enemies are spoken of in parallel with "the deep waters":

> Rescue me
> From sinking in the mire;

---

68. Nonetheless, he argues that this did figure as part of the ritual because the primeval conflict is often spoken about in the Old Testament without further explanation, suggesting it was a familiar concept. Oesterley, "Early Hebrew Festival Rituals," 128.
69. Eaton, *The Psalms*, 24.
70. Ibid.
71. Ibid.
72. Eaton suggests that the re-enactment in the temple of Yahweh's battle and victory could be that which is envisaged in Ps 48:9: "We have enacted your faithful love, in the midst of your temple O God." Ibid., 197.
73. Pss 3:1–3; 6:1–5; 7:1–2; 17:8–12; 18:6; 22:1–18 provide just a few examples.

4. Kingship in the Hebrew Scriptures: The Psalms

> Let me be delivered from my enemies
> And from the deep waters
> Do not let the flood sweep over me,
> Or the deep swallow me up,
> Or the Pit close its mouth over me. (Ps 69:14–15)

This suggests that the enemies are identified with, or in fact represent, the forces of Chaos. Goldingay also identifies the waters here and in Ps 93 and Ps 124 with the forces of Chaos.[74] This same theme is encountered in Ps 18:

> The cords (waves) of death encompassed me,
> the torrents of perdition assailed me;
> the cords of Sheol entangled me,
> the snares of death confronted me.
> In my distress I called upon the LORD;
> to my God I cried for help.
> From his temple he heard my voice
> And my cry to him reached his ears. (Ps 18:4–6)

The parallelism here between the enemies of the king, the flood, the deep waters, the mire and the pit leads to the conclusion that these are all aspects of the one threat. This theme is also evident in a number of other psalms:

> Why do the nations conspire,
> and the peoples plot in vain?
> The kings of the earth set themselves,
> And the rulers take counsel together,
> Against the LORD and his anointed, saying,
> "Let us burst their bonds asunder,
> and cast their cords from us." (Ps 2:1–3)[75]

---

74. Goldingay, *The Psalms*, 3:480.
75. Gillingham also regards this as a battle psalm. Gillingham, "The Messiah in the Psalms," 214. Longman, however, states: "We are somewhat at a loss to understand exactly what kind of historical background generated such a thought. There were few time periods when Israel or Judah under the Davidides had vassals who would contemplate throwing off their shackles." Tremper Longman III, "The Messiah: Explorations in the Law and Writings," in Porter, ed., *The Messiah in the Old and New Testament*, 18. Eaton, on the other hand, considers this to be part of the enthronement ritual of the Davidic kings which took place in the autumn festival when first installed and in subsequent years, possibly including a drama whereby "the divine election of the king, his empowerment, contest with hostile forces, salvation and exaltation were enacted." Eaton, *The Psalms*, 65. Collins also suggests that the *Sitz im Leben* of this psalm is the period of the monarchy, "in the context of an enthronement ceremony." Collins and Collins, *King and Messiah as Son of God*, 12.

You have put me in the depths of the Pit,
in the regions dark and deep,
Your wrath lies heavy upon me,
And you overwhelm me with your waves.

Your wrath has swept over me;
your dread assaults destroy me.
They surround me like a flood all day long;
From all sides they close in on me. (Ps 88:6–7, 16–17)

The floods have lifted up, O Lord,
the floods have lifted up their voice,
the floods lift up their roaring. (Ps 93:3)

Out of the depths I cry to thee, O Lord!
Lord, hear my voice!
Let thy ears be attentive
To the voice of my supplications! (Ps 130:1)

In these and a number of other psalms the king cries out to Yahweh to rescue him from the deep/the waves/Sheol/the pit;[76] he is bound with cords[77] and his feet are slipping.[78] He is surrounded by enemies who mock him;[79] he suffers shame[80] and humiliation;[81] he is abandoned by his family[82] and friends[83] as well as by Yahweh himself.[84] In some of the psalms the king weeps,[85] in others he is silent.[86] The king's affliction, at times identified with Yahweh's wrath,[87] has been brought on by Yahweh himself[88] or is on his behalf.[89] The people also scorn him, saying:

76. Pss 32:6; 42:5–7; 88:3–7; 116:3; 119:81–88; 124:2–5; 130:1.
77. Pss 2:3; 18:4; 116:3, 16; 140:5.
78. Pss 35:15; 37:24; 38:16–17; 69:2; 73:2.
79. Pss 22:7–8; 43:2; 89:51.
80. Pss 22:6–7; 69:7, 19; 89:45.
81. Pss 44:15; 69:12.
82. Ps 69:8.
83. Ps 41:9 reads: "Even my bosom friend in whom I trusted, who ate of my bread has lifted his heel against me." Cf. Ps 88:18.
84. Pss 22:1–2; 43:2; 88:14; 89:38, 46; 102:2.
85. Pss 6:6–8; 39:12; 42:3; 102:9; 116:8.
86. Pss 39:2, 9; 62:5.
87. Ps 88:7.
88. Pss 22:1–2; 32:4; 38:2; 39:9–10; 88:6–7; 89:38, 45; 118:18; 119:75.
89. Ps 69:7 reads: "It is for your sake that I have borne reproach, that shame has covered my face." Ps 69:9 reads: "It is zeal for your house that has consumed me; the insults of those who insult you have fallen on me." Ps 69:26 reads: "For they persecute those whom you have struck down, and those whom you have wounded, they attack still more." Eaton comments: "the royal leader is…bearing the hostility

4. Kingship in the Hebrew Scriptures: The Psalms 79

"Commit your cause to the LORD; let him deliver—let him rescue the one in whom he delights."[90] Nonetheless, Yahweh protects him: "For he will give his angels charge over you, to guard you in all your ways. On their hands they will bear you up, lest you dash your foot against a stone."[91] Although he makes both positive[92] and negative[93] confessions, Yahweh rescues the king because of his righteousness.[94] His subsequent rescue is then spoken of in terms of being "lifted up out of the waters," which again are identified with the king's enemies:

> He reached down from on high, he took me;
> he drew me out of mighty waters.
> He delivered me from my strong enemy,
> And from those who hated me. (Ps 18:16–17)

> He drew me up from the desolate pit (or tumult),
> out of the miry bog,
> and set my feet upon a rock
> making my steps secure. (Ps 40:2)

> If it had not been the LORD who was on our side,
> when our enemies attacked us,
> then they would have swallowed us up alive,
> when their anger was kindled against us;
> then the flood would have swept us away,
> the torrent would have gone over us;[95]
> then over us would have gone the raging waters. (Ps 124:2–5)

> Stretch out your hand from on high;
> set me free and rescue me from the mighty waters,
> from the hand of aliens. (Ps 144:7)

The king asks not only to be delivered but to be set on high,[96] that is, raised up,[97] "resurrected."

---

meant for the Lord himself. The psalm leant itself to messianic applications and, next to 22, is the most frequently cited psalm in the New Testament." Eaton, *The Psalms*, 256.
    90. Ps 22:8.
    91. Ps 91:11–12.
    92. Pss 25:21; 26:1–7; 41:4; 59:3–4.
    93. Pss 25:7, 11; 32:5; 38:3–4; 51:1–5; 73:13.
    94. Ps 18:20.
    95. Goldingay states: "…talk of waters and torrent suggest forces of more than natural significance, and/or the forces of chaos that assert themselves against order and against God." Goldingay, *Psalms*, 3:480.
    96. Where his feet will not slip, "in a wide place"; see Pss 18:33, 36; 26:12; 56:13; 121:3.

Were these themes to be isolated, it might suggest that the psalms in question arose from a particular historical situation.[98] However, in my examination of the psalms I have found that these themes are repeated in sufficient number that it would seem too coincidental to suggest that they all represent some type of similar historical threat.[99] I propose instead that they did, in fact, form part of a pre-exilic enthronement ceremony at the New Year festival, celebrated at the temple at the autumn[100] and/or spring equinoxes in which the myth of Yahweh's battle with the forces of Chaos prior to his subsequent act of creation[101] was re-enacted as a means of engendering "recreation" and the blessings of fertility for the new year.[102] Day, who produces a number of arguments in support of Mowinckel's view concerning the New Year festival, comments: "Mowinckel's view, which is not always properly understood, is that it is Yahweh's primeval victory at creation which is being celebrated, but in such a way that it is re-enacted and renewed in the present."[103] This is further suggested by the following:

> The voice of the LORD is over the waters;
> the God of glory thunders,
> The LORD, over mighty waters…
> LORD sits enthroned over the flood
> The LORD sits enthroned as king for ever. (Ps 29:3, 10)

97. Ps 3:3; 9:13; 27:5–6; 30:3; 41:10; 71:20; 86:13. Related themes are found in other psalms: "I have trusted in the LORD, I shall not slip" (Ps 26:1); "My foot stands on level ground" (Ps 26:12); "He shall set me high upon a rock" (Ps 27:5). In Ps 27:11 the LORD is asked to lead the king "on a level path."

98. This, in fact, is the direction taken by a number of commentators, although many different theories are put forward. For each individual psalm and in some cases a group of psalms, there appears to be no consensus of opinion about the situation being described. Ps 18 provides a useful example. In his commentary Goldingay sets out five different views about the origin of the psalm and suggests that the most plausible situation is that it was written in honour of David in the Persian period, although he does not categorically discount any of the others, thus highlighting the difficulty of attempting to apply particular historical circumstances to any one psalm. Goldingay, *Psalms*, vol. 1.

99. For a brief survey of scholars who have attempted to assign historical circumstances to the Psalms, see Eaton, *The Psalms*, 57.

100. Ibid., 29.

101. As evidenced in Ps 74:12–17.

102. "The vital importance of this time of year in ancient Palestine was that the new agricultural cycle was about to begin. Strongly felt was the need to renew the relationship with the Lord, master of all the forces of life and to seek his gift of winter rains, which did not in fact arrive with unfailing regularity. Without them the cycle could not begin and starvation was inevitable." Eaton, *The Psalms*, 23.

103. Day, *Psalms*, 81.

No definitive explanation is found for the Bronze Sea,[104] which stood in the original temple. However a number of commentators have hinted at a cultic use.[105] It is interesting to speculate therefore whether this represented the original waters of Chaos and whether it may have played a part in the enthronement ceremony. If this were so it might be suggested that a mimic representation may have taken place, one that re-enacted Yahweh's victory over the forces of Chaos. In it the king (bound with cords?) would be immersed in the water (of the Bronze Sea) and pushed across the width of the "sea" whilst being mocked, with his feet slipping and eventually being engulfed by the water. The persons, possibly priests, who surround and push the king, likely represented the nations or kings of the nations who in turn represent the forces of Chaos. The king is then rescued ("raised up") by "the LORD" (who at this point may be represented by the high priest) and subsequently enthroned.

This theory would cohere with the phenomenon identified above, that the king's distress is often spoken about in terms of being engulfed in water and his rescue spoken of in terms of being lifted from the water which is also identified with his enemies. This would fit quite closely with the situation outlined in these psalms, of which Ps 118 is a further example:

> Out of my distress I called on the LORD:
> the LORD answered me and set me in a broad place...
>
> all nations surrounded me
> in the name of the LORD I cut them off!
> They surrounded me, surrounded me on every side;
> In the name of the LORD I cut them off!

104. Although it is described along with its dimensions, no explanation of its purpose is given in 1 Kgs 7:23–25. In 2 Chr 4:2–5 we are also told of its vast proportions and that it could hold "two thousand baths," which according to Edersheim was the equivalent of two million gallons. Alfred Edersheim, *The Temple* (London: James Clarke, 1959), 56. However, in 2 Chr 4:6 we are told that the sea "was for the priests to wash in."

105. Although he rejects a cosmological interpretation of other aspects of the Temple, de Vaux states: "There is less certainty, however, in saying that the 'Sea' of bronze does not represent the primordial waters." De Vaux acknowledges that other scholars have identified this with the *apsû* of Mesopotamian temples. De Vaux, *Israel*, 328–29. It is also identified as such by F. J. Hollis, "The Sun Cult and the Temple at Jerusalem," in Hooke, ed., *Myth and Ritual*, 106. Johnson states: "It seems clear that the 'bronze sea' which figures so prominently in the furnishings of Solomon's Temple was intended as a replica of this cosmic sea, and, as such, must have been designed to play a prominent part in the ritual of the culture." Johnson, *Sacral Kingship*, 60.

> I was pushed hard so that I was falling,
> but the LORD helped me...
>
> I thank you that you have answered me
> and have become my salvation. (Ps 118:5, 10–11, 13, 21)[106]

Robinson in fact identifies a possible connection between the Bronze Sea and the pre-exilic ritual in the Temple in connection with the Chaos-monster myth, although he does not elaborate this suggestion.[107] Eaton suggests that the spring of Gihon, which features in the enthronement of Solomon (1 Kgs 1:32–40) was the location of the king's "baptism,"[108] and in conjunction with his further comments on Ps 110:3,[109] it may be conjectured that a baptism and anointing (1 Kgs 1:39) at the spring preceded, and prepared the king for, the ritual battle in the temple and his subsequent "victory" and enthronement.

The forces of Chaos are featured at other points in the Psalms, portrayed as Chaos Waters,[110] the primeval sea,[111] the Chaos dragon/Leviathan[112] or Rahab,[113] where they are also identified as Yahweh's enemies. Yahweh's battle with the Chaos Waters/monster (Pss 74:12–14; 89:9–10; 93:3–4; 104:6–7) precedes his act of creation (Pss 74:15–17; 89:11–12; 93:1–2; 104:5, 10–30), the establishment of the earth. This would suggest that the re-enactment in the ritual is understood to "ensure" re-creation, which is Yahweh's continuing gift of fertility, particularly connected with provision of water.[114]

---

106. Eaton rejects a post-exilic dating, and states: "the obvious interpretation that the central individual is the king can therefore be accepted. His fate is the focus of the people's light and salvation, the great cornerstone of the society, the target for the mythically pictured hostile nations. His peril and rescue, his rejection and reinstatement, can be understood as scenes from the ceremonies that dramatised the royal calling." Eaton, *The Psalms*, 404–5.

107. He cites Ps 104:9; Isa 57:20 and Jer 5:22, and states: "It may well be that it was this form of the myth which was represented in the pre-exilic ritual of Jerusalem, and the ceremonial may have included the pouring of water into that 'bronze sea' whose function has been the subject of so many conjectures." T. H. Robinson, "Hebrew Myths," in Hooke, ed., *Myth and Ritual*, 178.

108. Despite Ps 18's heading and its repetition in the context of 2 Sam 22, Eaton rejects the reading of a military victory and suggests instead the king's "baptism" possibly as part of "some great rite" in his installation. Eaton, *The Psalms*, 105.

109. Suggesting this line refers to the king's anointing and baptism. Ibid., 385.

110. Pss 77:16; 89:9.

111. Ps 104:6–9.

112. Pss 74:12–14; 104:26.

113. Ps 89:10.

114. Gray comments: "The theme of God's conflict with the unruly waters resulting in his establishment as King recurs in certain of the Psalms, e.g. xxix, 10;

4. Kingship in the Hebrew Scriptures: The Psalms

The expected outcome of the temple ritual is explored further below. However, it may be helpful to quote Ps 65, for this psalm provides useful information for the topic discussed here. In Ps 65 Yahweh's act of creation, understood as salvation, is coupled with his victory over the Chaos Waters, which in turn is identified with his enemies:

> By awesome deeds you answer us
> With deliverance
> O god of our salvation
> You are the hope of all the ends of the earth
> And of the farthest seas
> By your strength you established the mountains;
> You are girded with might
> You silence the roaring of the seas
> The roaring of their waves
> The tumult of the peoples. (Ps 65:5–7)

As a consequence, Yahweh himself waters the earth and blesses it with fertility:

> You visit the earth and water it.
> You greatly enrich it;
> The river of God is full of water;
> You provide the people with grain,
> For so you have prepared it.
> You water its furrows abundantly
> Setting its ridges,
> Softening it with showers,
> And blessing its growth.
> You crown the year with your bounty
> Your wagon tracks overflow with richness.
> The pastures of the wilderness overflow
> The hills gird themselves with joy,
> The meadows clothe themselves with flocks
> The valleys deck themselves with grain.
> They shout and sing together for joy. (Ps 65:9–13)

A further element introduced in Ps 74 is the destruction of the sanctuary,[115] which may represent the "desolation" (of the earth) before the restoration following the king's enthronement. The temple, in effect, stands for the whole cosmos, a feature we saw in the surrounding

---

xlvi, 2–4; lxxiv, 12–15; lxxxix, 8–18, and in the Prophets, explicitly in Nahum ii, 11 which in our opinion, taken in conjunction with Isaiah lii, 7, conclusively determines the *Sitz im Leben* of the liturgy of God as King in the New Year festival in Israel, as Mowinckel has consistently argued..." Gray, *The Legacy of Canaan*, 33.

115. Ps 74:3–7.

cultures. That is, the forces of Chaos threaten to destroy the cosmos and the plea is made for God to recapitulate his former triumph when he defeated the forces of Chaos and established the earth. Also, just as we saw in the surrounding cultures, we have, in the midst of the enthronement liturgy, the recitation of the story of Yahweh's act of creation:

> Yet my God my King is from of old,
> working salvation in the earth
> You divided the sea by your might;
> You broke the heads of the dragons in the waters.
> You crushed the heads of Leviathan;
> You gave him as food for the creatures of the wilderness.
> You cut openings for springs and torrents;
> You dried up ever-flowing streams.
> Yours is the day, yours also the night;
> You established the luminaries and the sun,
> You have fixed all the bounds of the earth;
> You made summer and winter. (Ps 74:12–17)

As well as the affliction spoken of in terms of being engulfed by water, the king suffers other afflictions. In Ps 69:21 the king says: "they also gave me poison for my food and for my thirst they gave me vinegar to drink." He is also stripped of his royal insignia.[116] In Ps 22 the king says:

> I am poured out like water
> and all my bones are out of joint;
> my heart is like wax
> it is melted within my breast...
>
> For dogs are all around me;
> a company of evildoers encircles me
> they have pierced my hands and feet.[117]
> I can count all my bones.
> They stare and gloat over me;
> They divide my clothes among themselves,
> and for my clothing they cast lots. (Ps 22:14, 16–18)

Despite suggesting a link between this psalm and the Servant Songs of Deutero-Isaiah, Mowinckel does not connect them with the king's enthronement. Eaton, on the other hand, does make this connection.[118] In

---

116. Ps 89:39, 44.
117. This is the translation given in the Septuagint, the RSV, NIV and Eaton's commentary. However, in the NRSV this line is translated: "my hand and feet have shrivelled."
118. Eaton suggests it represents a kind of liturgical drama which may have been enacted "at the year's turning point." Eaton, *The Psalms*, 119.

4. Kingship in the Hebrew Scriptures: The Psalms

Ps 34:20 we learn that, despite his affliction, none of the king's legs were broken, which leads us to identify the king with the Passover lamb of Exod 12:46/Num 9:12.

Having undergone his trial and overcome his enemies, the kingship of Yahweh is celebrated. In Pss 93:1; 96:10; 97:1 and 99:1, each of which is understood to be an enthronement psalm, the phrase *Yahweh malakh* occurs, a phrase which Mowinckel suggests indicates the immediacy of the event, that Yahweh has become king at this point[119] in the same manner as Absalom and Jehu in 2 Sam 15:10 and 2 Kgs 9:13,[120] both of whom are announced with trumpets. Johnson disagrees with this proposition.[121] Eaton, on the other hand, states:

> It is obvious from the context that it is an exciting and dramatic moment. Chaos-foes and evil powers have been defeated, and the Lord has entered as victor, the most high God, the Creator-King.[122]

This is also evident in Ps 45, where Yahweh's enthronement as king is a cause of joy for his people:

> God has gone up with a shout,
> The LORD with the sound of a trumpet
> "Sing praise to God, sing praises!
> Sing praises to our King, sing praises!
> For God is king of all the earth;
> Sing praises with a psalm!" (Ps 47:5–7)

According to the Targum, Ps 81, which also mentions the trumpet, was read during the Feast of Tabernacles. Verse 3 reads:

> Blow the trumpet at the new moon

Psalm 98 provides another example:

> O sing to the LORD a new song,
> For he had done marvellous things
> His right hand and his holy arm
> Have gained him victory.

---

119. Mowinckel, *The Psalms*, 107.
120. Ibid.
121. Johnson, *Sacral Kingship*, 61 n. 1.
122. Eaton also compares this to similar ceremonies in Babylonia and Assyria. Eaton, *The Psalms*, 23. Day, who is also of the opinion that the phrase infers something "new" has happened, particularly in the case of Pss 96 and 98, states: "It is difficult to suppose that the phrase *Yahweh malak* mentioned in connection with the new song in these psalms simply describes an eternal state ('Yahweh is king'), for there would be nothing new in that!" Day, *Psalms*, 79.

> The LORD has made known his victory;
> He has revealed his vindication in
> the sight of the nations...
>
> With trumpets and the sound of the horn
> Make a joyful noise before the King, the LORD... (Ps 98:1–2, 6)

Goldingay comments: "Yahweh's [right] hand and arm are pictured as semi-independent of Yahweh...so that they achieve things on Yahweh's behalf."[123] He also points out that trumpets and horns would be used to announce the arrival of a human king; thus they are also blown before King Yahweh.[124] Traditionally trumpets/horns (*shofarim*) are associated with New Year and with salvation. However, it could be suggested that v. 6 is indicating that at the point of enthronement the king "is" Yahweh, and it is to be noted that in the Septuagint this verse reads "make a joyful noise to the Lord before the King." The parallelism suggests that the king and the Lord, whilst two separate persons, are both present at the same place, adding strength to idea that the king at the enthronement represented or "embodied" the LORD, that is, Yahweh. Further parallels are seen in Ps 89, which deals with Yahweh's choice of David as his Anointed; just as Yahweh is first among the Gods (vv. 6–7), so David is first among the kings of the earth (v. 27); just as Yahweh ruled the sea (v. 9), so David will rule the sea (v. 25); just as Yahweh scattered his enemies (v. 10), so David's enemies will be scattered (vv. 22–23) suggesting that David now stands in Yahweh's place, administering his justice and maintaining (and re-creating) the conditions which Yahweh brought about at creation.

There are a number of places in the Psalms which are suggestive of a processional, similar to that identified in the surrounding cultures: Pss 24:7–10; 68:24–27; 98; 100; 132:8–9[125] (paralleled in 2 Sam 6). Furthermore, David's song of thanksgiving for the bringing up of the ark to the Tabernacle in 1 Chr 16:8–36 is formed for the most part from Pss 96:1–13; 105:1–15; 106:1, 47–48, including individual lines from other psalms. Another processional, Ps 118, includes lines which may have been spoken antiphonally:

---

123. Goldingay, *Psalms*, 3:121. Cf. also Ps 108:6.
124. Ibid., 3:122.
125. Gillingham suggests this is a liturgical composition concerned with bringing the Ark to Zion, with vv. 1–2, 3–5, 6–10 "suggesting some antiphonal responses between the cultic leader and the congregation." Gillingham, "The Messiah in the Psalms," 216–17.

> Open to me the gates of righteousness
> that I may enter through them
> and give thanks to the LORD. (v. 19)

And perhaps, as in other antiphonal psalms, the Priests within would utter the next line on behalf of *Yahweh*:

> This is the gate of the LORD;
> the righteous shall enter through it. (v. 20)

The king would then reply:

> I thank you that you have answered me
> and have become my salvation. (v. 21)

The priests would then respond:

> Blessed is the one who comes in the
> name of the LORD.
> We bless you from the house of the LORD. (v. 26)

That this is a festal procession is further confirmed in v. 27:

> the LORD is God
> and he has given us light
> Bind the festal procession with branches
> Up to the horns of the altar.

This is the final psalm in the Hallel (Pss 113–118), the prayer recited at the Feast of Tabernacles which according to the Mishnah[126] was associated with the torch dance, timed to reach the Eastern gate of the Temple at sunrise, suggesting that this rite was originally connected with the sun. Hollis makes a detailed argument for the significance of the siting of the Temple and its previous connection with the Jerusalemite cult (a sun-worship cult) appropriated by David.[127] The suggestion is that the festivals of Unleavened Bread (Massoth) and Tabernacles (Sukkot) were celebrated precisely at the time of the spring and autumn equinoxes respectively, when the rising sun flooded the Holy of Holies. As we have seen above, it is considered that the autumn equinox (and possibly that of the spring) is the point at which the enthronement of Yahweh took place, again suggesting a connection with the harvests and therefore fertility. Later tradition also connected the arrival of the Messiah with the spring festival of Passover[128] (which came to be conjoined

---

126. *M. Suk.* 5:2–4.
127. Hollis proposes that the Temple and the altar were built to align with the rising sun at the equinoxes. Hollis, "The Sun Cult," 90–91.
128. I consider the festival of Passover in more detail in Chapter 6.

to Massoth).[129] The Messiah was expected to enter Jerusalem from the east, over the Mount of Olives—that is, the very point where the sun rose at the equinoxes. This connection with the sun is further suggested by the wording of Ps 80, which was chosen as one of the particular psalms for Massoth, the festival celebrating the barley harvest. This psalm addresses Yahweh as the one who is "enthroned upon the cherubim" and entreats him to "shine forth," with the repeated refrain "let your face shine that we may be saved." Furthermore, at the Feast of Tabernacles, at which Ps 89 was recited, there came to be a public renunciation of the sun-cult.[130]

As well as the association with sun worship mentioned above, a number of other features of the festival—water libation[131] and the construction of *sukkoth*—are further suggestive of its connections with fertility and "re-creation." Psalms 120–34 were recited during the water libation at the festival on the 8th day, that is, on "the great day" of the festival. These psalms are also known as "Psalms of Ascent" or "Songs of the Steps"[132] and in later Rabbinic tradition these were also associated with life-giving water.[133] Shouts of Hosanna ("Save us")[134] accompanied the procession at Sukkot, at which Ps 118 was recited and *lulavim* waved (*m. Suk.* 3:1–2). The waving of the *lulav* has also been interpreted as a fertility rite.[135] This interpretation rests not just with the upward waving action of the ritual, but with the choice of materials with which the *lulav*

---

129. Morgenstern argues for the significance of Massoth and its connection with the original Canaanite cult festival, which featured the dying and rising vegetation deities. He proposes that King David also observed this festival and that it lay behind Jesus' visits to Gethsemane during this period. Julian Morgenstern, *Some Significant Antecedents of Christianity* (Leiden: Brill, 1966), 30–31.

130. *M. Suk.* 5:4 states: "Our fathers in this place stood with their backs to the Temple of the Lord and they worshipped the sun towards the east but we belong to the Lord and our eyes are directed to the Lord."

131. *M. Suk.* 4:9 states that two bowls were filled, one with wine and one with water; both had holes in (although of differing sizes so that the water and the wine would empty out at the same time).

132. According to Jewish tradition (*m. Suk.* 5:4), there were fifteen steps leading up to the inner court of the temple, corresponding to the fifteen psalms (Pss 120–134).

133. Rabbi Johanan relates the legend of David digging the pits under the Temple when the Deep (Tehom/Chaos Waters) rose and threatened to submerge the world. David eventually threw a sherd with the [ineffable] Name on it and it was subdued. David, however, decided it was better for the Deep to be nearer the surface of the earth to keep it watered and he therefore uttered the fifteen Songs of Ascent to draw the water nearer to the surface. See Raphael Patai, *Man and Temple in Ancient Jewish Myth and Ritual* (Edinburgh: Thomas Nelson, 1947), 56.

134. A theme also found in a number of the psalms of ascent.

135. Oesterley, "Early Hebrew Festival Rituals," 142.

is to be made. The four species are each connected in some way with fertility: the palm branch is linked with the tree of life; myrtle is associated with Astarte, goddess of fertility; the willow, which grows by the water, symbolizes moisture;[136] and the etrog represents the "fruit of goodly trees" (Lev 23:40).

Despite the abundant fertility themes, unlike the New Year festivals of the surrounding cultures there is little evidence in the psalms to suggest a hierogamy.[137] However, one of the instructions for the Feast of Tabernacles is that a *sukkah* should be built and lived in during the course of the festival. Although it has been suggested that the building of booths was common during harvests in this period, nonetheless the *sukkah* has also been identified with the "sacred grove" associated with the hierogamy in the surrounding cultures.[138] The continuing practice of constructing a *chuppah* as part of the wedding service may also be a reflection of this.[139] Later tradition aside, the reason given for the construction of *sukkoth* in Lev 23:36–41 is "so that your generations may know that I made the people of Israel live in booths when I brought them out of the land of Egypt." However, this does not explain why the booths must be made of the specific materials cited, particularly as they are to recall dwelling in the desert, a location where, presumably, these species would not have been available. Nor does it explain why these species are replicated in the *lulav*, each of which, as we saw above, is connected with fertility. And yet, Sukkot's connection with the enthronement of the king/Yahweh and its association with fertility/creation are clearly brought into connection with the Exodus.

We might also note that in Ps 77:15–20 the victory over the waters of Chaos is identified with the parting of the Reed Sea. Psalm 74 has

---

136. Ibid.
137. Though the setting for Ps 45 is a royal wedding, this is generally not interpreted as a hierogamy. In later tradition this psalm came to be interpreted messianically in *Targum Ketuvim* and the *Testament of Judah*. See Jocelyn McWhirter, *The Bridegroom Messiah and the People of God: Marriage in the Fourth Gospel* (Cambridge: Cambridge University Press, 2006), 108–9.
138. Oesterley, "Early Hebrew Festival Rituals," 139–40.
139. The *chuppah* is constructed by the groom and the ceremony begins with the words "Blessed be he that comes in the name of the Lord," that is, the traditional greeting of the coming king. Throughout the ceremony the blessings recited celebrate the kingship of God and his role as creator. The *ketubah* is read out (the covenant between the couple). The connection with the Temple is reinforced in the smashing of a glass, which is understood to commemorate the destruction of the Temple, with the *yihud* which immediately follows the ceremony "ensuring" Israel's continued fertility.

also been interpreted this way, with Egypt identified with the monster Rahab.[140] In Ps 105:44 the Exodus narrative is linked with the promise of "the land," and therefore the outcome of the Exodus is associated with the enthronement rituals that ensure the land's fertility. The Exodus is foundational in the *Heilsgeschichte* of Israel, and its inclusion in the Psalms may therefore merely reflect its significance as the major work of salvation of Israel by Yahweh. Alternatively, it may be proposed that its inclusion here stems from its association with the chaos myth, which, as we have seen, is also a prominent feature of the Psalms.

Rather than merely "being associated" with the chaos myth, I propose that, in fact, the Exodus narrative as a whole is a recapitulation of the myth underlying the enthronement ritual, with Moses in the role of the king. Moses is not only rescued from the water as a baby[141] and brought up in the royal household, but later he (and Israel, Yahweh's "son") is again rescued from the Sea of Reeds (identified, as we have seen, with the forces of Chaos), following which there is a psalm of thanksgiving. Moses then goes up to the mountain of God,[142] with the suggestion of apotheosis,[143] and in later tradition he "becomes king"[144] and takes part in a hierogamy.[145] Moses offers himself as atonement for the people, and mediates between them and God.[146] As a result he is given divine wisdom,[147] the people's destiny is fixed[148] and he builds the tabernacle (the blueprint for the later Temple, which in turn represents the cosmos).[149] The outcome of this role is guaranteed fertility (that is, the

140. See also Isa 30:7.
141. Goldingay notes that the verb *masa* used to describe Moses as one "lifted" out of the water (Exod 2:10) is the same verb used in Ps 18:16 to describe the king being lifted from the waters. Notably, these two occurrences are the only occasions when this verb is used. Goldingay, *The Psalms*, 1:266. Whilst Goldingay draws the conclusion that this is asserting a parallel between David and Moses, I would suggest it is demonstrating a link between the two waters, both understood as the waters of Chaos.
142. As the Ark/king goes up to Zion, the mountain of God, associated with the Temple.
143. Exod 34:29–35.
144. Moses is spoken of as king in later Rabbinic literature, in the mystical tradition and in the traditions of the Samaritans. Like the king, Moses is also referred to as the "faithful shepherd" in the work of the same title *Raya Mehemna*.
145. In the mystical tradition Moses "marries" the *Shekhinah*. See Gershom Scholem, *Major Trends in Jewish Mysticism* (New York: Schocken, 1961), 199.
146. Exod 32:30–32.
147. The Torah is given (Exod 34:29).
148. The covenant is made (Exod 34:10).
149. Exod 25:1–2.

miraculous provision of food and water in the desert)[150] and the entry into the "land flowing with milk and honey."[151] I would also suggest that royal ideology provides the underlying motif of the Joseph narrative which precedes and establishes the conditions for that of the Exodus.[152]

Outcome of the King's Role

At his enthronement the king is understood to be "seated at the right hand side of God" (Ps 110:1) and told that he will reign forever.[153] As a consequence, enemies,[154] both physical and spiritual,[155] are defeated. Once Yahweh is enthroned, he is king, not just of Israel, but of all the earth.[156] In thanksgiving for these new conditions, the people sing a "new song" (Pss 33:3; 40:3; 96:1; 98:1; 144:9; 149:1).

A further consequence of the king/Yahweh's reign is the dispensation of judgment, either directly (Pss 7:8; 67:4; 96:10, 13; 97:1–2) or through the king (Ps 72:1–2). But this judgment and justice (*mišpāṭ*), like *ma'at* in the surrounding cultures, has wider connotations—this is divine justice, incorporating peace, freedom from oppression (Ps 10:18), healing of the blind (Ps 146:8), relief for the poor (Pss 14:6; 74:21; 107:41; 109:31; 132:15; 140:12), orphans and widows (Pss 10:14; 68:5; 146:9) and the setting free of prisoners (Ps 146:7). In fact, these are conditions which very much replicate those expected outcomes of the king's role in the surrounding cultures: "The king is…upholding the divine order and his role is God-given. He is therefore part of the manifestation of God to humanity…"[157] Whilst the blessings are understood to come from Yahweh (Ps 145:5–10), it is the king who is the channel of these blessings to his people:

---

150. Exod 16:15; 17:6.
151. Exod 3:8.
152. Joseph is abandoned by his brothers, "killed," rescued from the pit and raised up into the royal household, as a result of which fertility ensues and Israel is rescued.
153. Ps 89:4, 36–37.
154. Pss 47:3; 68:1; 89:20–22; 110:1.
155. I suggested earlier that the enemies mentioned in the psalms represent not just the physical enemies, that is, the surrounding hostile nations, but also the spiritual enemies of Yahweh, and therefore of Israel, that is, the hostile spiritual forces who rule through the kings of those nations.
156. Pss 22:27–29; 47:2, 7–8; 86:9; 96:10; 100:1.
157. Dell, "The King in the Wisdom Literature," 185.

> Give the king your justice, O God,
> and your righteousness to a king's son...
>
> May he defend the cause of the poor of the people,
> give deliverance to the needy
> and crush the oppressor...
>
> May he be like rain that falls on the mown grass,
> Like showers that water the earth...[158]
>
> For he delivers the needy when they call,
> the poor and those who have no helper.
> He has pity on the weak and the needy
> And saves the lives of the needy...
>
> May there be abundance of grain in the land;
> may it wave on the tops of the mountains;
> May its fruit be like Lebanon;
> and may people blossom in the cities
> like the grass of the field.
> May his name endure for ever,
> his fame continue as long as the sun.
> May all nations be blessed in him;
> may they pronounce him happy. (Ps 72:1, 4, 6, 12–14, 16–17)

Therefore fertility[159] and its prerequisite, rain,[160] are not only a consequence of the king/Yahweh's enthronement (thereby "fixing" the destiny of the people), but the major outcome or blessing which is sought;[161] conversely, lack of rain or dry land is understood as a curse.[162] Whilst the conditions in these psalms are entreated for the present, the superabundant quality of them suggests they also contain an eschatological quality. Rain is also one of the desired results of the Feast of Tabernacles and, as we saw above, fertility forms a major theme of the psalms recited at Sukkoth.

---

158. Knohl comments: "...in the psalms we find one more connection to the reigning ideology of the ancient Near East. The King is the embodiment of the fertility of the land." Knohl, *The Divine Symphony*, 91.
159. Pss 65:11–13; 67:6; 104:10–28; 126:6; 144:12–15.
160. Pss 65:9–10; 68:7–9; 72:6; 84:6; 107:35–36; 147:8.
161. Ps 72:16 reads: "May there be abundance of grain in the land, may it wave on the tops of the mountains; may its fruit be like Lebanon; and may people blossom in the cities like the grass of the field."
162. Ps 68:6: "But the rebellious dwell in a parched land." Ps 107:33–34 reads: "He turns rivers into a desert, springs of waters into thirsty ground, a fruitful land into a salty waste, because of the wickedness of its inhabitants."

Conclusion

In this brief survey of the biblical Psalms it has emerged that there was a developed royal ideology in ancient Israel which at many points resembled that discerned in the texts of the surrounding cultures. Here the king, closely identified with Yahweh, played a central role in an enthronement ceremony that was understood to recapitulate Yahweh's original battle with the forces of Chaos prior to his act of creation and enthronement as king over the earth. The *raison d'être* of this ritual was the establishment of Yahweh's *mišpāṭ* (the right order of the cosmos), salvation (encompassing the defeat of Israel's/Yahweh's enemies), healing of the sick, protection of the vulnerable and in particular "*re*-creation," dependent upon the rains and consequent fertility. This is confirmed by Gray, who also acknowledges the importance of the festivals in this respect:

> We agree with Mowinckel, that the messiah of apocalyptic was unknown in pre-Exilic Israel. This figure, however, was a development of the earlier historical king, the anointed of Yahweh, who represented the people before God and mediated the divine blessing to the community. The installation of such a prince was itself a manifestation and warrant of the triumph of Cosmos over Chaos, and the king's ascendancy was the counterpart of the Kingship of God, a conception which is expressed in the royal psalms 2 and 110. Again the good order of God was sustained by the regular seasonal festivals, where the king played a vital role.[163]

We will now consider the development of the person and role of the Anointed in the books of the Prophets.

---

163. Gray, *The Legacy of Canaan*, 35.

Chapter 5

KINGSHIP IN THE HEBREW SCRIPTURES: THE PROPHETS

Introduction

In the previous chapter I considered the role of the king in the book of Psalms. In order to expand my understanding of the concept of the king in the Hebrew Scriptures (as the source of the Anointed), I will now turn my attention to the Prophets.[1]

A large number of the biblical prophets wrote in the exilic or post-exilic periods—meaning, effectively, in the period post-monarchy. Consequently, an examination of these books reveals that whilst many of the themes of sacral kingship are still visible, these are fragmentary, as we witness a move away from the king as the central character in the drama of salvation. This fragmentation is a natural corollary of the cessation of the New Year enthronement festival (following the demise of the monarchy), coupled with the subsequent elevation of Torah in this period, with the consequence that what was once possible to "achieve" cultically was now able to be "achieved" through adherence to Torah. In Deut 11:13–15 (which came to be an integral part of the Shema), we read:

> If you will only heed his every commandment that I am commanding you today—loving the LORD your God, and serving him with all your heart and with all your soul—then he* will give the rain for your land in its season, the early rain and the later rain, and you will gather in your grain, your wine, and your oil; and he*[2] will give grass in your fields for your livestock, and you will eat your fill.

Thus, the responsibility for fertility is also understood to rest with the individual, not with a central figure in the cult, whether king, high priest or even (though outside the cult) prophet, as we shall observe below.

---

1. I am following the Christian canon of the Hebrew Scriptures when designating books as Prophetic.
2. In the Samaritan, Septuagint and Vulgate versions "he" is used; in the Hebrew "I" is used.

Nonetheless, until the destruction of the Temple in 70 C.E., I would argue that both "methods" existed side by side. The Day of Atonement eventually replaced the pre-exilic New Year festival with its enthronement ritual, as the means by which the nation's sins could be atoned for in an annual festival during the new year period, through the person of the Anointed in the cult.[3] This dual concern is apparent in the writings of the Deuteronomist: "By upholding both the Davidic promise and David as a paradigm of loyal conduct, the Deuteronomist balances two concerns—legitimating the Davidic monarchy and exhorting his audience to observe Yhwh's commands."[4]

In the present chapter, therefore, whilst I will examine the person and role of the king in the Prophets, in order to understand the development of the Anointed, I will also consider the role of the prophet as well as that of the figures of the "Servant" and the "Son of Man,"[5] which I propose represent a development of certain aspects of the king's role. In addition, I will continue to examine these under the heading of "king." Since limitations of space prohibit any lengthy discussion of variant exegeses of the texts selected, I shall highlight only some of the most significant controversies surrounding them (suggesting further reading where appropriate). My aim here is to identify the development of the royal ideology in the prophets as a small but integral part of the overall discussion on the role of the king.

The Person of the King

Despite emanating for the most part from the exilic and post-exilic periods, there are still a large number of references to kings and kingship in the Prophets.[6] Moving back to pre-exilic times,[7] it is notable that

---

3. The transformation of this festival into the post-exilic Day of Atonement will be considered more fully in the following chapter.
4. Knoppers, "David's Relation to Moses," 101.
5. This will be dealt with more fully in the following chapter when the book of Enoch is examined.
6. Here I am conscious of Mason's statement on the difficulty of defining what is post-exilic, not only because of final editing of texts during the post-exilic period, but also because of passages which are now thought to be exilic or post-exilic additions to pre-exilic works. Rex Mason, "The Messiah in the Postexilic Old Testament Literature," in Day, ed., *King and Messiah*, 338–39.
7. Collins discusses this passage and Isa 9:7 and states: "It is now generally accepted that both passages have their primary frame of reference in the Assyrian period, in the late 8th century BCE." Collins and Collins, *King and Messiah as Son of God*, 36.

in First Isaiah[8] we find the announcement of the birth of a future king (Isa 7:14) in terms that are suggestive of divinity: his name is to be Immanuel[9] "God with us" and the statement that he will be born of a virgin ἡ παρθένος[10] (according to the Septuagint) may be further suggestive of this.[11] It has been proposed that Anat, the Canaanite goddess and consort of Baal, was also understood to be Yahweh's consort.[12] Thus the king here announced could be understood as offspring of the Gods. There are a number of propositions for the identity of the Immanuel figure. One proposal is that he is the child of King Ahaz,[13] whilst other suggestions include Hezekiah[14] or "another royal figure that will replace the Davidic dynasty."[15] Isaiah 9:6–7 also describes this future king in

8. Duhm's division of the book into three parts—chs. 1–39, 40–55, 56–66, representing (with some variation) pre-exilic, exilic and post-exilic phases of writing—has had a major influence. Childs, however, discusses more recent interpretations that have identified much greater levels of inter-textuality within Isaiah. Such inter-textuality raises difficulties in dating different sections of the book, leading Childs to conclude: "A growing consensus now suggests that the heart of the entire redactional process lies with Second Isaiah, whose influence reshaped First Isaiah and largely determined the form of Third Isaiah." Brevard S. Childs, *Isaiah* (Louisville, Ky.: Westminster John Knox, 2001), 3.

9. Whether this in fact constitutes a name is discussed by Mowinckel, *He That Cometh*, 18.

10. "The Greek word *parthenos* does not necessarily mean *virgo intacta* any more than the Hebrew עלמה, but it is not the usual translation equivalent. In most cases עלמה is rendered in the LXX by the Greek νεᾶνις, 'young woman.' παρθένος most often corresponds to בתולה 'virgin.' The translation choice, then, is remarkable..." Collins and Collins, *King and Messiah as Son of God*, 59.

11. Brown discusses the translation in the MT and in the LXX and proposes that the choice of *parthenos* by the LXX translator "represented a deliberate preference for understanding the young woman of Isa 7:14 as a virgin." Raymond E. Brown, *The Birth of the Messiah* (New York: Doubleday, 1993), 148. Childs also discusses variant interpretations of the word, and, whilst he does not draw any clear conclusion, does suggest that the usage here with the definite article may denote "a specific maiden either present or known from tradition." He also points out that all other occurrences of *'almah* (with the exception of Prov 30:19) do appear to be virgins. Childs, *Isaiah*, 66.

12. This is thought to be confirmed by a fifth-century B.C.E. Jewish Aramaic papyri from Elephantine in Egypt. The background to this and the dating of its origins are considered by Day, *Yahweh and the Gods*, 144.

13. Collins and Collins, *King and Messiah as Son of God*, 36.

14. The identification of Immanuel with Hezekiah is also the traditional Jewish position. Timothy D. Finlay, *The Birth Report Genre in the Hebrew Bible* (FAT 2/12; Tübingen: Mohr Siebeck, 2005), 178.

15. Ibid.

terms which may suggest divinity: "For a child has been born for us, a son is given to us; authority rests upon his shoulders; and he is named 'Wonderful Counsellor, Mighty God, Everlasting Father, Prince of Peace'."[16] According to Bright, this follows the pattern of a dynastic oracle[17] of which Mic 5:2 provides a further example:

> But you, O Bethlehem of Ephrathah
> who are one of the little clans of Judah
> from you shall come forth for me
> one who is to rule in Israel,
> whose origin is from of old
> from ancient days.

The final lines of this announcement suggest the pre-existence of the king and, like Isa 7:14, came to be understood as an announcement of the Messiah in later Judaism.[18] Isaiah 9:6–7 and 11:1–6 are also understood messianically within *Targum Jonathan*.[19] However, according to Chester, it was as a consequence of the Assyrian crisis and the failure of the monarchy that these prophecies were reinterpreted messianically.[20] A number of features came together during this period—the exile, the reforms of Josiah and the emergence of the Deuteronomists—all of which undermined the legitimacy of the monarchy,[21] with its final demise occurring as a consequence of the Exile. A corollary of this was the attachment of greater significance to the kingship of Yahweh. Discussing Isa 1–39, Williamson states:

---

16. According to Childs, these are royal titles of kingship and the description of his reign makes it absolutely clear that his role is messianic. Childs therefore comments, "The language is not just of a wishful thinking for a better time, but the confession of Israel's belief in a divine ruler." Childs, *Isaiah*, 81. Collins, on the other hand, states, "Despite the problems in the chronology, it is highly probable that the child whose 'birth' is proclaimed in Isaiah 9 is Hezekiah. The proclamation dates from the king's enthronement, if not his actual birth." Collins and Collins, *King and Messiah as Son of God*, 41.

17. *Targum Jonathan*, see Levey, *The Messiah*, 93.

18. Mic 5:2 is quoted in Matt 2:6 as a text announcing the birth of the Messiah and applied to Jesus' birth. It is also associated in *Targum Jonathan* with the Messiah.

19. See Levey, *The Messiah*, 45.

20. "After Isaiah's death, his Immanuel prophecies and programme were reinterpreted by his disciples (within chs. 7–9, and beyond) and, more significantly, these messianic prophecies were preserved for posterity, and the expectations of their fulfilment postponed to the future." Andrew Chester, *Messiah and Exaltation* (Tübingen: Mohr Siebeck, 2007), 201.

21. Collins and Collins, *King and Messiah as Son of God*, 34.

In those parts of the book that are widely agreed to come from the exilic period or later, God's kingship comes strongly to the fore, while conversely, human kingship disappears completely from view, at least so far as Israel is concerned.[22]

This is particularly evident in Ezekiel, with the first chapters introducing the vision of God's throne chariot,[23] imagery that was to become a dominant feature of the spiritual experiences of the Jewish mystics, the traditions of whom, in turn, came to rely heavily on kingship motifs.[24] Furthermore, it is in Ezekiel that Yahweh condemns "the shepherds of Israel" (Ezek 34:1–10) and says "I myself will be the shepherd of my sheep" (Ezek 34:15). Joyce comments: "The theme of God's kingship is particularly important because of the discernible pattern whereby the downgrading of human royal rule in Ezekiel mirrors the upgrading of the royal sway of God."[25] Further references to God's kingship are found in Isa 6:5; 43:15; 44:6; Jer 8:19; 46:18; 48:15; 51:57, and Mal 1:14, and numerous other places throughout the Prophets.

Nonetheless, the Davidic kingship is still envisioned; directly following the criticism of the former kings, and the statement that he himself will be the shepherd, Yahweh states: "I will set up over them one shepherd, my servant David, and he shall feed them; he shall feed them and be their shepherd" (Ezek 34:23). This text suggests that, despite the failure of particular monarchs, the line of David has still retained its significance. The condemnation of the past "shepherds" is also found in Jer 23:1–2 and 50:6, with a corresponding promise that Yahweh will:

---

22. H. G. M. Williamson, "The Messianic Texts in Isaiah 1–39," in Day, ed., *King and Messiah*, 238–39.

23. Kutzko discusses the different hypotheses for the setting of Ezekiel. Ultimately, however, he takes the traditional stance that it emanates from the Babylonian exile, accepting the dating of the opening chapter, traditionally understood to point to Ezekiel having been part of the first deportation in 597 B.C.E.: "although…the book may even have been redacted in the early post-exilic period." John F. Kutzko, *Between Heaven and Earth: Divine Presence and Absence in the Book of Ezekiel* (Biblical and Judaic Studies 7; Winona Lake: Eisenbrauns, 2007), 15–18.

24. A number of the features of the throne, such as the sea of crystal, are not only reproduced in the Jewish mystical tradition, but also in the throne vision of the Christian apocalypse; the description of the throne itself, with its living creatures, also features in the temple vision of Isaiah and is understood to be representative of that which existed in the First Temple. See Margaret Barker, *The Revelation of Jesus Christ* (Edinburgh: T. & T. Clark, 2000), 21.

25. Paul M. Joyce, "King and Messiah in Ezekiel," in Day, ed., *King and Messiah*, 335.

raise up for David a righteous Branch and he shall reign as king and deal wisely and shall execute justice and righteousness in the land. In his days Judah will be saved and Israel will live in safety. And this is the name by which he will be called: "The LORD is our righteousness." (Jer 23:5–6)

The appellation "shepherd" is applied to the king/Yahweh and kingship is spoken of using this metaphor in other sections of the prophets: Isa 56:11; Jer 3:15; 6:3; 10:21; 12:10; 22:22; 23:4; 25:34–36; Ezek 34:2, 7–10; Mic 2:12–13; 5:4; Nah 3:18; Zech 11:7–8.

In Isa 9:2–7 the announcement of the king's birth/enthronement[26] includes the promise that there will be no end to the throne of David and in Jer 30:9 we have the assurance that Israel will serve "David their King" whom Yahweh will raise up for them, an assurance that is confirmed in Ezek 34:23. This is well past the time of David and may therefore suggest more than the provision of a mere successor.[27] Commenting on the polemic against royal leaders in the later chapters of Ezekiel, Joyce states:

> These texts remind one of the so-called "law of the King" of Deuteronomy 17, from much the same period of Israel's history: they share with that material what might be described as a dialectical critique of monarchy, allowing it a place within the divinely ordained polity, but only when radically subordinated to the will of God and to the needs and interests of the community of the people of God.[28]

In the surrounding cultures there was an association with the king and the Tree of Life and here the monarchy is also spoken of in terms which may be reminiscent of that. In Isa 11:1 the future hope of Israel will be a "shoot from the stump of Jesse and a branch out of his roots."[29] The term "branch" also features in Isa 4:2, as well as in Jer 23:5 and Jer 33:14–15, where again it is expressly connected with the Davidic monarchy. In Zech 3:8 the "Branch" is connected not only with the title "servant," but

---

26. Collins comments: "These three texts (Psalms 2, 110, Isaiah 9) have all been plausibly related to enthronement ceremonies in ancient Judah." Collins, *The Scepter and the Star*, 23.

27. Equally, it could be argued that it represents nothing more than the continuation of a particular dynasty.

28. Joyce, "King and Messiah in Ezekiel," 336.

29. Williamson discusses this term and the possibility that this implies the fall of the Davidic monarchy, but suggests that as the writer goes "back beyond David to Jesse," rather than implying the fall of the house of David, he instead suggests that the new ruler will be a "second David." Williamson, "The Messianic Texts in Isaiah 1–39," 263.

also the high priest.[30] The term "Branch" in this passage is also understood as a messianic designation in later Rabbinic Judaism.[31] In Dan 4:12 Nebuchadnezzar, although a foreign king, is spoken of as the tree which sustains all life: "Its foliage was beautiful, its fruit abundant, and it provided food for all. The animals of the field found shade under it, the birds of the air nested in its branches, and from it all living beings were fed." In the allegory of Ezek 17 the king of Judah is the topmost shoot of a cedar tree (Ezek 17:3). In Isa 53:2 it is said of the Servant that "he grew up before him like a young plant, and like a root out of dry ground."

Whilst there are several instances of the term "Most High,"[32] this does not seem to be paralleled with Yahweh in the Prophets (as was the case in the Psalms). Having said this, it is to be noted that in Isa 45:7 the "dual aspect" of God as the giver of both bad and good is attributed to Yahweh, whereas in Lam 3:38 this is attributed to the Most High. However, in Amos 4:11 there *is* a parallelism between Yahweh and *elohim*. Here Yahweh states: "I overthrew some of you as when God overthrew Sodom and Gomorrah." The word used here for God is *elohim*; Yahweh does not say "when *I* overthrew," indicating that two distinct gods or aspects of God are meant here (as I suggested in the previous chapter). This is further confirmed in the original incidence recorded in Gen 19:24, where in fact it is Yahweh who is said to have rained brimstone and fire on Sodom and Gomorrah, whereas in Gen 19:29 it is God (*elohim*)— again suggesting that the names are at times interchangeable, as "aspects" of the one being.

The correlation of Yahweh/the king and the sun also appears in the Prophets, as evidenced in Isa 9:2 and 60:1. In Isa 60:19 it is said that Yahweh will replace the sun. In Ezekiel's description of the new temple

---

30. Mason discusses the various proposals about the figure, in particular whether it refers to Zerubbabel. He states: "From such obscure and varied material it is hard to form a final judgment and impossible to be dogmatic about any conclusions we do reach." Mason, "Messiah in the Postexilic Old Testament Literature," 348. Tollington states: "I suggest that Zechariah adopts the motif צמח to point away from current historical figures towards a future leader for the community… Thus it seems that the motif צמח is used by Zechariah to indicate a future Davidic ruler who will be raised up by Yahweh and on whom a new dynasty will be founded." Janet E. Tollington, *Tradition and Innovation in Haggai and Zechariah 1–8* (Sheffield: Sheffield Academic, 1993), 172. See Wolter H. Rose, *Zemah and Zerubbabel: Messianic Expectations in the Early Postexilic Period* (Sheffield: Sheffield Academic, 2000), for a fuller discussion on the identity of the Branch.

31. *Targum Jonathan*. See Levey, *The Messiah*, 97.

32. Isa 14:14; Lam 3:35; Dan 3:26; 4:17, 34; 5:18; 7:27.

5. Kingship in the Hebrew Scriptures: The Prophets

we are told that the glory of the God of Israel "was coming from the East" (Ezek 43:1–5). It is also the east gate through which the Messiah is expected to enter at Passover, having first come over the Mount of Olives—all of which is further suggestive of sun imagery.[33] In Ezek 44:1–3 we learn that the east gate is to remain shut and only the prince, "because he is a prince, may sit in it to eat food before the LORD." Therefore, although there is still a royal figure in Ezekiel's vision of the new Temple, one who functions in the cult, nonetheless this is a *nasi* ("prince") and not a *melek* ("king"), and it is Yahweh himself who enters the east gate. Further sun imagery applied to Yahweh is found in Hab 3:3–4 and Mal 4:2.

A number of minor themes identified in the surrounding cultures and in the Psalms also appear here. In Isa 28:16, Yahweh says he is laying a "foundation stone," a "cornerstone" in Zion, and in Zech 10:4 Yahweh says the cornerstone will come "out of Israel." However, in Isa 8:14 Yahweh is called a "rock one stumbles over." In Jer 2:13 the people of Israel have forsaken Yahweh, "the spring of living water," and instead dug cisterns for themselves, "broken cisterns that cannot hold water."[34] In Jer 17:13 Yahweh is "the fountain of living waters" and in Jer 17:8 those who trust in Yahweh "shall be like a tree planted by water, sending out its roots by the stream." In Isa 26:19 Yahweh is associated with dew, which is linked with resurrection. In Isa 42:5 Yahweh "gives breath to the people on earth," though in Lam 4:20 it is Yahweh's anointed who is called "the breath of our life." Yahweh's name is also significant; it is holy (Isa 57:15); associated with healing (Mal 4:2) and protection (Zech 13:9). In Isa 44:6 Yahweh is designated "the first and the last." However, a new theme is introduced in the Prophets whereby a forerunner will announce the coming of Yahweh himself (Isa 40:3) to his temple (Mal 3:1), and in Mal 4:5 we are told that this messenger will be Elijah, from which source the later doctrine developed that Elijah would be not the forerunner of Yahweh, but of the Messiah. Again, this is suggestive of a correlation between Yahweh/the Anointed.

---

33. I discussed this more fully in Chapter 4.
34. "Jeremiah depicts God as a fertility god… Embedded in the broken cisterns is the allusion to the Baals which are generally associated with fertility. No rain from the heavens (v. 12), out of relationship with the fountain of living water (v. 13b), and in possession of broken cisterns (v. 13c)—Israel's fate is sealed. The people are doomed to die." Carol J. Dempsey, *Jeremiah: Preacher of Grace, Poet of Truth* (Interfaces Series; Minnesota: Liturgical, 2007), 15.

The connection between the role of the king and the high priest also continues in the Prophets. In Zechariah we encounter both roles of the Anointed—king and high priest—separated into two individuals: Joshua the high priest and Zerubbabel the ruler after the exile. This is a concept which was later developed at Qumran.[35] However, in Zech 6:11 it is Joshua who is given the crown, a detail that would seem to indicate that, as high priest, he had also taken over the king's role.[36]

The title "Son of Man," applied sparingly to the king in the Psalms, is applied to the prophet Ezekiel 87 times. However, in Daniel this term is also applied to a heavenly figure in the apocalyptic vision of Dan 7, whose identity is the source of intense scholarly debate. This vision has interesting parallels with the book of Enoch[37] and with the mythology encountered in the previous chapter. In Dan 7:2–3 four beasts arise out of the great sea which was stirred up by four winds from heaven.

Collins comments:

> ...the imagery of this vision, which sets the sea and its monster over against a "rider of the clouds" and a white-headed "Ancient of Days," has old associations with kingship. The imagery is rooted in ancient Canaanite mythology, where a rebellious deity, Yamm (sea) rises up against Baal, the rider of the clouds and god of fertility and rain, while El, the High God, is a venerable white-headed figure. The royal ideology of pre-exilic Israel derived much of its imagery from this Canaanite mythology... The "one like a son of man" in Daniel takes the place occupied by Baal in the Canaanite myth, and by the Davidic king in the mythology of pre-exilic Israel.[38]

Despite the equation of the Son of Man's role with that of the Davidic king, Collins states that this figure should be identified as the archangel Michael.[39] However, Grabbe suggests that if this were the case "Michael would still be functioning as a representative of the Jewish people." He comments further:

---

35. There is speculation whether in fact at Qumran two separate figures are expected or whether the reference is to just one figure who is both royal and priestly. See Collins, *The Scepter and the Star*, 74–77.

36. According to Laato, there is a distinction here between "the ideal figures of the future (the Branch and the Priest) and the figures of the historical present (Zerubbabel and Joshua)." Antti Laato, *A Star is Rising: The Historical Development of the Old Testament Royal Ideology and the Rise of the Jewish Messianic Expectations* (Atlanta: Scholars Press, 1997), 202.

37. I will consider this in Chapter 6.

38. Collins, *The Scepter and the Star*, 36–37.

39. Ibid., 37.

5. Kingship in the Hebrew Scriptures: The Prophets

It is almost universally agreed among scholars that "one like a son of man" in Daniel 7 represents "the people of the holy ones of the Most High," as Dan. 7:27 states. This may originally have been the community or group responsible for Daniel, the *maskilim* of other parts of the book... In later interpretation, these people are taken to be the Jewish people.[40]

However, according to Walton, it is the Most High who is identified with the Son of Man figure:

In Daniel 7 the kingdom is handed over to the קדישין, identified as the People of the Most High, but it is the Most High who is seen as having possession of the everlasting kingdom and who is obeyed and served (7:27). It is clear from the comparison of the wording of v. 27 with v. 14 that the Most High must be identified with the son of man. The argument has been made that the one like the son of man is most easily identified as Michael. If this is so, the text thus avoids setting up a second divine king succeeding to the head of the pantheon as portrayed in the ancient Near Eastern exemplars. At the same time, if this is so, it is the only place in the OT where the kingdom is ruled by an angelic figure rather than a messianic figure.[41]

In this vision Daniel sees "one like a Son of Man" coming with the clouds of heaven and being presented to the Ancient of Days.[42] Lacocque suggests a correspondence between the latter and El:

...the Danielic "Ancient of Days" plays the role of El in mythology, and the "Son of Man" that of Baal. But the author did not detract from monotheism. Under his pen, the "Ancient of Days" is none less than YHWH, and the "Son of Man" is, according to the context (Daniel 8–12), Michael, the patron angel of Israel... As the heavenly patron of Israel, the "Son of Man" is enthroned as a king and thus occupies the place of the Davidide in the enthronement festival when the Temple was standing.[43]

An alternative suggestion is that the vision may refer to the Day of Atonement ritual:

---

40. Lester L. Grabbe, *Judaic Religion in the Second Temple Period* (London: Routledge, 2000), 282.
41. John Walton, "The Anzu Myth as Relevant Background for Daniel 7?," in *The Book of Daniel: Composition and Reception* (ed. John J Collins, Peter W. Flint and Cameron VanEpps; 2 vols.; Boston: Brill, 2002), 1:82.
42. With respect to Daniel's vision of the "one like a Son of Man" being given dominion, glory and kingship (7:14), Collins comments "it is natural enough, then, to infer that the figure on the clouds is the king of a restored Jewish kingdom." Collins, *The Scepter and the Star*, 36.
43. Lacocque, "Allusions to Creation in Daniel 7," in Collins, Flint and VanEpps, eds., *The Book of Daniel*, 1:122.

> In Daniel's vision, thought to be closely related to the royal rites of Psalm 2, the Man came in clouds (of incense?) before the One on the heavenly throne and "was offered in sacrifice to him" (Dan. 7:13). The word usually rendered "was presented before him" (*qrb*, literally "brought near") is the term used for making a temple offering [and is implied in the Greek of Theodotion at this point]. Given the temple context of this vision, "offered as a sacrifice" is the more likely meaning. The one offered is then enthroned and given power "over all peoples, nations and languages."[44]

If this were the case, as we shall see in Chapter 6, this would furnish a high priest/Son of Man equation. However, as we saw above, Lacocque proposes that the setting is that of an enthronement festival with the Son of Man as king, and that what is depicted is a transfer of power:

> The insistence in this chapter on kingship (the setting of thrones; the exercise of judgment; the granting of universal dominion) definitely leads in that direction. During a crowning ceremony, God confers upon the "Son of Man" kingship, the divine kingship, so that the final judgment upon the beasts be imbued with ultimate authority. In other words, the mythic scene of the assembly of the gods conferring royal authority to Marduk or to Baal, is here replaced, as may be expected by the one God charging his lieutenant to wage divine authority.
>
> In the background is King David (cf. Psalms 2 and 110, texts that show the Davidic king enthroned alongside YHWH).[45]

This would seem to be confirmed, in that Dan 7:14, which states that the Son of Man's dominion is "an everlasting dominion that shall not pass away," and that his kingship is one that "shall never be destroyed," parallels what has earlier been said of the Most High God (Dan 6:26). This indicates a correspondence between the Son of Man figure, the Most High and, as this is also promised of the Davidic monarchy (Ps 89:29), the king/Anointed,[46] suggesting that "Son of Man" may well be a title of the king/Anointed.[47]

The designation of the king as Servant found in the Psalms and the surrounding cultures also continues here (Ezek 34:23). Notably, within the book of Isaiah a separate Servant figure appears, the identity of whom, like the "one like a Son of Man," in Daniel also remains controversial.[48] The problem stems from the fact that the nation, Israel, is at

---

44. Barker, *The Revelation*, 382.
45. Lacocque, "Allusions to Creation in Daniel 7," 126.
46. Ibid., 122.
47. Cf. Collins, *The Scepter and the Star*, 37.
48. The question of the Servant's identity has been an ongoing subject of scholarly debate and the source of numerous volumes. Goldingay discusses the various suggestions and produces an extensive bibliography on the subject. See John

times addressed as Yahweh's servant, whereas in other sections an individual is clearly envisaged. The servant has therefore been variously identified as the people Israel, the prophet of Second Isaiah or an unknown figure.[49] As Blenkinsopp notes:

> In addition to a general reference to the Jewish community as a whole, the term אבד (אבדים) stands both for an individual prophetic figure (in 49–54[55]) and for a specific group cherishing eschatological beliefs and alienated from the official leadership (in 55[56]—66).[50]

Oswalt's suggestion is that,

> Section (41:1–42:9) is introducing the entire servant concept, which involves comforting the fearful servant [Israel] and proclaiming the ministering servant [the individual], after which Chs 42–48 are devoted to developing the first element. When that topic is completed, Chs 49–55 address the ministry of the ideal servant.[51]

However, a closer examination of the figure reveals a number of parallels with the figure of the king. In Isa 42:1 we learn that Yahweh has put his spirit on the Servant, he has been chosen (Isa 41:8; 42:1; 49:7), he has been "called from the womb" (Isa 49:1), hidden away (Isa 49:2)[52] and is to be exalted (Isa 52:13). It is interesting to speculate, therefore, given that Second Isaiah emanates from the period of Exile, when the monarchy had effectively come to an end, whether the Servant is in effect a "substitute" for the king, a precursor of the exalted heavenly figure of the much later Daniel and *1 Enoch*.

When we examine the individual prophets themselves a number of similarities with the king are also evident. In Jer 1:5–10,[53] the prophet's

---

Goldingay, *The Message of Isaiah 40–55: A Literary-theological Commentary* (London: T&T Clark International, 2005), 469–520.

49. See Bernd Janowski and Peter Stuhlmacher, eds., *The Suffering Servant: Isaiah 53 in Jewish and Christian Sources* (trans. Daniel P. Bailey; Grand Rapids: Eerdmans, 2004) for discussions on the identity of the Servant and different interpretations of this passage.

50. Joseph Blenkinsopp, "The Servant and the Servants in Isaiah and the Formation of the Book," in *Writing and Reading the Scroll of Isaiah: Studies of an Interpretive Tradition* (ed. Craig C. Broyles and Craig A. Evans; 2 vols.; Leiden: Brill, 1997), 1:170.

51. John N. Oswalt, *The Book of Isaiah Chapters 40–66* (NICOT; Grand Rapids: Eerdmans, 1998), 108 n. 9.

52. In later Jewish tradition the Messiah was understood to have been hidden away by God (see the *Book of Zerubbabel*).

53. Yahweh says to Jeremiah, "Before I formed you in the womb I knew you and before you were born I consecrated you" (Jer 1:5), and the role for which he has been consecrated is spoken of in terms reminiscent of those of the king: "See, I have

call is couched in terms similar to that of the dynastic oracle in Isa 9:2–7. The prophets are recipients of God's spirit (Ezek 2:1; Dan 5:14) and mediate between the people and God as the king had done (Isa 6:7–9; Jer 1:7; Ezek 2:3).

The Role of the King

As shepherd (king), Yahweh promises to seek out the lost sheep, to gather in those who have been scattered "from the peoples and from the countries," to bind up the crippled, strengthen the weak and to judge "between sheep and sheep and between rams and goats" (Ezek 34:11–17). He will "feed his flock like a shepherd" (Isa 40:11), gather in exiles (Jer 31:10) and fight Israel's enemies (Zech 14:1–3). This is to occur "on the Day of the Lord."

Nonetheless, at a number of places in the Prophets there is still a role for the king to play. As we saw above, in Ezek 34:23 it is said that the Davidic king will feed Yahweh's people and be their shepherd. In Isa 11:4 the Davidic king, the shoot from the stock of Jesse (Isa 11:1), will judge the poor with righteousness and "decide with equity for the meek of the earth." Cyrus, king of Persia, is named as Yahweh's shepherd (Isa 44:28) and his anointed (Isa 45:1)[54] and through him Yahweh says that he will rebuild Jerusalem and lay the foundations for the Temple (Isa 44:28) and make Yahweh's salvation and name universally known (Isa 45:6). The correlation of the king's presence and that of Israel's well-being is made explicit in Hos 3:4–5; Mic 4:9 and Jer 17:25,[55] although in the latter this is brought into conjunction with the keeping of the Sabbath. And yet, it is not just the presence of the king/Anointed that ensures Yahweh's blessings, but also his function in the cult, as highlighted in Haggai. Yahweh has not blessed the people, despite the existence of the Anointed(s), because there is no Temple:

> You have looked for much, and lo, it came to little; and when you brought it home, I blew it away. Why? Says the LORD of hosts. Because my house lies in ruins, while all of you hurry off to your own houses.

---

set you this day over nations and over kingdoms to pluck up and to break down, to destroy and to overthrow, to build and to plant" (Jer 1:10). Jeremiah is also the one whom Yahweh afflicts (Jer 20:7).

54. Even though Cyrus does not "know Yahweh" (Isa 45:5).

55. Jer 17:25: "But if you listen to me, says the LORD, and bring in no burden by the gates of this city on the Sabbath day, but keep the Sabbath day holy and do no work on it, then there shall enter by the gates of this city kings who sit on the throne of David."

5. Kingship in the Hebrew Scriptures: The Prophets

Therefore the heavens above you have withheld the dew and the earth has withheld its produce and I have called for a drought upon the land and the hills, on the grain, the new wine, the oil, on what the soil produces, on human beings and animals and on all their labours. (Hag 1:9–10)

This same thought is expressed in Amos 9:11–15. The Temple is also a significant feature in Ezekiel; although the vision of the *Merkabah* enabled Ezekiel to explain how Yahweh could be present without the Temple, nonetheless the fact that Ezekiel describes the vision of the new Temple suggests that the Temple is still an integral part of Yahweh's presence and so blessings:[56] "and the name of the city from that time on will be: *the LORD is Here*" (Ezek 48:35).[57] Joyce discusses the frequent use of *nasi* ("prince") in Ezekiel, where it appears 33 times, with over half of these occurrences appearing in chs. 40–48. The use of this term is understood to represent a downplaying of the royal role, as its use elsewhere always relates to "authorities in subordination to a greater authority."[58] This is evident in Ezek 34:23–24, where although David is to be "shepherd and servant," in the same verse it is made clear that Yahweh will be their God and David here is called *nasi*, not *melek*. It is interesting to note that the most frequent use of *nasi* occurs in the chapters dealing with Ezekiel's vision of a new Temple, the *nasi there* officiating in the cult, suggesting that despite the earlier condemnation of royal leaders, and despite the use of the term *nasi* instead of *melek*, the place of a royal figure in the cult is still deemed essential, albeit in a diminished role.

Nonetheless, as noted above, in the post-exilic period the king's role as Anointed was taken over by the high priest and the Day of Atonement came to replace the New Year festival and enthronement ritual. In the final chapter of Jeremiah[59] we read of the fall of Jerusalem and the destruction of the temple vessels, amongst which was the Bronze Sea (Jer 52:17).[60] There is no evidence that this feature was reinstated in the

---

56. "The book of Ezekiel structurally revolves around the Jerusalem temple and the divine כָּבוֹד." Kutzko, *Between Heaven and Earth*, 1.

57. "Following the throne vision in chap. 1 and the indictment of Israel in chaps. 6–9, the divine presence of God in the temple mounts its cherubim throne and leaves the Jerusalem temple (11:22–25): from divine presence to divine absence. The book concludes with the return of the *kābôd* to the restored sanctuary (43:1–9): from divine absence to divine presence." Ibid., 2.

58. Joyce, "King and Messiah in Ezekiel," 330.

59. Jeremiah spans the latter part of the seventh and early part of the sixth century B.C.E., thus covering the fall of Jerusalem, the destruction of the temple and the exile to Babylon.

60. I proposed in Chapter 4 that this was used as part of the pre-exilic enthronement ceremony.

Second Temple and its absence may provide a further reason for the "translation" of the pre-exilic New Year festival and enthronement ceremony.

As noted above, it has been proposed that the Day of Atonement forms the backdrop for the passage in Dan 7:9–14, where the Son of Man is presented to the Ancient of Days. Zechariah 3 also features "Day of Atonement" motifs; Joshua the high priest stands before the angel of the LORD, his "filthy garments"[61] are removed and he asks for a clean turban.[62] In Zech 3:6–8 Joshua is given the right of access into the heavenly council and in Zech 3:9 Yahweh says "I will remove the guilt of this land in a single day," which is the expected outcome of the Day of Atonement.[63] As we saw above, Joshua is not only the high priest but also an Anointed and the one on whom the crown is placed. Whether or not he is to be identified as the Branch remains a matter of debate, the other contenders being Zerubbabel or a future messianic figure.[64]

As noted above, in Isaiah a figure emerges who, despite being nominated as Yahweh's servant and despite being chosen and anointed, is not designated king. Nonetheless, the role attributed to the Servant closely resonates with elements of the king's role in the surrounding cultures and in the Psalms, suggesting that this figure may in fact be a substitute for that of the king. This suggestion may be strengthened by the fact that the Servant figure emerges in the exilic and therefore post-monarchic work of Deutero-Isaiah.

Duhm designated four particular sections of Deutero-Isaiah in which the servant features prominently as "Servant Songs."[65] The servant's

---

61. That is, his iniquity, a feature which is also found in the book of Enoch and in the New Testament book of Revelation. I will consider the symbolism of the high priest's clothing and its removal on the Day of Atonement in Chapter 6.

62. The turban is connected with atonement because on it is inscribed the holy Name (Exod 28:36–38).

63. Klein notes the similarity of language between this passage and Lev 16, which deals with the Day of Atonement regulations. George L. Klein, *Zechariah* (NAC; Nashville: B. & H. Publishing, 2008), 60.

64. See Eugene H. Merrill, *Haggai, Zechariah, Malachi: An Exegetical Commentary* (Washington: Biblical Studies, 2003), 126–27.

65. These comprise Isa 42:1–4; 49:1–6; 50:4–9; and 52:13–53:12. Oswalt comments: "Although scholars have widely accepted his general thesis that the songs are separate pieces, they have agreed little about the actual limits of the 'songs' and even less about their date and authorship. Since the 1940s there has been a definite trend to link them more and more closely with chs. 40–55 as a whole, and some have gone so far as to argue that they cannot be separated from their context in any way." Oswalt, *The Book of Isaiah*, 107. (T. N. D. Mettinger, *A Farewell to the Servant Songs: A Critical Examination of an Exegetical Axiom* [Scriptora Minora 13; Lund:

main role in the first song is to bring "justice" to the nations: "He will not grow faint or be crushed until he has established justice in the earth; and the coastlands wait for his teaching" (Isa 42:4). This closely parallels the king's role in Ps 72:1–2[66] and, in fact, Oswalt identifies this function of the servant with kingship.[67] The servant is given as a covenant (Isa 42:6). Furthermore, in the second song the servant is to be a light to the nations so that Yahweh's salvation "may reach to the end of the earth" (Isa 49:6), and he is to gather in the exiles (Isa 49:5–6), a task attributed to the Messiah in later Judaism.[68] In the third song the servant undergoes a trial which closely parallels that of the king in the Babylonian ritual:

> I gave my back to those who struck me,
> and my cheeks to those who pulled out the beard,
> I did not hide my face,
> from insult and spitting. (Isa 50:6)

Following my proposal that the New Year festival "translated" post-Exile into the Day of Atonement, it is interesting to note that the tractate in the Mishnah concerning this day (*m. Yoma* 6:4) makes the following

---

Gleerup, 1983], ranks among the exponents of this thesis.) Nonetheless, Oswalt concludes: "However one may evaluate Duhm's conclusions, one cannot fault his observations: there is an atmospheric change at these four places in the text." Oswalt, *The Book of Isaiah*, 107.

66. It is stated in 2 Kgs 11:12 that at the enthronement of the king (David) he was given a book of testimonies, a book which some scholars suggest was the Book of the Law (with which he had to familiarise himself). Whether or not this is so, it was part of the king's role to guard the righteousness of the people. In many ways, we can recognize the Judges as being precursors of the kings. Notably, when each Judge died, the people turned away from "right religion" that is from the religion of *Yahweh* and began again to worship the Baals and Asherahs and "to do what was right in their own eyes." It would appear, therefore, that part of the Judge's role, later taken over by the king, was to oversee the right practice of the religion. The extension of this right practice of religion from Israel to the nations is also envisaged here in a universalism which is seen at other points in the Prophets.

67. "As a number of commentators have pointed out, the language here is that of presentation, similar to that used of Saul to Samuel (1 Sam. 9:17). It is also the language applied to God's particular appointees, such as Abraham (Gen. 26:24), Moses (Exod. 14:31), and David (2 Sam. 3:18). It is particularly common with reference to the kings. That is significant to this passage because of the common understanding in the ancient Near East that kings were particularly commissioned to establish judicial order (*mišpāṭ*) in their realms, as this Servant is expected to do in the whole world (v. 4)." Oswalt, *The Book of Isaiah*, 109.

68. Cf., for example, Benediction 10 of the Amidah; see *The Authorised Daily Prayer Book of the United Hebrew Congregations of the Commonwealth* (Centenary ed.; Great Britain: Kuperard, 1968), 76–86.

statement about the scapegoat: "And they made a causeway for it because of the Babylonians who used to pull its hair, crying to it 'Bear [our sins] and be gone! Bear [our sins] and be gone!'" I would suggest that the ritual described in the Mishnah represents part of the disintegration of the New Year festival, with the scapegoat suffering the humiliation originally associated with the king at the festival, a humiliation which is also evident in the role of the Servant in the above quotation from Isaiah.

Like the king in the Psalms, the Servant in the fourth song is despised and rejected (Isa 53:3/Ps 22:6–7); innocent himself (Isa 53:9/Ps 26:1–7), he suffers vicariously for the sins of the people; "he was bruised for our iniquities," "with his stripes we are healed" (Isa 53:4–6, 8, 10–12). The suffering is inflicted upon him by Yahweh (Isa 53:4, 10/Ps 38:2) and, although oppressed and afflicted, he remains silent (Isa 53:3–7/Ps 62:5). "By a perversion of justice he was taken away" (Isa 53:8). When he dies his grave is made alongside the wicked and with a rich man (Isa 53:9). It is through his death that atonement is made for the people (Isa 53:5–12).

As in the Psalms, there is a declaration of innocence: "the Lord GOD helps me; who will declare me guilty?" (Isa 50:9/Ps 18:20–21) and a reversal of fortune takes place: "for the Lord God helps me; therefore I have not been confounded" (Isa 50:7/Ps 18:16–19). The servant is to "act wisely";[69] he will be "exalted," "lifted up" (Isa 52:13/Ps 40:2–3).[70] Kings "will shut their mouth" because of him (Isa 52:15), and it is said that he will "startle" many nations (Isa 52:15). An alternative suggestion for the uncertain Hebrew word often translated as "startle" is "sprinkle"—the act that the high priest carried out following his emergence from the Holy of Holies, having offered the blood sacrifice on the Day of Atonement.[71]

Although not identified as a "Servant Song,"[72] Isa 61:1–4 is also understood to be spoken by the servant who is anointed and who has the

---

69. Oswalt discusses the translation of the Hebrew (*śkl*) and states: "It is instructive that this same verb is used of the Davidic Messiah, called the Branch, in Jer 23:5." Oswalt, *The Book of Isaiah*, 378.

70. Oswalt comments: "One must not overlook the significance of these words (*rwm* and *nś*) used four times in combination in this book (and no place else in the OT). In the other three places (6:1; 33:10; 57:15) they describe God's exaltation." Ibid.

71. "A hint of that which is to come may be contained in the word 'startle' (52:15) which if the Heb. is retained should be rendered 'sprinkle' (cf. Lev 4:6, etc.)—a cultic term, which would suggest the servant's mediatorial and atoning role; cf. Isa 53:10." Douglas R. Jones, "Isaiah II and III," in Black, ed., *Peake's Commentary*, 527.

72. "The similarities between [Isa] 42:1–9 and 61:1–3 have long been noted." Oswalt, *The Book of Isaiah*, 109 n. 10.

spirit of the Lord God upon him. His role involves bringing good tidings to the poor, releasing prisoners (or opening the eyes of the blind) and proclaiming "the year of the LORD's favour and the day of vengeance of our God and to comfort those who mourn." Collins discusses various arguments against the interpretation of these passages evincing the notion of a suffering messiah figure, and he notes that even though these passages are understood messianically in the Targum, the suffering element is understood to refer to the temple.[73] Collins therefore concludes:

> The view that Isa 52:13–53:12 was interpreted with reference to a suffering messiah by some Jews before the rise of Christianity is associated above all with Joachim Jeremias. Subsequent scholarship has largely moved away from that position and admits that it is difficult to demonstrate either the notion of a suffering servant in Judaism or the influence of Isaiah 52:53 in the New Testament.[74]

I suggested above that as part of the democratisation of the king's role, the Prophets also take on a central mediatorial role between Yahweh and the people. This is evident in a number of places, such as Jer 20:7–10, where there is a lament similar in style to that of the king in the Psalms, in which the prophet pleads to Yahweh and complains of his humiliation and desertion by his friends before he is rescued by Yahweh (Jer 20:11–13). A similar lament is also found in Jer 11:18–20, again couched in language reminiscent of the king's lament. Notably, the simile of Jer 11:19—"But I was like a gentle lamb led to the slaughter"—is used of the servant in Isaiah (Isa 53:7), a fact that further reinforces the parallel with the king's role. Jeremiah 11:19 continues: "I did not know it was against me they devised schemes saying: 'Let us destroy the tree with its fruit.'" Again, this is suggestive of the tree of life/Anointed identification found in the surrounding cultures and elsewhere in the Prophets, here connected with the suffering of the prophet. This is also a feature of Ezekiel, where the prophet suffers and is humiliated (Ezek 4:4); the affliction is caused by Yahweh.[75]

Importantly, it is in Jonah that the similarities between the prophet's and the king's roles become most explicit. In the Psalms, the nations rise

---

73. Collins dismisses Jeremias' suggestion that this is in reaction to the Christian interpretation of the passage as alluding to a suffering messiah. Collins, *The Scepter and Star*, 123–25. It is interesting that all the other verses in this section of Isaiah are rendered quite literally in the Targum, apart from this one.

74. Ibid., 123.

75. Yahweh says to Ezekiel: "Then lie on your left side and place the punishment of the house of Israel upon it; you shall bear their punishment for the number of the days that you lie there."

against the king: he undergoes a trial inflicted by Yahweh, one which involves him being immersed in water, an action that parallels the dangers associated with the Chaos Waters; he cries out to Yahweh, who rescues him by lifting him up out of the waters. In Jonah, the nations rise against the prophet and he undergoes a trial inflicted by Yahweh, one which involves him being immersed in waters that might also be taken to parallel the Chaos Waters; he cries out to Yahweh, who rescues him by lifting him up out of the waters (Jon 1–2). The parallel with the king's role in the Psalms is particularly evident in Jonah's lament:

> I called to the LORD, out of my distress
> And he answered me;
> Out of the belly of Sheol I cried
> And you heard my voice
> You cast me into the deep,
> Into the heart of the seas
> And the flood surrounded me
> All your waves and your billows passed over me. (Jon 2:2–3)

Before Jonah is sacrificed, lots are cast—the same happened before the sacrifice in Psalms (Ps 22:18) and the sacrifice on the Day of Atonement (Lev 16:7–10). Like the king in the Psalms, Jonah is cast out from Yahweh's presence: "I am driven away from your sight; how shall I look again upon your holy temple?" (Jon 2:4). As in the Psalms, it is Yahweh who has caused the affliction (Jon 2:3), even though in the narrative Jonah offered himself up and it was the sailors who cast him in. As a result of the sacrifice, the Chaos Waters are subdued.[76] Like the king in the Psalms, Jonah calls in distress, pleading to Yahweh for help, and it is Yahweh who lifts him up from the deep (*Tehom*) where he has been for three days:[77] "out of the belly of Sheol I cried" (Jon 2:2), "you brought up my life from the Pit" (Jon 2:6). As a consequence, not only are the sailors saved, but also the Ninevites. Such an action makes clear that Yahweh's salvation is also "for the nations."[78] Finally, like the kings in

---

76. A phenomenon also associated with Yahweh (Ps 89:9–10) and the king (Ps 89:25). Fossum cites an instance from the Talmud (*B. Bat.* 73a) which associates the Name of God with quieting stormy seas. See Jarl E. Fossum, *The Image of the Invisible God: Essays on the Influence of Jewish Mysticism on Early Christology* (Göttingen: Vandenhoeck & Ruprecht, 1995), 128.

77. I noted in Chapter 3 that Marduk's sojourn in the underworld also lasted for three days and that Jesus, according to the New Testament, rose from the grave after three days. In addition, Jesus expressly identified his role with that of Jonah.

78. Although universalism is evident right from the beginning of the Hebrew Scriptures, forming part of Abraham's call (Gen 12:3), and though it features throughout the prophets, Jonah is the first Hebrew Prophet to be sent to a Gentile

5. Kingship in the Hebrew Scriptures: The Prophets

the surrounding cultures, and as was the practice at the Feast of Tabernacles, Jonah builds a *sukkah* (Jon 4:5).

The chaos myth is also evident in other places in the Prophets. In Zechariah the myth is linked to the promise of redemption (Zech 10:8–9) and spoken of in terms of a new Exodus (Zech 10:11): "They shall pass through the sea of distress and the waves of the sea shall be struck down."[79] In Isa 51:9 the Exodus narrative is directly linked not only with the Chaos myth at creation—

> Awake, awake, put on strength, O arm of Yahweh,[80] awake as in days of old the generations of long ago! Was it not you who cut Rahab in pieces, who pierced the dragon? Was it not you who dried up the sea, the waters of the great deep; who made the depths of the sea a way for the redeemed to cross over?

—but also with the promise that Yahweh will once again redeem his people in a new Exodus: "So the ransomed of the LORD shall return, and come to Zion with singing; everlasting joy shall be upon their heads; they shall obtain joy and gladness and sorrow and sighing shall flee away" (Isa 51:11). Mettinger comments: "Here we are confronted with a development that seems to be uniquely Israelite: the historicisation of the battle motif."[81] Mettinger attributes the application of the battle motif (*Chaoskampf*) to the Exodus, to the change in calendar from the autumn reckoning to a spring reckoning,

> and a related move of emphasis in the liturgical year from Tabernacles to Passover. When Passover became the main festival, motifs that were originally connected with the celebrations of the autumnal New Year were naturally transferred to the major festival of the spring.[82]

nation. It is interesting to note, therefore, that the book of Jonah is read today as part of the modern Day of Atonement service because of its universalism, and yet also because of its *Chaoskampf* motifs. This is particularly noteworthy in light of my proposition that the Day of Atonement took over from the pre-exilic enthronement festival.

79. "The author of Zech. 10:11 uses language associated with this event [the Exodus] but in a way that echoes earlier Canaanite mythology. Just as Ba'al struggled with the sea god, Yam, so Yahweh, though his name does not appear here, will attack the sea and defeat it." David Peterson, *Zechariah 9–14 and Malachi* (Louisville, Ky.: Westminster John Knox, 1993), 78.

80. As we saw in Chapter 4, the "arm of Yahweh" (Ps 98:1–2) is again personified and acts as the agent of salvation.

81. Tryggve N. D. Mettinger, "In Search of the Hidden Structure: YHWH as King in Isaiah 40–55," in Broyles and Evans, eds., *Writing and Reading the Scroll of Isaiah*, 1:149.

82. Ibid.

Although concerning foreign kings and not prophets, similar themes are found in Ezek 28:1–10, in which the king of Tyre considers himself a god. There, Yahweh casts him down into the Pit where he will "die the death of the slain in the heart of the seas," and this will be "at the hands of the nations." A very similar idea is found in Isa 14 concerning the king of Babylon, also designated "the Day Star, son of Dawn," who attempts to make himself "like the Most High" but who has "fallen from heaven" and is cast down to *Sheol*/the Pit.[83] In Zech 12:10 it is an anonymous figure who will suffer on "the day of the LORD" and it is the people themselves who have "pierced" him. The mourning for him by the women is likened to the mourning for a fertility deity (Zech 12:11). However, in Zech 13:7–9 we learn that Yahweh's shepherd, "the man who stands next to me," will be afflicted "on that day," leading to the conclusion that the one who is pierced is Yahweh's shepherd, that is, the king/Anointed. Later tradition interpreted the figure of Zech 12:10 as the Messiah, the son of Joseph, who is slain.[84]

In Jeremiah we also find a feature which may be indicative of the democratization of the ideology of the hierogamy found in the surrounding cultures. In Jer 2:2 Israel is Yahweh's bride (Jer 2:2), though she is likened to a bride who has been unfaithful (Jer 3:20). This bride has worshipped other "gods" who are not real gods but idols. She has prostituted herself and the consequence of her betrayal of Yahweh is the withholding of the rain (Jer 3:3; 14:1–9; 23:10), the antithesis of the hierogamy in the enthronement ceremony.[85] Conversely, the giving of water and fertility as a consequence of Israel's *right* relationship with Yahweh is found in Hos 2:8–9. Yahweh says of Israel,

> She did not know that it was I who gave her the grain, the wine and the oil, and who lavished upon her silver and gold which they used for Baal. Therefore I will take back my grain in its time and my wine in its season and I will take away my wool and my flax which were to cover her nakedness.

---

83. In Luke 10:18 Jesus sees Satan fall from heaven. Paradoxically, Jesus is called the "Day Star" in 2 Pet 1:19.

84. In *b. Suk.* 52 the Messiah ben Joseph is killed in battle (the Messiah ben David is expected to return in triumph). This doctrine is thought to have developed following the defeat and death of Bar Kokhba, the messianic pretender who died in battle ca. 132 C.E.

85. "Depraved Israel has become like a whore, even though God planted it as a choice vine from the purest stock. The harlotry image is associated with Baal worship, and the vine image recalls Isaiah 5. Both are related to fertility, with Baal being the god of fertility and Israel's god often assuming that *persona* as creator and LORD of creation." Dempsey, *Jeremiah*, 17.

In the absence of a king,[86] Israel has to "wed herself to Yahweh" and be faithful to him (Hos 2:16–17), the consequences of which are spoken of in terms reminiscent of the creation myth in Gen 1:20–25, thereby suggesting "re-creation." In Amos 3:2 Yahweh says to Israel: "You only have I known of all the families of the earth." This is the same verb used in Genesis when Adam *knew* Eve, suggesting an intimacy between Yahweh and Israel, one that is reminiscent of the hierogamy. In the surrounding cultures the hierogamy between the god/king and goddess/queen produced "sons of god"; in Hos 1:10 it is the Israelite people, as a result of their union with Yahweh, who produce "children of the living God."

Finally, in the Psalms we found evidence of a procession involving the king at the Feast of Tabernacles, a feast which I contended was celebrated as a New Year festival, and which also involved the king's/Yahweh's enthronement. In Isa 62:10 we read:

> Go through, go through the gates, prepare the way for the people; build up, build the highway, clear it of stones, lift up an ensign over the peoples. The LORD has proclaimed to the end of the earth: Say to daughter Zion, "See your salvation comes; his reward is with him."

Further, in Zech 9:9, we read:

> Rejoice greatly, O Daughter Zion! Shout aloud, O daughter Jerusalem! Lo, your king comes to you; triumphant and victorious is he, humble and riding on a donkey, on a colt, the foal of a donkey.

All of this speaks of the entry of a peaceful king into Jerusalem, the most likely setting for which is the New Year festival, possibly the Feast of Tabernacles. The reference to the festival in Zech 14:16–19 would seem to confirm this.

Outcome of the King's Role

Although the mediator of Yahweh's blessing changes through the Prophets and is at times represented directly by Yahweh himself, at others by the "Immanuel" figure, yet others by Cyrus the Persian king as well as the Servant and Son of Man figures, even so, the reinstatement of

---

86. Even though Israel set up kings and princes they were not chosen by Yahweh, and therefore Yahweh did not bless them with fertility. Hos 8:4 records: "They made kings but not through me, they set up princes but without my knowledge." According to Hos 9:2, therefore, the "threshing floor and wine vat shall not feed them and the new wine shall fail them."

the Davidic king is still expected, albeit in a diminished role. Indeed, the desired or projected outcomes of the reign of Yahweh, whether directly or through a Davidic king, form a pattern which can be traced throughout the Prophets with a certain degree of uniformity. Whether these outcomes relate to an annual "Day of the LORD" when Yahweh judges his people and decides their destiny,[87] or whether these relate to a projected time in the future as some of the more supernatural and/or apocalyptic outcomes might suggest, is open to question.[88]

Boda's comments may be pertinent here:

> Those who define "eschatology" in ahistorical, cosmic, cataclysmic, final ways, restrict eschatology to late apocalyptic writings in the Hebrew Bible... However, those who understand eschatology as a future hope that envisions the breaking in of a new era have a greater openness to the presence of this phenomenon in the Old Testament.[89]

I would suggest, therefore, that whilst in many cases specific historical situations are being addressed, nonetheless these are often set within a wider theological framework. That is to say, what Yahweh has done in the past, he is expected to recapitulate in the present, with a hoped-for final consummation in the future. Therefore, whilst there was a direct correlation between the giving of rain, and hence fertility, with the cultic role of the Anointed, the observance of the festivals and later the observance of Torah, nonetheless this annual recurrence of fertility was also understood as a recapitulation of the original act of salvation—that is, creation,—with a final act of "re-creation" also expected ("a new heavens and new earth," Isa 65:17). The intimate connection between salvation/righteousness and rain/showers (and therefore the renewal of creation) bears witness to this fact: "Shower, O heavens, from above and let the skies rain down righteousness; let the earth open, that salvation may spring up, and let it cause righteousness to sprout up also" (Isa 45:8). Therefore, although there are a number of figures in the Prophets who are the mediators of Yahweh's kingdom, the expected outcomes of their mediation all represent variations of a similar theme.

As a consequence of the birth/enthronement of the Immanuel figure—"the shoot from the stock of Jesse"—the promise is made that the Davidic kingdom will last forever (Isa 9:7). He will "judge the poor with righteousness and decide with equity for the meek" (Isa 11:4). He will

---

87. That is at the autumnal New Year festival or the post-exilic Day of Atonement.
88. See, e.g., Isa 13:9–13 and 26:19.
89. Boda, "Figuring the Future," 43.

gather in the exiles (Isa 11:12) and the earth will be "full of the knowledge of the LORD" (Isa 11:9). However, more supernatural conditions are also expected: "The wolf shall live with the lamb; the leopard shall lie down with the kid. The cow and the bear shall graze, their young shall lie down together and the lion shall eat straw like the ox" (Isa 11:6–7). As noted above, whilst some of these promises may be taken to relate to the historical period in which they are set (although projected into the near future), the supernatural quality of some of them would suggest an eschatological expectation, especially when introduced by the formulaic "On that day," as in Zech 14:8, "On that day living waters shall flow out from Jerusalem," and in Zech 14:9, "the LORD will become king over all the earth; on that day the LORD will be one and his name one."

The servant is the one who will announce the "Day of the LORD" (Isa 61:1) and the most significant outcome of his role is atonement (Isa 53:5, 8, 11–12). He will bring justice, not just to Israel but also to "the nations" (Isa 42:3), and he will be a "light to the nations" so that Yahweh's salvation will reach "to the ends of the earth" (Isa 49:6). As a consequence, the poor will be helped and the blind healed/prisoners released (Isa 42:7; 61:1–2). As a result of Cyrus' role, the exiles can return to Jerusalem and the temple can be rebuilt (Isa 44:28).

In Ezekiel the main frame of reference is the kingship of Yahweh, as a result of which the exiles are gathered in (Ezek 34:12), the injured will be healed and the weak strengthened (Ezek 34:16). Yahweh will judge "between sheep and sheep, between rams and goats" (Ezek 34:17). There will be "a covenant of peace" (Ezek 34:25), Israel will be safe from her enemies and Yahweh will bless them with rain and fertility (Ezek 34:26–27), which will result in fecundity (Ezek 34:29). Yahweh promises to be with them (Ezek 34:31). Nonetheless, the Davidic monarchy still has a role to play. Whether or not it is incidental, it is to be noted that the verses promising rain and fertility (Ezek 34:26–29) follow on from the promise of the reinstatement of "David" (Ezek 34:23). In this connection Wright comments:

> There is some mystery as to how we should hold together the idea of God himself being his people's shepherd and the role of a Davidic "prince" in their midst. Already in historical Israel, of course, there was a strong connection between human royalty and divine kingship, as seen in some of the psalms.[90]

---

90. Christopher J. H. Wright, *The Message of Ezekiel: A New Heart and a New Spirit* (Leicester: InterVarsity, 2001), 280.

This connection is also apparent in Zechariah, where the promises of rain and fertility (Zech 10:1) also follow on from the announcement of the king's entry into Jerusalem: "Ask rain from the LORD in the season of the spring rain, from the LORD who makes the storm-clouds, who gives showers of rain to you, the vegetation in the field to everyone" (Zech 9:9). The promise of atonement (Zech 13:1), however, follows on from the announcement of mourning over the one "whom they have pierced" (Zech 12:10–11), a figure who, from the context, as suggested above, would appear to be the king.[91] Therefore, as we saw with Ezekiel, whilst Yahweh himself is king and it is he who promises the blessings, nonetheless this is still in conjunction with the human agency of the king. Notably, in Zech 14:17 Yahweh's gift of rain and fertility are also attendant on the observation of the Feast of Tabernacles—not just by Israel, but by "all the families of the earth." Again, Yahweh promises to be with his people, to return and take up his place in Zion, and again the consequence of this is fertility:

> For there shall be a sowing of peace, the vine shall yield its fruit and the ground shall give its produce and the skies shall give their dew; and I will cause the remnant of this people to possess all these things. (Zech 8:12)

Rain as a gift from Yahweh is also explicit in Jer 14:22, where Jeremiah asks: "Can any idols of the nations bring rain? Or can the heavens give showers? Is it not you, O LORD our God? We set our hope on you for it is you who do all this." In Jer 3:2–3 it is because of the people's sin that the rain has been withheld; in Amos 4:1, 6–9 it is the oppression of the poor and needy; and in Hos 2:1–13 it is Israel's unfaithfulness to Yahweh that causes him to withhold the rain and the harvests. Therefore, it is Israel's own moral actions, rather than cultic worship, which affect Yahweh's giving or withholding of rain.

The giving or withholding of rain and subsequent fertility is therefore a major recurring theme throughout the Prophets. Other recurring expected outcomes include atonement[92] and the universal acknowledgment of Yahweh as God,[93] which is often spoken of in terms of Yahweh

---

91. "The 'one whom they have pierced' has been identified with a range of historical figures from Josiah to Simon Maccabee. More probably, it refers to some incident that is no longer known to us, near the time of composition." Although Collins notes that though some scholars find in this passage "a martyrdom of the eschatological good shepherd or Davidic King," he considers that "There is nothing in the text...to confirm that the one who was pierced was a king." Collins, *The Scepter and the Star*, 33.
92. Isa 43:25; 53:11; Jer 31:34; 33:8; Ezek 36:25; Zech 13:1.
93. Isa 11:9–10; 45:23; 54:5; 56:6–8; Zech 2:11.

5. Kingship in the Hebrew Scriptures: The Prophets 119

ruling as king (Zech 14:9). This kingship involves a kingdom without end,[94] and a king who, for Daniel, is promised to the "one like a Son of Man" (Dan 7:13). There will be peace (Mic 4:3–4; Zech 8:12) with Israel/Yahweh's enemies, both physical and spiritual, destroyed.[95] Yahweh will punish the host of heaven and the kings of the earth (Isa 24:21), and they will be gathered together as prisoners in a pit, where, "after many days," they will be punished (Isa 24:22; 34:2), thus providing a link with the Azazel/watcher myth in the book of Enoch, which forms the background to the scapegoat ritual of the Day of Atonement. We know from later texts (*1 En.* 67; Jude 1:6) that the fallen angels are to be gathered together in a pit, and I would suggest that this further confirms the correspondence between the fallen *elohim* and the kings of the *goyim*, the former ruling through the latter, just as Yahweh rules through the king of Israel. Thus Israel's enemies are not just physical (*goyim*) but spiritual (*elohim*). This is further confirmed in Isa 17:13, where the *goyim* are spoken of directly in terms of the Chaos Waters[96] which are identified elsewhere with Leviathan, who will also be punished "on that day" (Isa 27:1).

Although the earth will be judged by Yahweh, in Jer 23:5–6 this justice will be administered by a king in the line of David. This justice encompasses Yahweh's vengeance and the satisfaction of his wrath, spoken of as his "cup of wrath" (Jer 25:15; Zeph 2:3; 3:8). A further consequence is that those exiled or dispersed from Israel will be gathered in,[97] spoken of as a recapitulation of the Exodus. In Jer 16:16 the metaphor of fishing is used for the in-gathering of the exiles: "I am now sending for many fishermen, says the LORD, and they shall catch them."

A new song will be sung to Yahweh (Isa 42:10),[98] which in turn is connected to the "new thing" that Yahweh is bringing about. This "new thing" is spoken of in supernatural terms connected with water (Isa 43:19). There is to be a redemption of Israel (Isa 44:23), one which will be everlasting (Isa 45:17). There will be a new heaven and a new earth (Isa 65:17; 66:22), as well as a New Jerusalem (Isa 54:11) and a new

---

94. Isa 9:7; Ezek 37:25; Dan 2:44.
95. Zeph 3:19; 14:3.
96. Isa 17:13: "The nations roar like the roaring of many waters, but he will rebuke them, and they will flee away."
97. Isa 11:11; 16:14; 35:8–10; 43:5–6; Mic 4:6–7; Zeph 3:20. Cf. Jer 16:14 and 23:1–7.
98. Mettinger, commenting on the similarity between this section of Isaiah and the YHWH Malak psalms, which also contain the theme of a new song, states: "The idea of the Divine Warrior, who vindicates his kingship in a new victory over the forces of chaos, is something that gives a profound unity to the whole book of Isaiah 40–55." Mettinger, "In Search of the Hidden Structure," 150.

temple (Ezek 40–48). A cornerstone will be laid (Isa 28:16) which, it could be conjectured, is connected to the building of temple. There will also be a new covenant (Jer 31:31) and the servant in Isaiah will be given as a covenant to the people (Isa 42:6; 49:8); this is a covenant of peace (Isa 54:10).

Finally, the outpouring of Yahweh's spirit, once reserved for the few (kings, prophets and other specific individuals),[99] is now promised to all Israel (Isa 44:3; Ezek 36:26–27; Joel 2:28). This may represent a further democratization of the king's role. There will be a resurrection of the dead (Ezek 37:1–10; Isa 26:19), which in Isaiah is carried out by dew (Isa 26:19), and sorrow and death will be eradicated (Isa 25:8; 30:9; 35:10; Hos 13:14). There will be no more weeping (Isa 65:19); the deaf will hear and the blind will see (Isa 29:18–19; 35:5); the lame will walk and the dumb will speak (Isa 35:6; Zeph 3:19).

Conclusion

In the Prophets, then, whilst we witness the same concern with the necessities of life—the giving of rain, the harvest, the protection from enemies, peace, healing and general welfare of Israel; all of which may be encompassed in the term *mišpāṭ*[100]—nonetheless there is a development in the means by which and agent through whom these blessings were to be attained. Whilst a role is still allocated to the king in his cultic function, once the monarchy came to an end this role was then taken over by the high priest on the Day of Atonement.[101] Furthermore, a number of factors came together which gave rise to an element of democratization of the king's role, one whereby the prophets and, to an extent, the people themselves, through keeping Torah, were responsible for obtaining Yahweh's blessings. However, an important development was the emergence

---

99. E.g. Exod 31:1–4.

100. "*Mišpāṭ* is the order of compassionate justice that God has created and upon which the wholeness of the universe depends. In Israel, God revealed *mišpāṭ* in the form of the *tôrāh* (note that in Isa 42:4 *mišpāṭ* and *tôrāh* form a synonymous parallel). Those who repudiate God's *mišpāṭ* introduce evil into the world. God acts through God's servants to nullify the power of evildoers and to restore the harmony that arises where God's *mišpāṭ* is acknowledged and observed. *Mišpāṭ* is not a parochial concept. As seen in formulations of the blessings and curses of the covenant like Deuteronomy 28 and Hosea 4:1–3, the chaos or harmony that results from disobedience or obedience affects the entire universe, inclusive of human history and natural phenomena alike." Hanson, *Isaiah 40–66*, 42–43.

101. Although this did not figure prominently in the prophets, this will be considered in depth in the following chapter.

5. Kingship in the Hebrew Scriptures: The Prophets

of the servant figure in Isaiah, a figure who, I propose, acted as a "substitute" for the figure of the king after the monarchy effectively came to an end with the Exile.[102] The servant's role matched closely that of the king in the enthronement ceremony identified in the surrounding cultures and in the Psalms, as did the expected outcomes of that role—atonement and its consequent blessings. Furthermore, whilst disparate, enthronement themes *were* found throughout the prophets and in particular emerged in the works of Deutero-Isaiah, Zechariah and Jonah, with the kingship of God still forming a major theme throughout the Prophets.

In the following chapter I will consider the role of the Anointed in the non-canonical Jewish literature of the Second Temple period, that is, the literature of the period that spanned from the end of the writing of the Old Testament/Hebrew Scriptures up to the writing of the New Testament.

---

102. Deutero-Isaiah was a prophet of the Exile and, whilst Zerubbabel features in Zechariah, post-exile the role of the king was effectively taken over by the high priest.

Chapter 6

THE ANOINTED IN THE SECOND TEMPLE PERIOD:
THE HIGH PRIEST

Introduction

In this chapter I will be examining the role of the Anointed in the period following the return from Exile. Since the high priest took over the sacral role of the king post-exile, in the first section of this chapter I will be considering the role of the high priest and in particular his role on the Day of Atonement, which I believe came to replace the pre-exilic New Year festival at the autumnal equinox. I will also examine the festival of Passover, which takes place at the vernal equinox and is considered by some also to have been a New Year festival. I will suggest that each of these festivals (including Sukkot, which I considered in Chapter 4) represents elements that were originally connected with the pre-exilic New Year festival at which the kingship of Yahweh was celebrated, which nonetheless may have been celebrated twice yearly, thereby representing the two "new years" corresponding with the two major harvests at the vernal and autumnal equinoxes—the two major crisis points in the year. In order to do this, I will be looking at works included in the Old Testament Apocrypha and Pseudepigrapha, as well as the writings of Philo and Josephus, with brief reference also to the Dead Sea Scrolls. As in the previous chapters, I will consider material from the Mishnah, which, whilst it emanates from a later period (ca. 190 C.E.), nonetheless deals with matters of the Second Temple and is also thought to contain earlier material. I will also consider a number of messianic texts from Qumran in which a Davidic Messiah continues to feature.[1] Primarily, I

---

1. A number of works deal with this topic; cf., for example, Mowinckel, *He That Cometh*; Neusner, Green and Frerichs, *Judaism's and Their Messiahs*; Charlesworth, ed., *The Messiah*; Collins, *The Scepter and the Star*; Collins, *King and Messiah as Son of God*.

6. The High Priest

will be concentrating on how the sacral kingship strand of the concept developed and will therefore limit my examination to those texts which are relevant to my enquiry.[2]

The Person of the High Priest

An important source of information concerning the high priest in this period is that of "P," thought to date from the Exile or soon after.[3] In the post-exilic period, the high priest became *the* Anointed. Although a number of scholars suggest that this also included the taking over of the monarch's role as political head,[4] Rooke has argued against it.[5] What is not disputed, however, is that the high priest took over the position and central role in the cult, one formerly occupied by the king as *the* Anointed.[6] This development involved the taking over of the accoutrements of the king[7] and the hereditary nature of the kingship.[8] The death of the high priest marked the end of an epoch, as had formerly the death of the king (Isa 6:1), and was also the trigger for the release of those who had sought refuge for manslaughter (Num 35:28). At Qumran both a priestly *and* a royal Messiah were expected (1QS 9.11), although there is some debate whether this relates to two persons or two aspects of the one person.[9] However, it could be argued that Melchizedek, the messianic

---

2. See Grabbe, *Judaic Religion*, for a comprehensive chronological survey of texts of this period.
3. Deborah W. Rooke, *Zadok's Heirs: The Role and Development of the High Priesthood in Ancient Israel* (OTM; Oxford: Oxford University Press, 2000), 12.
4. Rooke gives examples of scholars who take this position, ranging from Wellhausen (1885) right up to Redditt a century later. Rooke cites only one example (Morgenstern in 1938) who suggests otherwise. Ibid., 1–5.
5. Ibid. 328. Rooke does acknowledge that there were two periods when the two offices were vested in the one person—the time of the monarchy and the Hasmonean period. Rooke notes, however, that during these periods "this high priesthood was a function of the political leadership role rather than the leadership role being a function of the high-priestly role." Ibid., 329.
6. See de Vaux, *Ancient Israel*, 400; Grabbe, *Judaic Religion*, 32.
7. See de Vaux, *Ancient Israel*, 400. Rooke states: "Three items in particular from the high priest's garments are often regarded as 'royal' elements and made the basis for speculation that the high priest moved into the place of the monarch during the post-exilic period." Rooke, *Zadok's Heirs*, 19.
8. Edersheim, *The Temple*, 94.
9. Collins discusses the evidence in the scrolls and concludes that two messiahs were expected, one royal and one priestly. Collins comments: "This binary messianism had, of course, its biblical precedent in Zechariah's 'two sons of oil,' and indeed

figure of 11Q13, also represents both high priest and king (as did the original figure in Gen 14:18–24).

Although in "P," as may be expected, there is no indication of the divinity of the high priest, nonetheless there is the idea that the high priest has a special status that sets him apart from all others, even the other Aaronic priests, who in turn are of a higher "rank" than the Levitical priests. This was evident in the rite of anointing. The Anointing oil was poured on Aaron (Exod 29:7; Lev 8:12) but only sprinkled on his sons (Exod 29:21; Lev 8:30): "this would allow for all priests to be anointed while at the same time distinguishing one in particular as *the* anointed priest."[10] Other stipulations also suggest an attempt to maintain the high priest's ritual purity and separateness from the profane. He could not marry the widow of a priest,[11] but only "a virgin of his own people" (Lev 21:14), and he could have nothing to with death and its rituals.

There are, however, hints in other texts of this period that the high priest was "in some way" understood to have an angelic/divine nature. One of the texts cited in this respect is that of Hecataeus of Abdera,[12] quoted in Diodorus,[13] who states that when the high priest (*archierea*), who is a messenger (*aggelos*) of God's commands, "expounds the commandments to them," the people fall down to the ground and do reverence to him.[14] According to Fletcher-Louis, the high priest is understood here to somehow embody or represent the creator God, and this is reflected in his role in the cult which we will consider below.[15]

At Qumran, in 11QMelchizedek, Melchizedek is an "exalted figure," a "god-like being" who will atone for the sins of the people; in col. 2.9 Melchizedek's name is substituted for that of "the Lord" "in the year of

---

the model of dual leadership can be traced further back, to the roles of king and High Priest in the pre-exilic community, and even to Moses and Aaron in the Pentateuch." Collins, *The Scepter and the Star*, 77.

10. Rooke, *Zadok's Heirs*, 20.

11. Ibid., 25.

12. Hayward discusses the difficulty in dating the text. C. T. R. Hayward, *The Jewish Temple: A Non-Biblical Sourcebook* (London: Routledge, 1996), 18–20; however, in Grabbe's view the text belongs in the Early Greek period, ca. 300 B.C.E., which is the period attributed to the text by Josephus (*C. Ap.* 1.183). Grabbe, *Judaic Religion*, 37.

13. Diodorus Siculus, *Biblotheca Historica* XL, 3.5, which Grabbe confirms as "almost universally accepted as authentic." Ibid., 37.

14. Ibid., 38. Cf. also Crispin Fletcher-Louis, *All the Glory of Adam: Liturgical Anthropology in the Dead Sea Scrolls* (Leiden: Brill, 2002), 69.

15. Fletcher-Louis, *All the Glory*, 71.

the Lord's favour" (Isa 61:2).[16] Psalm 82:1 is applied to Melchizedek: "Elohim [God] takes his stand in the assembly of El, in the midst of Elohim [gods] he judges." The text is fragmentary but has been restored to read "our god is Melchizedek." Collins comments "this may seem to be a very bold restoration, but in fact Melchizedek had already been identified with the Elohim, or god, of Ps 82. In the view of this interpreter, the Most High god is El. Elohim is a lesser deity, an angel, if you prefer."[17] Melchizedek has also been associated with the figure who claims to be enthroned in heaven in 4Q491 (the "Self-Exaltation Hymn"), who, it has been suggested, may in fact be the eschatological high priest.[18] Although in the text as we have it Melchizedek is not expressly entitled "priest," the association with the figure in Gen 14:8 would suggest this. Furthermore, as Collins has stated, the fact that "his activity culminates on the Day of Atonement" is also suggestive of this.[19]

Aristeas[20] speaks in awe of the "other-worldliness" of the high priest on his return from the Holy of Holies: "The overall appearance of these things created awe and confusion so as to make one think that he has come close to another man from outside the world,"[21] which again suggests a change in status in the high priest as he functions in the cult. Hayward suggests that the high priest "may even have the character of an angel."[22] Furthermore, it is proposed that within the cult the high priest in his "garments of glory" represented the Glory of God.[23] This was also a feature of later tradition: "The rabbis record the tradition that Aaron's garments are those of God himself" (*Gen. Rab.* 38:8; cf. *y. Yoma* 7:3, 44b; *Lev. Rab.* 21:11).[24]

Philo[25] also suggests that the high priest is bordering on divinity when he enters the Holy of Holies:

---

16. James C. VanderKam and Peter W. Flint, eds., *The Meaning of the Dead Sea Scrolls: Their Significance for Understanding the Bible, Judaism, Jesus and Christianity* (London: T&T Clark International, 2002), 225.

17. Collins and Collins, *King and Messiah as Son of God*, 80. John Collins discusses the various challenges to this reading on pp. 80–82.

18. Ibid., 85.

19. Ibid., 83.

20. The date of this work remains a matter of debate, though the majority view places it in the second century B.C.E.; see Hayward, *The Jewish Temple*, 26–27.

21. *Letter of Aristeas* 99, cited ibid., 30.

22. Ibid., 36.

23. Fletcher-Louis, *All the Glory*, 67.

24. Ibid., 363.

25. A Hellenistic Jewish writer ca. 20 BCE–50 CE, most of whose writings are commentaries on the Pentateuch. See Grabbe, *Judaic Religion*, 90.

if one is to speak the real truth, he is a sort of nature bordering on God, inferior indeed to him, but superior to man; "for when," the scriptures say, "the high priest goes into the Holy of Holies he will not be a man." What then will he be if he is not a man? Will he be God?... [B]ut he touches both these extremities...[26]

In addition, Philo also speaks of the high priest in terms of the concept of corporate personality: "...but when he is looked at by himself he becomes numerous; he is a tribunal, an entire council, the whole people, a complete multitude, the entire race of mankind."[27] This is further confirmed in those passages that state that the high priest not only represents the world symbolically through the garments and accoutrements that he wears,[28] but that he becomes "a little world himself."[29] The breastplate, which the high priest wore, was also significant; on it were engraved twelve precious stones representing the twelve tribes of Israel—thus, in effect, the high priest represented the people of Israel to God. Thus, just like the king, the high priest represents God to the people, but also the people to God. Effectively, then, the high priest replaced the king as mediator between the nation and God. According to both Philo[30] and Josephus,[31] the twelve stones also represented the zodiac; the two stones on the high priest's shoulders represented the sun and the moon, according to Josephus,[32] and the two hemispheres, according to Philo.[33]

In Sir 50:5–7 Simon the high priest[34] is spoken of in exalted terms, ones which also associate him with sun imagery:

26. Philo, *On Dreams* 2.18.188.
27. Philo, *On Dreams* 2.18.188.
28. Philo, *The Special Laws* 1.16.84, states: "He is also commanded to wear another robe also, having very beautiful embroidery and ornament upon it, so that it may seem to be a copy and representation of the world." See also Philo, *On the Life of Moses* 2.26.133.
29. Philo, *On the Life of Moses* 2.26.134. Alternatively, it could be suggested that he represents not humanity per se, but the whole cosmos, a concept which I believe lies behind the "seamless robe" of both Aaron and Jesus. It is said that Jesus was "slain from the foundation of the world" (Rev 13:8). As it is also said that the world is created through him (John 1:3), this resonates very closely with what is said of Marduk splitting Tiamat's body and using it to create the world. This is further strengthened when the materials used to make up the high priest's robe are considered, which I discuss below.
30. Philo, *The Special Laws* 1.17.97.
31. Josephus, *Ant.* 3.7.7 §§185, 186.
32. Josephus, *Ant.* 3.7.7 §§185, 186.
33. Philo, *The Special Laws* 1.16.86.
34. The high priest Simon II belonged to the House of Zadok. Hayward comments "The probability is overwhelming that the House of Zadok through the

> How glorious he was when the people gathered round him,
> As he came out of the inner sanctuary (or the house of the veil).
> Like the morning star among the clouds,
> Like the moon when it is full;
> Like the sun shining upon the temple of the Most High,
> And like the rainbow gleaming in glorious clouds.[35]

Sirach 50:8–10 makes use of terms which suggest an association with fertility:

> Like the roses in the days of the first fruits,
> Like lilies by a spring of water,
> Like a green shoot on Lebanon on a summer day;
> Like fire and incense in the censer,
> Like a vessel of hammered gold
> Adorned with all kinds of precious stones;
> Like an olive tree putting forth its fruit,
> And like a cypress towering in the clouds.[36]

According to Fletcher-Louis, in the Hebrew version of Sir 50:5–7 the high priest emerging from the inner sanctuary would evoke for the Jewish reader not just the high priest, but also God emerging as divine warrior to serve his people.[37]

In the *Testament of Levi*[38] we find a passage about the Anointed and his priestly role that uses language which creates similar allusions:

> Then shall the Lord raise up a new priest…
> And he shall execute a righteous judgment upon the earth
> for a multitude of days.

---

centuries evolved a particular understanding of its part in God's dispensation for Israel; of a sense of its own eternal worth as the chosen high priestly dynasty and of the profound significance of the Temple Service for which it was ultimately responsible before God." Hayward, *The Jewish Temple*, 39.

35. According to Hayward there is almost universal agreement on the dating of Sirach to the first quarter of the second century B.C.E. The translation used here is that of the NRSV.

36. "There is no doubt that Sirach viewed the High Priest Simon as the main mediator of God's blessing in his own time (50:1–21)." Collins, *The Scepter and the Star*, 34.

37. Fletcher-Louis, *All the Glory*, 83.

38. This forms part of the work known as the *Testaments of the Twelve Patriarchs*, a work which Horbury dates to the second century B.C.E. Horbury, "Messianism in the Old Testament Apocrypha," in Day ed., *King and Messiah*, 408. See Grabbe, *Judaic Religion*, 101–3, for a discussion of dating and provenance, as well as a short bibliography.

> And his star shall arise in heaven as of a king,
> Lighting up the light of knowledge as the sun the day,
> And he shall be magnified in the world.
> He shall shine forth as the sun on the earth,
> And shall remove all darkness from under heaven,
> And there shall be peace in all the earth...[39]

Despite the interest in a high priestly redeemer figure, other texts are still concerned with a Davidic redeemer. Importantly, these figures are still spoken of in exalted terms. In 4Q246, the Messiah is directly designated "Son of God" and "Son of the Most High" (col. 2.1).[40] The "Son of God" figure appears in column 2 of this Aramaic fragment, which states:

> "Son of god" he shall be called, and they will name him "Son of the Most High"... "he will be great" (v. 7), "His [or its] kingdom is an everlasting kingdom and all his [or its] ways truth. He [or it] will judge the earth with truth and will make peace. The sword will cease from the earth and all cities will pay him [or it] homage. The great God will be his [or its] strength." (vv. 7–8)[41]

According to Brooke, this text was written at a time when

> several compositions are implying an increased interest in the expectation of an eschatological king, specifically a Davidic figure (4Q174; 4Q252; 4Q285). Thus it seems to me likely that the scribe who copied the actual manuscript would have thought of the Son of God figure as referring to a Jewish king.[42]

However, as Brooke points out, the majority "of the surviving column 2 can be interpreted as giving pride of place to the people of God and it is God himself who wages war for them."[43] John Collins draws on analogies made between this text and Dan 7 as a means of resolving this problem:

---

39. *T. Lev.* 13:2–50, cited in Mowinckel, *He That Cometh*, 288.
40. VanderKam, *The Meaning of the Dead Sea Scrolls*, 336.
41. Collins comments on the correspondence between this passage and the infancy narrative in Luke and concludes: "It is difficult to avoid the conclusion that Luke is dependent in some way, whether directly or indirectly, on this long lost text from Qumran." Collins, *The Scepter and the Star*, 155. VanderKam also comments: "Here one cannot simply dismiss the parallel as one title that happens to surface in two texts; on the contrary, the entire contexts have striking similarities." VanderKam, *The Dead Sea Scrolls Today*, 179.
42. George J. Brooke, "Kingship and Messianism in the Dead Sea Scrolls," in Day, ed., *King and Messiah*, 447.
43. Ibid.

6. The High Priest

> In Daniel 7, the eternal kingdom is explicitly given both to the "one like a son of man" and to the people of the holy ones. In the same way, the tensions in 4Q246 can be resolved if the "son of God" is understood as a messianic king, so that the kingdom is given simultaneously both to him and to the people.[44]

John Collins therefore concludes that 4Q246 refers to a Jewish messiah and that the figure called "son of God" might be understood as an interpretation of Daniel's "one like a Son of Man."[45] He comments: "If this were so, this would be the earliest instance of the messianic interpretation of the 'one like a son of man,' which is attested in the *Similitudes of Enoch*, well established in *4 Ezra*, and dominant in later Judaism."[46]

The hope for a Davidic king is also evident in the florilegium 4Q174, which states:

> *I will raise up your seed after you* (2 Sam 7:12). *I will establish the throne of his kingdom [for ever]* (2 Sam 7:13). *[I will be] his father and he shall be my* son (2 Sam 7:14). He is the Branch of David who shall arise with the Interpreter of the Law [to rule] in Zion [at the end] of time.[47]

Although *2 Baruch* is dated slightly later than the period under discussion (ca. 100 C.E.), the messiah here is also a heavenly figure, though, as Grabbe notes, he is "hardly divine" (cf. *2 Bar.* 29–30; 39:7–40:3; 70:9; 72–74).[48]

Encountered throughout the previous chapters is the idea that other deities mentioned are in fact aspects of the one supreme deity, aspects which eventually came to be seen as separate personalities. I propose that this is also evident in the rationale behind the two goats in the ritual of the Day of Atonement (considered below). It has been proposed that the goat for Yahweh was sacrificed as a substitute for the high priest, suggesting therefore that it represents the high priest, who in turn represents Yahweh.[49] The other goat, for Azazel, would therefore represent Azazel the chief of the *elohim*, the fallen angel also known as Semihaza and understood as Yahweh's adversary. The fact that the goats had to be

---

44. Collins and Collins, *King and Messiah as Son of God*, 71.
45. Ibid.
46. Ibid., 72.
47. Geza Vermes, *The Complete Dead Sea Scrolls in English* (London: Penguin, 1997). 494.
48. Grabbe, *Judaic Religion*, 119.
49. The name on the high priest's turban is understood to be the *Tetragrammaton*, implying that the high priest in effect represents Yahweh. See Margaret Barker, *The Risen Lord* (Edinburgh: T. & T. Clark, 1996), 62–63.

identical for the ritual suggests some correspondence between what they represented, leading to the possibility that Azazel and Yahweh were understood to represent the dual aspect of the Most High.[50] I mentioned in Chapter 4 that in the Rabbinic tradition *elohim* and Yahweh were understood to represent the two major aspects of the Most High (his justice and his mercy, respectively).[51] In the mystical tradition, when God's mercy is distanced from his justice, the latter becomes evil.

The Role of the High Priest

In order to understand the role of the high priest, the Anointed in the post-exilic period, it is necessary first to understand the significance of the temple. It becomes clear in the writings of this period that the temple is understood not just to be important to Israel, but that it has a cosmic significance which not only links it with Eden and the original creation of the world, but also supports the world's continued existence. This rationale is particularly evident with regard to the major festivals, and in particular the festival of Sukkoth, which is associated with rain, dew and fertility. However, glimpses of this viewpoint are also evident in the biblical material itself, where the temple plays a major part in Israel's well-being. At the dedication of the temple following the installation of the Ark (1 Kgs 8), Solomon blesses the people and then relays the benefits of the temple, namely, atonement and fertility.[52] Again, this is associated with the Feast of Tabernacles: "And all the men of Israel assembled to King Solomon at the feast in the month Ethanim, which is the seventh month" (1 Kgs 8:2). In *Liber Antiquitatum Biblicarum*,[53] the feast of Tabernacles (Sukkot) is associated with the original covenant with Noah and hence fertility, the cycle of the seasons and in particular the gift of rain and dew is bound up with this festival (*L.A.B.* 13:7).

The temple itself was understood to be a "copy" of the original tabernacle, the pattern and furnishings for which were given directly by God to Moses (Exod 25:9, 40: 26:30). In turn, the temple was understood to be a copy of the universe:

---

50. Barker discusses this in detail in her *Risen Lord*, 75–76.
51. The blood of the "Yahweh goat" is sprinkled on the *kapporet*, often translated "mercy seat."
52. As a result of prayers in the temple, sins will be forgiven, and all the rain will be given; also, famine, pestilence, blight, mildew, locust and caterpillars will be removed, and enemies will be dealt with and sicknesses healed.
53. Dated mid- to late first century C.E.

When Moses received the instructions to build the tabernacle, it was to be done, like the original creation which he had seen,[54] in six days. On the seventh day the people were to rest because in six days the Lord made heaven and earth (Exod 3:17). A short account of building the tabernacle appears in Exod 40:17–32 and if we compare this with the account of the creation in Genesis 1, bearing in mind that both passages probably passed through the hands of editors and reformers, remarkable similarities are still apparent.[55]

Fletcher-Louis comments: "The Temple was far more than the point at which heaven and earth met. Rather, it was thought to correspond to, represent, or, in some sense, to *be*, 'heaven and earth' in its totality."[56] This correspondence is also evident in the discussions of the future temple found in the Temple scroll 11QT 29.9, where the building of the new temple is equated with the renewal of heaven and earth at the end of days.[57]

The personnel of the temple, and in particular the high priest, also participate in this cosmic significance by carrying out the daily rituals and the annual cycle of festivals, religious acts intimately bound up with the agricultural cycle. An inter-textuality is identified between Sir 50, Exod 25–31, Exod 35–44 and Gen 1, suggesting that in the cult the high priest "plays the lead role in the re-enactment of creation," which is the cult's "defining dramatic performance."[58] Therefore, the work that Simon carries out in the temple is analogous to that assigned to Moses by God for the tabernacle, which in turn replicates God's own work in creation.[59] This suggests that the high priest represents Yahweh, and in Ben Sira the high priest Simon is, by allusion, identified with the Glory of the LORD in Ezekiel's vision.[60] According to Hayward, "It is entirely likely therefore that the high priest's completion of the order, *kosmos* of the

---

54. "[T]he *Book of Jubilees*…says that Moses on Sinai was told to record the six days of the creation, including the details of Day One which are omitted from the account in Genesis (*Jub.* 2.1–3)." Barker, *Revelation*, 18.
55. Ibid.
56. Fletcher-Louis, *All the Glory*, 62.
57. Wachholder, cited in ibid., 64.
58. Ibid., 81.
59. "It is possible that Moses had seen a vision of a heavenly temple which he had to copy on earth, but most indications are that he saw a vision of the whole creation, and this is what the tabernacle and temple were to replicate." Barker, *Revelation*, 17.
60. "Simon is 'like the rainbow which appears in the cloud (50:7b)'… This is an explicit reference to the 'likeness of the Glory of the LORD' in Ezekiel 1:28, who is also 'Like the bow in a cloud on a rainy day'." Fletcher-Louis, *All the Glory*, 72–73.

daily sacrifice, referred to in 50:19, belongs to the same sort of continuum as God's ordering of the works of creation."[61]

This cosmological understanding of the temple is also found in the writings of Philo and Josephus:

> Both Josephus and Philo explore at some length the cosmic symbolism of the Tabernacle/Temple and its paraphernalia (Philo *Mos.* 2:71–145; Josephus, *Ant.* 3:123, 179–187). Both agree that the woven work of the tabernacle and the temple veil are made from four materials symbolizing the four elements—earth, water, air and fire (*War* 5:212–3; *Ant.* 3:138–4; *Quaestiones in Exodum* 2:85, cf. *Mos.* 2:88). Both regard the seven lamps as symbolic of the planets (*Mos.* 2:103; *B.J.* [i.e. *War*] 5:146, 217). Both consider the High Priest's garments to be yet another extended cosmic metaphor (*Mos.* 2:117–126, 133–135, 143; *Ant.* 3:180, 183–187).[62]

It is therefore clear that within the temple-as-microcosm theology, the high priest's role was to maintain the stability of the cosmos, just as it had been the role of *the* Anointed, the king, in the pre-exilic period. Through his presence and actions in the cult, and through the cycle of festivals, the blessings of Yahweh, and in particular those of rain and fertility, were made available not only to Israel, but to the nations:

> In its earliest history this temple mythology has to be understood in the context of ancient Near Eastern mythology related to kingship, the divine conflict with the forces of chaos and the foundation of city and temple… Despite scholarly neglect we do find that this mythology is everywhere present in the post-biblical literature.[63]

The major cultic role that seems to have been exclusive to the high priest was his officiating at the Day of Atonement rituals. Although there is no scholarly consensus concerning the inception of the Day of Atonement,[64] there is evidence to suggest that it was a post-exilic festival.[65]

---

61. Hayward, *The Jewish Temple*, 80.
62. Fletcher-Louis, *All the Glory*, 65.
63. Ibid., 64.
64. It appears in the Torah without any etiological explanation. Miller comments: "The fact that this ritual is not mentioned in any clearly preexilic texts or referred to in major postexilic texts that tell of other cultic matters, such as Ezekiel, Ezra, and Nehemiah, has led most scholars to assume that the Day of Atonement ritual was instituted in the postexilic period." Patrick D. Miller, *The Religion of Ancient Israel* (LAI; Louisville, Ky.: Westminster John Knox, 2000), 115.
65. G. Buchanan Gray, *Sacrifice in the Old Testament* (Oxford: Clarendon, 1925), 306. Kraus disagrees. Although he recognizes the differing strata and traditions in Lev 16, he nonetheless concludes that it was part of the autumn festival "from the earliest period and points back even as far as the desert period." Hans

6. *The High Priest*

Whether or not this is the case, its prominence in the post-exilic community[66] would suggest that either it had become more significant during this period or that it was a product of this period. Eichrodt, who posits a pre-exilic dating, suggests that it formed part of the pre-exilic New Year festival which incorporated a celebration of the king's enthronement. Eichrodt therefore suggests that in the wake of the demise of the monarchy the importance of the Day of Atonement grew. Without a king to play the central part in the ceremony (in particular the enthronement), and without the bronze laver,[67] the enthronement ceremony could not have taken place.[68] Rooke comments:

> The present ceremony may well be connected with the New Year rites, given that it comes within a few days of the feast of Tabernacles and that P marks the first of the seventh month as a feast day (Lev. 23: 24–5) and the tenth of the seventh month—Yom Kippur itself—as the day when the Jubilee year is to be declared (Lev. 25: 9).[69]

She concludes: "as far as the high priest is concerned the rites once again demonstrate his close connection with the Tabernacle... and his representative function on behalf of the people as a whole."[70] Rooke understands this role as comparable to that of the king:

> This very close connection between priest and people is reminiscent of that between monarch and people, in that the pre-exilic nation's fortunes rose and fell with the integrity or otherwise of their kings, and the king was an embodiment of the people he ruled. To that extent, therefore, the anointed priest can be said to be functioning here in a royal role.[71]

Again, this would suggest that the Day of Atonement was post-exilic, or that its prominence grew after the Exile at a time when the nation's fate now rested on the execution of this festival. It could equally be

---

Joachim Kraus, *Worship in Israel: A Cultic History of the Old Testament* (trans. Geoffrey Buswell; Oxford: Blackwell, 1966), 69.

66. Falk comments: "the lack of reference to the Day of Atonement in pre-exilic material and its increasing importance throughout the Second Temple period suggest that it either originated in the post-exilic period or had not previously been calendrically fixed." Daniel K. Falk, *Daily, Sabbath, and Festival Prayers in the Dead Sea Scrolls* (Leiden: Brill, 1998), 72.

67. That is, if the ritual I have suggested in Chapter 4 did indeed take place.

68. See E. O. James, "Initiatory Rituals," in Hooke, ed., *Myth and Ritual*, 160, and Grabbe, *Judaic Religion*, 317.

69. Rooke, *Zadok's Heirs*, 24.

70. Ibid.

71. Rooke does, however, qualify that this is a sacral, not a political role. Ibid., 23.

argued that the Day of Atonement retreated into the background during the period of the monarchy only to re-emerge following its demise. Certainly, the instructions to sprinkle the blood of the goat on the *kapporet* would seem to suggest the presence of the Ark, which was absent from the Second Temple.

According to the instructions in Exod 28:30, Aaron, as high priest, is to bear the sins of Israel and to bear the name of Yahweh (Exod 28:36). Via the priestly blessing, he "puts" the name of *Yahweh* onto the people as a means of protection.[72] In Exod 28:31 we learn that Aaron's robe was to be seamless and made up of four colours (Exod 28:5), colours which, according to later tradition, represented the four elements of the material world.[73] In contrast, according to Lev 16:4, when he entered the Holy of Holies, the high priest is to wear only linen garments which are "holy garments" after he has bathed. Again, in later tradition the "linen robe, made of the finest flax,"[74] is thought to be suggestive of the heavenly world. According to Josephus,[75] in the cosmology of the temple there were three areas; the first two corresponding to the land and the sea, "areas accessible and common," and the third division for God, "because heaven is inaccessible to men."[76] The high priest, therefore, according to this understanding, when entering the Holy of Holies, was leaving behind the material world (by taking off his vestments made up of colours and elements representing the material world) and ascending (in his linen robe, representing the heavenly garments) into the heavenly presence of God, seated on his throne.[77] In order to do so the high priest had to go through the veil, which itself was made up of the same elements representing the material world, which again suggests that this separated the material world from the heavenly. The high priest wore a turban bearing a gold plate engraved with the words "holy to the Lord" (Exod 28:36–38; Lev 6:4). As we saw above, later tradition suggests that in fact the high priest, in some way, represented Yahweh.

Having offered a bull as a sin offering for himself, the high priest takes the two goats selected for the offering and cast lots, "one lot for the

72. Via the priestly blessing Num 6:22–27.
73. Josephus, *Ant.* 3.8.9.
74. Philo, *On Dreams* 1.216–17.
75. Josephus is thought to have lived 37–ca. 100 C.E.
76. Josephus, *Ant.* 3.7.7.
77. This is the experience described by Isaiah (Isa 6:1–13) and Ezekiel (Ezek 1:4–3:12), both of whom were from priestly families. This was also the foundational text for the mystical tradition, a central feature of which was ascents to the throne of God. Furthermore, this may also be what is represented in Ps 11:4, "the LORD is in his holy temple, the LORD's throne is in heaven."

6. *The High Priest*

LORD and the other lot for Azazel." He then kills the goat "for Yahweh" and takes its blood into the Holy of Holies to make atonement. It has been proposed that the goat which was sacrificed, in fact, was a substitute for the high priest and therefore the high priest is, in effect, offering his own blood as atonement.[78] According to Barker, "The meaning of this is clear: the LORD himself renews the creation every year by the gift of his own life. The creation was renewed by the creator."[79] When he emerges from behind the veil, in clouds of incense,[80] he then places his hands on the goat "for Azazel" thereby transferring the sins of Israel onto the goat which subsequently undergoes ritual humiliation[81] and is then sent away into the wilderness (Lev 16:15–22). Only when this has occurred, and the crimson thread tied to the door of the sanctuary turned white, is atonement completed.[82] Taken together, the two halves of this ceremony provide a close parallel to the suggested events of the enthronement ceremony involving the king, albeit in a different sequence—the "death" and ascension to the throne (of God)[83] preceding the ritual humiliation and abandonment. Furthermore, as mentioned above, the stipulation that the goats must be identical further indicates that they represent one figure, which I suggest is that of the servant/king, who in the cultic rites undergoes ritual humiliation, is abandoned, "dies" and is resurrected and then ascends to the throne (of Yahweh), as a result of which atonement is made for the people.

It has been proposed that when the flesh of the goat for Yahweh is eaten by the priests, as was the custom, this in fact represents the flesh of Yahweh. Furthermore, as the high priest represented Yahweh,[84] and thus the goat was a substitute for himself, it has been suggested that the high

---

78. Barker has argued for this reading on the basis both of Origen's understanding of the text and the fact that the Hebrew preposition *l* can mean "as" as well as "for," meaning that the goats could therefore be chosen "as Yahweh" and "as Azazel." This reading also does away with the objection that the latter could be conceived as an offering "to Azazel," the chief of the fallen angels. Barker, *Revelation*, 45.
79. Ibid., 46.
80. Ibid., 169. This may also be what is implied in Sir 50:6 (quoted above), although Hayward dismisses the suggestion that the event described here is Yom Kippur. Hayward. *The Jewish Temple*, 50.
81. *M. Yoma* 6:4 "and they made a causeway for it because of the Babylonians who used to pull its hair, crying to it, 'Bear [our sins] and be gone! Bear [our sins] and be gone'!"
82. *M. Yoma* 6:8.
83. Ps 110:1.
84. He bore the name of the LORD on his turban. See n. 49.

priest may have offered the flesh of the goat to his fellow priests using words very similar to those of Matt 26:26.[85]

Whilst much of this ritual can be seen to parallel that of the Anointed identified in the preceding chapters, there is nothing in the ritual of the Day of Atonement itself to suggest a hierogamy, with the possible exception of the symbolism surrounding the high priest's robes.[86] Nonetheless, there is evidence from Judg 21:19–21 that "fertility" dances took place in the vineyards during this New Year period and later tradition associates these with the Day of Atonement.[87]

Although the Passover came to be associated with the Feast of Unleavened Bread (*Massoth*), which was closely connected with the barley harvest and with the sun, it is thought that its origins were that of a nomadic festival and as such associated with the moon. Indeed, the Passover is in essence a night celebration, with many of its injunctions confirming that.[88] The Passover sacrifice was killed at the ninth hour in the temple and the sacrificial meal began just before nightfall and had to be completed and the remains burned before sunrise. However, some scholars dispute this,[89] and in the texts of the Second Temple period the two festivals are combined.[90] Scholarly discussion aside, the biblical text does state that the festival is to take place on the night of the full moon following or nearest to the spring equinox (Deut 16:1), a detail which suggests the possibility that it may have been regarded as a New Year festival. This is strengthened by the injunction in Exod 12:2: "This month shall be for you the beginning of months; it shall be the first month of the year for you."

---

85. Barker, *The Risen Lord*, 76–77.

86. Cf. Edersheim, *The Temple*, 325.

87. "Rabban Simeon b. Gamaliel said: 'There were no happier days for Israel than the 15th of Ab and the Day of Atonement, for on them the daughters of Jerusalem used to go forth in white raiments…all the raiments required immersion. And the daughters of Jerusalem went forth to dance in the vineyards. And what did they say? "Young man, lift up thine eyes and see what thou wouldest choose for thyself"'" (*m. Ta'anit* 4:8). The biblical quotations given associate this with King Solomon and the "crown wherewith his mother hath crowned him in the day of his espousals," as well as with the building of the temple, both of which are enthronement themes.

88. The ordinances for both festivals are given together in Exod 12.

89. "In contrast to the majority of scholars, both Segal and Engnell maintained that Passover was never an amalgam of two separate feasts." Tamara Prosic, *The Development and Symbolism of Passover until 70 CE* (London: T&T Clark International, 2004), 60.

90. "Where our sources for the Second Temple period are explicit, they show them to be combined into a unit." Grabbe, *Judaic Religion*, 141.

6. *The High Priest*   137

The Paschal offering was usually a one-year-old male lamb without blemish (Exod 12:5–6). One theory suggests that Paschal victims were originally firstlings of sheep or goats substituted for a yet earlier annual sacrifice of firstborn children.[91] According to Robinson,

> We may find a further suggestion in the death of the eldest sons of Egypt. This surely goes back to an age when the firstborn was still held to be demanded in sacrifice by the superhuman powers of fertility, and it is interesting to note the hint that the Egyptian firstborn were a surrogate for the eldest in Israel (Exod 12:15f.). Since all the firstborn in Egypt had been slain, *Yahweh* could, in the future, be content with an animal victim in place of the sons of Israel.[92]

This is also Prosic's position:

> the governing idea behind the connection between Passover sacrifice and firstlings and firstborn in Exodus legislation, regardless of how indirect and secondary that connection might be, is fertility. On the night of Passover in Egypt Yahweh implicitly appears in the aspect of a fertility god. That hidden meaning of Yahweh in the story of the tenth plague, on the other hand, suggests that before it was transformed into a commemoration, Passover belonged to the category of festivals dedicated to the fertility cult, and the gods and myths of that particular cult.

She therefore concludes: "In the biblical texts, fertility is the ultimate way in which the blessing of Yahweh is manifested."[93]

In Deut 16 the rites concerning the Passover lamb and unleavened bread are understood as a memorial, "so that all the days of your life you may remember the time of your departure from Egypt" (Deut 16:3b), and according to Exod 12:23 the blood of the Passover lamb was smeared on the doorposts on the night of the tenth plague so that "when the LORD goes through the land to strike down the Egyptians, he will see the blood on the top and sides of the door-frame and will pass over that doorway, and he will not permit the destroyer to enter your houses and strike you down."

However, it has been suggested that this was already an ancient apotropaic rite practised before the historicizing of the Passover and its association with the Exodus, used to keep at bay evil spirits connected with the moon.[94] Furthermore, the explanation for the observance of the Passover given in the Hebrew Scriptures suggests that underneath it lay a much older tradition:

    91. Gray, *Sacrifice*, 364.
    92. Robinson, "Hebrew Myths," in Hooke, ed., *Myth and Ritual*, 193.
    93. Prosic, *The Development and Symbolism of Passover*, 59.
    94. Robinson, "Hebrew Myths," 191.

> That the Paschal victim was to be eaten was directly commanded in the law of Deut 16:1–9 and it is clearly implied that the Paschal meal was already an ancient rite; in other words Deuteronomy certainly does not institute a new rite, but modifies the existing and long practised rite of eating the Paschal victim.[95]

The modifications, it is proposed, are the two prohibitions found in Exodus; one, which forbade eating the victim raw (Exod 12:9) and the other which forbade the breaking of its bones (Exod 12:46). This may also represent the rationale behind the injunction not to imbibe blood in Lev 17:11, "for the life (*nephesh*) of a creature is in the blood"; *nephesh* also means spirit. As Gray argues,

> A legal prohibition is commonly directed against what is, or has been actual practice. It has therefore been inferred that at one time the Paschal victim was eaten raw and that the bones having been broken and pounded for the purpose, were eaten as well as the flesh.[96]

This has in turn been compared with other Near Eastern sacrificial ceremonies in which the victim is eaten raw, including its blood and bones[97] and in which the participants, in so doing, are understood not only to enter into communion with their god but are understood to imbibe "the life" or spirit of the victim which represents or "is" the god.[98] If this rationale does underlie the original Passover, then this would mean that the unblemished male firstborn sacrificed in fact represents the God, whose blood affords protection and whose flesh provides communion.

Finally, when we consider the material from Qumran, we find that the high priest's role on the Day of Atonement also provides the background for the Melchizedek figure of 11QMelchizedek.[99] In this text, it is expected that the heavenly high priest will effect atonement on the tenth Jubilee: "And this thing will [occur] in the first week of the Jubilee that follows the nine Jubilees. And the Day of Atonement is the e[nd of the] tenth [Ju]bilee, when all the Sons of [Light] and the men of the lot of Mel[chi]zedek will be atoned for." In the text it is also stated that Melchizedek will judge the holy ones of God (quoting Ps 82:1–2), and

---

95. Gray, *Sacrifice*, 368.
96. Ibid.
97. See ibid., 368–69.
98. See ibid, 369.
99. "The extant part of the text begins with a citation of Lev 25:13 and Deut 15:2, verses that deal with the year of jubilees and the year of release; to them is added Isa 61:1 ('to proclaim liberty to the captives'), which is understood to address the last days." VanderKam, *The Dead Sea Scrolls Today*, 53.

6. The High Priest

that "this is the day of [Peace/Salvation] concerning which [God] spoke [through Isa]iah the prophet" (quoting Isa 52:7; other quotations include Dan 9:25 and Isa 6:2–3). Barker comments:

> Daniel's prophecy of the Great Atonement, which would put an end to sin and destroy both Jerusalem and the temple, reckons seventy weeks of years from "the going forth of the word to restore and rebuild Jerusalem" (Dan 9:25). Seventy weeks of years, 490 years, can also be reckoned as ten Jubilees, and in the Melchizedek text (11QMelch) there is a similar expectation of the Great Atonement and Judgement after ten Jubilees.[100]

In the Messianic Apocalypse (4Q521 fragment 2 ii) it is the messiah who again has the central role; and here it is expected that heaven and earth will obey the messiah and that his role will involve: "releasing captives, giving sight to the blind and raising up those who are bo[wed down]…for he will heal the wounded, give life to the dead and preach good news to the poor and he will [sat]isfy the [weak] ones and lead those who have been cast out and enrich the hungry."[101]

In 4Q541 a "suffering messiah" has been identified[102] based on two fragments, 9 and 24. Fragment 9 reads:

> He will atone for all the children of his generation and he will be sent to all the children of his [pe]ople. His word is like a word of heaven and his teaching is in accordance with the will of God. His eternal sun will shine, and his light will be kindled in all the corners of the earth, and it will shine on the darkness. Then the darkness will pass away [fro]m the earth, and thick darkness from the dry land. They will speak many words against him, and they will invent many [lie]s and factions against him and speak shameful things about him. Evil will overthrow his generation… His situation will be one of lying and violence [and] the people will go astray in his days, and be confounded.[103]

This reading has, however, been challenged: "The obvious implication is that he is a priest and makes atonement by means of the sacrificial cult. He does not atone by his suffering and death, as is the case with Isaiah's servant."[104] According to Collins:

---

100. Barker, *Revelation*, 48–49.
101. Cited in Collins, who notes the dependence on Ps 146 and Isa 61:1–2. Collins, *The Scepter and Star*, 117.
102. Collins cites Jean Starcky and Emile Puech as proponents of this reading. Ibid., 123.
103. Ibid., 124–25.
104. Ibid., 125.

the Christian belief in such a figure, and discovery of prophecies relating to him, surely arose in retrospect after the passion and death of Jesus of Nazareth. There is no evidence that anyone in first-century Judaism expected such a figure, either in fulfilment of Isaiah 53 or on any other basis.[105]

Grabbe is of a similar opinion:

One of the topics that arises perennially is the question of whether there was a "suffering messiah" concept in pre-70 Judaism. The concept has been of great interest to both Old Testament and New Testament scholars and has produced an enormous amount of scholarly literature. As far as we can tell, the servant of Isaiah 40–55 was not a messianic figure in its original context; on the other hand, one or two people have thought they could find a messianic interpretation (or hints of it) in some of the Qumran scrolls. So far this has not produced good evidence for a "suffering messiah." Another issue concerns the attempt to find a "pierced messiah" in 4Q285; this has been more or less resolved in a consensus among Qumran scholars that no such figure in fact exists in this text.[106]

The Outcome of the High Priest's Role

In 1 Kgs 8:31–53 the result of prayer in the temple will be the condemnation of the guilty and the innocent being declared not guilty; when Israel confesses her sins in the temple, she will be saved from her enemies; and when the people pray towards the temple and ask forgiveness of their sins, the rain will come and all that hampers fertility will be erased. The mirror image of this concept is found in the Mishnah: *Rabban Simeon b. Gamaliel* says in the name of R. Joshua, "Since the day that the Temple was destroyed there has been no day without its curse; and the dew had not fallen in blessing and the fruits have lost their fatness."[107] This confirms that not only was the temple service intimately linked with fertility but also confirms the continuing significance of the temple even after its demise in 70 C.E. This is further confirmed in another Mishnaic tractate in *m. Aboth*, where the Zadokite high priest Simon the Righteous is cited as saying: "The world stands upon three things: The Torah, The Temple Service and deeds of loving kindness." Hayward comments: "For Simon's statement to make sense, the Temple and its Service must not only have been highly esteemed in themselves, but also have been considered to possess profound significance."[108]

---

105. Ibid., 126.
106. Grabbe, *Judaic Religion*, 290.
107. *M. Sotah* 9:12.
108. Hayward, *The Jewish Temple*, 1.

As we saw above in the 4Q521 text, the outcomes expected of the Messiah are the release of captives, healing of the blind and wounded, raising of the dead, bringing good news to the poor, leading "the holy ones" and "enriching" the hungry.[109] In 4Q246 the Messiah is expected to judge the earth and make peace (4Q246 5–10). The high priest's role in the *Testament of Levi* anticipates similar outcomes, as well as a universal acknowledgement of "the Lord."

The complex ritual of the Day of Atonement is understood to make atonement for the sins of Israel and to fix the destiny of the people for the following year (Lev 16:33–34). However, the sacrifice is made not only on behalf of Israel but also on behalf of "the whole race of [hu]mankind,"[110] as well as the whole earth.[111] Further desired results may be inferred from the prayer that the high priest uttered on his retreat from the Holy of Holies, a prayer which refers to freedom from captivity, "a year of cheapness, of fullness, of intercourse and trade; a year with abundance of rain, of sunshine, and of dew."[112]

One of the outcomes of the Passover is also the removal of sin: "That man who is clean and not on a journey and yet fails to perform the Passover—that soul shall be cut off from its kinsmen; because he presented not *Yahweh*'s offering, that man shall bear his sin" (Num 9:13).[113] Oesterley cites three further desired outcomes: the increase of flocks and herds; protection from evil spirits and communion with the deity.[114] The results of the Passover therefore correspond with those of the New Year/Enthronement ceremony: fertility and protection for the ensuing year. It is interesting therefore to note that in the present-day Amidah, in the period leading up to Pesach, Benediction 9 includes the words "Bestow dew and rain for blessing,"[115] and that the themes throughout this prayer are those of fertility and messianism,[116] with dew personified.[117] The deep (*Tehom*, the word used in the creation myth [Gen 1:2]

109. VanderKam and Flint, eds., *The Meaning of the Dead Sea Scrolls*, 333.
110. Philo, *The Special Laws* 1.17.97.
111. Philo, *The Special Laws* 1.17.97.
112. Cited from the Talmud in Edersheim, *The Temple*, 314.
113. Leaven, in later rabbinic tradition, is associated with sin. It is the custom at Passover to remove all leaven from the house and burn it. Exod 12:19 stipulates that "for seven days no leaven shall be found in your house."
114. Oesterley, "Early Hebrew Festival Rituals," 118.
115. *The Authorised Daily Prayer Book*, 82.
116. These include the restoration of Jerusalem, the gathering in of exiles and the release of captives.
117. Each verse ends with the phrase "this is the blessing of Dew." Notably, "Dew" is written with a capital letter, suggesting it is a proper noun. In Chapter 4 I discussed the identification of the king in Ps 110 as "Dew."

and associated with the Chaos Waters) is also said to "yearn for dew"; thus we have the forces of Chaos themselves longing for the messianic redemption that the dew will bring.

Key outcomes of the king's enthronement in the New Year festivals of Israel's surrounding cultures were justice, the establishment of *ma'at* and the fixing of destinies. In the Hebrew Scriptures, *mišpāṭ* and the fixing of destinies are also expected outcomes. From the Mishnah we learn that there are four "New Year" days on which the world is judged, each of which is connected with fertility and/or the enthronement of kings:[118]

> At four times in the year is the world judged; at Passover, through grain; at Pentecost, through the fruits of the tree; on New Year's Day all that come into the world pass before him like legions of soldiers, for it is written, *He that fashionneth the hearts of them all that considereth all their works*; and at the Feast [of Tabernacles] they are judged through water.[119]

Danby therefore concludes: "God's verdict on the world is shown by the richness or meagreness of the harvest."[120]

Conclusion

We have seen that the high priest in the post-exilic period has become *the* Anointed and as such is spoken of in highly exalted terms, bordering on divinity. Furthermore, in his cultic function he is even identified with God himself. The climax of the high priest's status is the central role he plays in the Day of Atonement festival. In relation to this festival we found a number of elements identified both in the cultic role of the Anointed in the surrounding cultures and in the Hebrew Scriptures: one element of the ritual involved the sacrifice of a substitute for the Anointed, following which, in the Israelite tradition, the Anointed, although not abandoned, did ascend completely alone to the throne of Yahweh. The humiliation experienced by the Anointed among Israel's neighbouring cultures and by the Anointed in the Hebrew Scriptures is here experienced in the other half of the ritual by the scapegoat, the goat "for" Azazel which, together with the goat "for" Yahweh, may have represented the dual aspect of the high god. Atonement made, the high priest emerges in triumph, with the destiny of the people fixed for a further year. Rain, fertility and peace were assured, for Israel and for the nations.

118. *M. Rosh Ha-shanah* 1:1.
119. *M. Rosh Ha-shanah* 1:2.
120. *The Mishnah* (trans. Herbert Danby; London: Oxford University Press, 1933), 188.

Furthermore, there is evidence to suggest that the original rationale behind the Passover sacrifice involved the sacrifice of a firstborn male without blemish. This sacrifice was understood to be a substitute for the people.[121] In addition, it was also understood to "be" God, whose blood warded off evil and whose body provided communion with his people. It was the means whereby the spirit of the God could be imbibed by the people.

There was, however, still the expectation of a Davidic Messiah in the Dead Sea Scrolls, although this appears to be a more exalted figure spoken of as "Son of God" and "Son of the Most High," a figure who was expected to release captives, open the eyes of the blind, lift up the oppressed, heal the wounded, raise the dead and bring good news to the poor. In the following chapter I will consider a further development of the texts of this period—the emergence of the Son of Man, a figure who also had an exalted heavenly messianic status.

---

121. That is the firstborn who would otherwise have originally been sacrificed to ensure fertility.

Chapter 7

THE ANOINTED IN THE SECOND TEMPLE PERIOD:
THE SON OF MAN

As well as the high priest taking over the title and to some extent the role of the Anointed, there emerged, within the texts of this period, another figure, one who was also associated with the title Anointed—that of the Son of Man. In this chapter I will consider the Son of Man figure in the literature of the Second Temple period, chiefly as he is portrayed within the book of Enoch, but also with brief reference to other works, including the book of Daniel.¹ The same thematic approach will be adopted here as elsewhere in this work.

The Son of Man

I considered the Son of Man briefly in Chapter 5 since this figure appears in the book of Daniel in the Hebrew Scriptures. However, the Son of Man figure also appears in two texts of this period; predominantly in *1 Enoch*, in the section known as the *Similitudes*,² but also briefly in *4 Ezra*. The date of the Similitudes of Enoch is still disputed; some scholars date it prior to the Christian era, whilst others suggest the latter end of the first century C.E. However, following the Third Enochic Seminar, Boccaccini has stated that the vast majority of specialists in Enochic Literature and Second Temple Judaism agree on a dating of the *Similitudes* to the turn

---

1. I discussed Daniel in Chapter 5. The late dating of Daniel (ca. 175 B.C.E.) brings it into the same time frame as the other works considered here.
2. According to Nickelsburg, the *Similitudes* (*1 En.* 37–71) consist of three parables: chs. 38–44; 45–57 and 58–69, introduced by ch. 37 as a "vision of wisdom," and closing with what has been discerned as two epilogues—one in 70:1–4 and the second in 71:1–17. George W. E. Nickelsburg, "Discerning the Structure(s) of the Enochic Book of Parables," in *Enoch and the Messiah Son of Man: Revising the Book of Parables* (ed. Gabriele Boccaccini; Grand Rapids: Eerdmans, 2007), 24.

of the era.³ Closely linked to the question of dating is that of the authorship of the *Similitudes*. One of the major problems surrounding this text is that, despite the presence of other parts of this work at Qumran, no trace has been found of the *Similitudes* (chs. 37–71);⁴ because it is in this section alone that the Son of Man figure is found, it has been suggested that this was either a Christian work or that it was a work that had been subject to Christian interpolation. However, this theory has for the most part been rejected.⁵ In this respect, Grabbe, who notes that the book contains "no indication of the fall of the temple or the post-70 situation," states that "there is nothing that must be Christian within the book, and most scholars accept that it is a Jewish work."⁶

The "Son of Man" figure has long been the subject of intense scholarly debate. As Chialà states, "In 1557 Théodore de Béze published a study on the Son of Man, and from then until the present day a steady stream of articles and monographs has kept the debate alive."⁷ Chialà goes on to comment:

> Each single interpretation obviously has its own unique features, but it is possible to group them into two general categories… [There] are those who understand it as a Christological title and others for whom it is simply a redundant substitute for a personal pronoun or for the noun "man."⁸

Collins, who gives a useful survey of the subject and outlines the main areas of discussion,⁹ comments: "For much of the twentieth century, scholars sought to explain this usage of 'Son of Man' with reference to an individual, supernatural figure, by appeal to a supposedly widespread myth of a Primal man of Iranian origin."¹⁰ He then explains that the

---

3. Held at Camaldoli, Italy, in 2005. See Boccaccini, ed., *Enoch and the Messiah*, 15–16.

4. However, as Charlesworth has pointed out: "cumulatively, perhaps we possess only about 10 to 20 percent of the manuscripts that were in the Qumran caves before, or in, June 68 C.E." Charlesworth, "Can We Discern the Composition Date of the Parables of Enoch?," in Boccaccini, ed., *Enoch and the Messiah*, 456.

5. "[I]n 1977, during a congress of specialists on 1 Enoch, no one agreed with Milik that the work is Christian." Ibid., 451.

6. Grabbe, *Judaic Religion*, 97.

7. Chialà, "The Son of Man: The Evolution of an Expression," in Boccaccini, ed., *Enoch and the Messiah*, 153.

8. Ibid. In this essay Chialà surveys the different interpretations of the expression and its chronological development, tracking it from Jeremiah to the *Testament of Abraham*.

9. Collins and Collins, *King and Messiah as Son of God*, 75. For a comprehensive bibliography, see Grabbe, *Judaic Religion*, Chapter 13.

10. Collins and Collins, *King and Messiah as Son of God*, 75.

Urmensch theory, particularly associated with the "History of Religion School" (the latest exponent of which was F. H. Borsch), was definitively repudiated by Carsten Colpe. Nonetheless, Colpe "affirmed the existence of a 'Son of Man' concept in Judaism around the turn of the era."[11] Although for Collins "the Son of Man" was not a fixed title in first-century C.E. Judaism, he does state: "There were, however, some widely held assumptions about the nature of the figure in Daniel's vision, and these go beyond what is explicit in the biblical text."[12]

The Person of the Son of Man

In the first part of *1 Enoch*, it is Enoch himself who is the central figure around which the narrative revolves. This purports to be the same Enoch who is mentioned briefly in Gen 5:21–24, a figure who, in later tradition, is identified with Metatron,[13] who in turn is identified with Michael.[14] Both of these figures are understood to be "heavenly high priests," and in *1 En.* 71:14 Enoch is associated with the Son of Man. Collins comments: "It is generally held that this passage identifies Enoch with the Son of Man whom he has seen in his visions. There is sharp disagreement, however, as to whether this identification was intended through the *Similitudes*."[15] There are understood to be two epilogues to the *Similitudes* and it is proposed that the second epilogue may have been added specifically to identify Enoch as the Son of Man by means of reaction against the Christian use of the title. According to Collins, "There is good reason… to suppose that the passage that contains the apparent identification of Enoch and the Son of Man is a secondary addition."[16] Furthermore, the Son of Man is a pre-existent heavenly figure (*1 En.* 48:6),[17] whereas Enoch is mortal, raised up from earth and eventually given immortality (*1 En.* 12:1). As Collins has noted: "In the body of the Similitudes, there

---

11. Ibid., 75–77.
12. Ibid., 78.
13. In the *Hekhalot* texts, Enoch is identified with the angel Yahoel (the first of 70 names of Metatron). In the Babylonian Talmud, Metatron is also identified with the *malak Yahweh*.
14. Cf. *Re'uyoth Yehezkel*. See also Hannah, who discusses the possibility that Metatron is Michael's esoteric name. Darrel D. Hannah, *Michael Traditions and Angel Christology in Early Christianity* (Tübingen: Mohr–Siebeck, 1999), 118.
15. Collins and Collins, *King and Messiah as Son of God*, 91.
16. J. J. Collins, "Enoch and the Son of Man: A Response to Sabino Chialà and Helge Kvanvig," in Boccaccini, ed., *Enoch and the Messiah*, 221.
17. "For this reason he was chosen and hidden in his presence before the world was created and forever."

is no suggestion at all that the Son of Man ever had an earthly career," which would obviate his association with Enoch.[18] Additionally, Collins argues that it is "possible to construe the Ethiopic text of *1 En.* 71:14 so that it does not require that the two figures [Enoch and the Son of Man] be identified."[19]

In later tradition it would appear that Metatron/Enoch came in effect to replace the Son of Man figure of the earlier Enochic works, the latter being a figure who, it may be surmised, had been abandoned because of his, by then, obvious Christian connections,[20] yet this figure was sufficiently important to the Enochic mindset that his presence could not be eliminated. Instead, he was translated into a figure that would be more acceptable to Rabbinic Judaism, once it had been made clear that this was not a "second power" in heaven. Nonetheless, in *3 Enoch*, God writes the "letters by which heaven and earth were created" upon a crown (*3 En.* 13:1) that he places upon Metatron, a figure who in *3 En.* 12:5 was called "the lesser YHWH."[21]

And yet, as Collins has pointed out, none of the titles attributed to the Son of Man in the Parables ("Messiah," "Righteous One," "Chosen One"), including the title Son of Man itself, are present in the later text (apart from "Chosen," which is applied once to Metatron).[22] Furthermore, he proposes that *1 En.* 71:14 was a secondary expansion and concludes:

> The identification was presumably not introduced by the Ethiopic translator, and so the expansion of the text would be dated relatively early, perhaps in reaction to the Christian identification of Jesus with the Son of Man. But none of this requires that Parables was originally composed with the identification in mind, and many of us would still argue that the composition of the text is more easily explained if chap. 71 is recognised as an addition.[23]

Although Kvanvig accepts the identification of Enoch and the Son of Man, he nonetheless identifies obstacles to such a reading.[24]

---

18. Collins and Collins, *King and Messiah as Son of God*, 93.
19. Collins, "Enoch and the Son of Man," 222.
20. Although citing a few exceptions, Chialà states: "Once the Christian era had begun, there was no longer any mention of the Son of Man in Judaism, not even among the specific group of Jews who wrote the Second Book of Enoch, and later the Third Book of Enoch." Chialà, "The Son of Man," 177–78.
21. Cited in Charles A. Gieschen, "The Name of the Son of Man in the Parables of Enoch," in Boccaccini, ed., *Enoch and the Messiah Son of Man*, 245.
22. Collins, "Enoch and the Son of Man," 222.
23. Ibid., 223.
24. Helge S. Kvanvig, "The Son of Man in the Parables of Enoch," in Boccaccini, ed., *Enoch and the Messiah Son of Man*, 212.

In contrast to the prominent role given to Enoch in the first part of *1 Enoch*, in the *Parables or Similitudes*, the central figure is the Son of Man (*1 En.* 26:26–29; 46:1–6; 48:2–7; 62:5–9, 14; 63:11; 70:1; 71:17), a heavenly figure expressly identified as the Anointed (*1 En.* 48:10; 52:4). This figure is also identified with "the Elect One"[25] (*1 En.* 40:5; 45:3; 49:2; 51:3; 61:8; 62:9) and the "Righteous One" (*1 En.* 38:2), terms that are also applied to the Anointed in the Hebrew Scriptures.[26] Kvanvig states: "the use of various titles with differing backgrounds does not mean that there are several figures involved. They all refer to the same eschatological figure."[27]

Although the title "Son of God" is not directly applied to the Son of Man in Enoch, nevertheless "His appearance is 'like one of the holy angels,' and his enthronement indicates a rank higher than that of any angel."[28] Thus the Son of Man figure in *1 Enoch* has the appearance of a man, though he is in fact a heavenly figure (*1 En.* 46:1) who stands in a special relationship to God:

> And yet although he is supernatural and divine, nevertheless as "the Elect One" he stands as the representative and head of "the elect ones," that heavenly company of righteous men who will one day inherit the kingdom which God has promised to his chosen people.[29]

The Son of Man is therefore a mediator between God and the people. Even so, the Son of Man is not just a heavenly being in the same way as the angels—he was pre-existent and exalted: "and in that hour that Son of Man was named in the presence of the Lord of Spirits, and his name before the Head of Days. Even before the sun and the constellations were created, before the stars of heaven were made, his name was named before the Lord of Spirits" (*1 En.* 48:2–3). His pre-existence is also evident in *1 En.* 62:7: "For from the beginning the Son of Man was hidden, and the Most High preserved him in the presence of his might, and he revealed him to the chosen." In *1 En.* 48:5 it is said that kings will prostrate themselves before him. Collins comments: "Whether this obeisance indicates divinity, or what degree of divinity might be debated...but he

---

25. A title also applied to the king/servant in the Hebrew Scriptures (Isa 4:28; 42:1, 6; 45:1–4; 48:14).

26. David Syme Russell, *The Method and Message of Jewish Apocalyptic, 200 BC–AD 100* (London: SCM, 1964), 327.

27. Kvanvig, "The Son of Man," 188. He suggests the oracles about the Servant of the Lord in the book of Isaiah as the most likely background for "Chosen One" and "Righteous One."

28. Collins and Collins, *King and Messiah as Son of God*, 94.

29. Russell, *The Method and Message*, 328.

sits like the Lord on a throne of glory and this surely bespeaks divine status in some sense, although it does not rule out the possibility that the figure in question is an exalted human being."[30]

Although it is the name of the Lord of Spirits "by which the righteous shall be victorious" and "the others" shall be saved (*1 En.* 40:6),[31] nonetheless the name of the Son of Man is also significant; it was named before all the created order (*1 En.* 48:3), which may suggest he played a part in creation. In fact, we learn that it was this name that was the source of creation (*1 En.* 69:16–26).[32] Furthermore, although for the most part quite distinct, there are areas of *1 Enoch* that would suggest a correspondence between the Son of Man/Elect figure and that of the Lord of Spirits (the usual name for God here),[33] not least of which is the suggestion that they both possess the Divine Name.[34] Both are said to punish the kings of the earth (*1 En.* 46:4–5; 62:10–11); both are said to be worshipped by the kings of the earth (*1 En.* 62:6–7; 63:1); both are the cause of the shame of the kings of the earth (*1 En.* 62:10; 63:11); both are full of righteousness (*1 En.* 58:4; 71:14–16) and will bring righteousness; both will judge between the righteous and the wicked (*1 En.* 51:3–4; 69:27).

Furthermore, in *1 En.* 62:14 we read: "And the Lord of Spirits will abide over them, and with that Son of Man shall they eat and lie down and rise up for ever and ever." Whilst this may represent two distinct persons, the use of parallelism may also suggest correspondence (as it

30. Collins and Collins, *King and Messiah, as Son of God*, 94.
31. The name of the Lord of Spirits plays a key role; people pray in the name of the Lord of Spirits. In *1 En.* 40:6 sinners deny the name; in *1 En.* 41:2 the elect ones are those who called on his glorious name. In *1 En.* 57:3 we learn his name is mighty 41:61 and in *1 En.* 50:2–3 we learn that the righteous shall be victorious in his name and that through his name they shall be saved.
32. In later rabbinic tradition the name of the messiah is listed among the things that preceded the creation of the world. See Collins, *The Scepter and the Star*, 181.
33. According to Gieschen this reflects the Hebrew title "YHWH Sabaoth." Gieschen, "The Name of the Son of Man," 239.
34. Gieschen puts forward a number of arguments to support his contention that the Lord of Spirits and the Son of Man both possess the Divine Name YHWH. Amongst them he cites *1 En.* 48:5—"all those who dwell on earth shall fall and worship before him [the Son of Man]; they shall glorify, bless and sing the name of the Lord of the Spirits"—on which he comments: "They will use the name of the Lord of the Spirits in worshiping the Son of Man because *both* possess the same Divine Name." Gieschen, "The Name of the Son of Man," 240 (original emphasis). Collins, however, questions whether *proskynesis* here should be defined as "worship" and sees a distinction between the honours paid to the Son of Man and those paid to the Lord of Spirits. Collins and Collins, *King and Messiah as Son of God*, 100.

does in the Hebrew Scriptures),³⁵ leading to the conclusion that the Son of Man and the Lord of Spirits (God) are, in some way, understood to be one. Based on *1 En.* 46:1–7, Gieschen suggests that the "one like a Son of Man" in Dan 7 is identified as the Glory of YHWH in Ezekiel (1:26–28).³⁶ The Son of Man figure is also closely associated with the fountain of righteousness and the fountains of wisdom (*1 En.* 48:1–2).

Whilst some scholars identify a correspondence between the Son of Man in Daniel and the Servant of Deutero-Isaiah,³⁷ others have identified a synthesis between the latter and the Son of Man in the *Similitudes of Enoch*.³⁸ We saw in Chapter 5 that the Suffering Servant is said to be righteous (Isa 42:1); he is the righteous one who will make many "to be accounted righteous" (Isa 53:1); he is chosen by God (Isa 42:1); he has been called and named from the womb (Isa 49:1); he is hidden (Isa 42:1); he is to be a light to the nations (Isa 42:6); and the kings of the earth will fall down and worship him (Isa 49:6). In *1 En.* 58:4; 71:14–16, the Son of Man is righteous; he is chosen by God (*1 En.* 46:3; 48:5); he was named before creation (*1 En.* 48:3); he was hidden (*1 En.* 62:7); he is to be a light to the nations (*1 En.* 48:4); the kings of the earth will fall down and worship him (*1 En.* 62:7).

As may be expected there is also a close correspondence between the Son of Man figure in Daniel and in *1 Enoch*, thereby indicating a correspondence between all three figures—the Son of Man in Daniel and in Enoch as well as the Suffering Servant in Isaiah—suggesting therefore that they are all representations of the one figure or idea. Gieschen also suggests that *1 En.* 48:2–3, in which the Son of Man is named, is related to the naming of the servant in Isa 49:1, although, as he admits, the setting is now prior to creation, rather than "from the womb."³⁹ I suggested

---

35. A similar instance may be found in *1 En.* 70:1. See also *1 En.* 48:2–5 and 53:6.

36. Gieschen, "The Name of the Son of Man," 240.

37. Black and Bruce maintain that Daniel's visions may have been dependent originally on the Servant passages in Deutero-Isaiah and that "the Son of Man in the one is representative of the Suffering Servant in the other." This is based on both similarity in language and correspondence of ideas, even extending to the concept of vicarious suffering "so prominent in Deutero-Isaiah" and which is "perhaps not completely absent" from Daniel. M. Black and F. F. Bruce, cited in Russell, *The Method and Message*, 337.

38. William Manson has compared words and phrases written of the two figures, as well as those used for the Davidic Messiah. According to Manson, the commonalities show that each is chosen by God, is called the Lord's Anointed, is endowed with wisdom and righteousness, is a light to the Gentiles and receives the homage of kings. See ibid., 339.

39. Gieschen, "The Name of the Son of Man," 240.

in Chapter 5 that the person and role of the Servant of Deutero-Isaiah replicated that of the Anointed in the Psalms and in the surrounding cultures. Here, the correspondence with the Son of Man figure further suggests a messianic context. The correspondence between Daniel and Enoch is strengthened even more by the close similarity in their visions.[40] Enoch saw: "One, who had a Head of Days, and His head was white like wool, and with Him was another being whose countenance had the appearance of a man, and his face was full of graciousness, like one of the holy angels" (*1 En.* 56:1). In *his* vision Daniel saw thrones "set in place" and the Ancient of Days taking his seat: "His clothing was as white as snow; the hair of his head was white like wool" (Dan 7:9).

There then follows a description of his throne, which corresponds with the one Enoch describes earlier: "His throne was flaming with fire and its wheels were all ablaze. A river of fire was flowing coming out from before him" (Dan 7:9–10). In *1 En.* 12:18–22 Enoch states:

> I looked and saw [therein] a lofty throne; its appearance was as crystal and the wheels thereof as the shining sun, and there was the vision of cherubim and from underneath the throne came streams of flaming fire so that I could not look thereon. And the Great Glory sat thereon and His raiment shone more brightly than the sun and was whiter than any snow…ten thousand times ten thousand (stood) before him.

And again in Daniel we read: "Thousands upon thousands attended him; ten thousand times ten thousand stood before him. The court was seated, and the books were opened." In *1 En.* 47:3 we read: "In those days I saw the Head of Days when he seated himself upon the throne of His glory and the books of the living were opened before Him." In Daniel's account of his vision he then sees "one like a Son of Man coming with the clouds of heaven and approaching the ancient of Days." This Son of Man is then given "authority, glory and sovereign power; all peoples, nations and men of every language, worshipped him. His dominion is an everlasting dominion that will not pass away and his kingdom is one that will never be destroyed" (Dan 7:9–14). In *1 En.* 47:3 we read that the Son of Man's glory is "for ever and ever, and his might unto all generations."

The very close similarity in style and content suggests the possibility that one is dependent on the other. Chialà acknowledges the dependence of *1 Enoch* on Daniel but also notes the development which has taken place: "In the Book of Parables, what was only a symbol or metaphor in

---

40. Collins states: "It is beyond doubt that the *Similitudes of Enoch* allude to Dan 7:9–10, 13–14." Collins, *The Scepter and the Star*, 177.

the book of Daniel—at least in chap. 7—becomes a character to whom precise traits and functions are attributed."[41] Furthermore the use of the demonstrative with the "Son of Man" is understood to be indicative of the use as a title (with the exception of *1 En.* 62:7 and 69:27).[42] Rather than representing a circumlocution, therefore, as suggested by the Jewish writers discussed above (Chapter 2), it would appear the Son of Man title referred to a quite distinct and detailed figure that was well known in Jewish circles prior to the time of Jesus.

The motif of kingship runs throughout *1 Enoch*, with God being spoken of in numerous places as "King," "Eternal King," "King of Kings,"[43] and the figure of the Son of Man/Elect One also being spoken of in terms suggestive of kingship. In *1 En.* 45:3, for instance, we are told that "on that day," which is an end-times designation, "Mine Elect One" shall sit on the throne of glory.[44] Furthermore, *1 En.* 48:10 takes us back by allusion to Ps 2 in the Hebrew Scriptures, to a psalm that speaks of the enthronement of the Anointed king, as God's son.[45]

Whilst there is no equation of the Son of Man (the Anointed) with the title "Shepherd" such as is found in the surrounding cultures and the Hebrew Scriptures, in *1 En.* 66–70 Israel is spoken of in apocalyptic language as "sheep," with God being referred to as the "Lord of the sheep." Furthermore, the kings of the nations are alluded to as the "70 shepherds" (*1 En.* 89:59), and it may be suggested that the stars (who are bound) therefore correspond to the *elohim*, that is, the fallen angels who ruled through these kings, to which I have alluded earlier.[46] The story of the fallen angels (*elohim*) in Gen 6 is expanded in *1 Enoch* and I suggest that there is a direct correspondence between the *elohim* of Gen 6; Deut 32:8, and *1 En.* 6 and that the kings of the *goyim* (ruled by the fallen *elohim*) therefore represent both physical and spiritual enemies of Israel.

---

41. Chialà, "The Son of Man," 159.
42. Collins comments: "Where the demonstrative is lacking, it is usually rendered superfluous by the context." Collins, *The Scepter and the Star*, 180.
43. *1 En.* 63:4.
44. *1 En.* 62:5; 69:27. See also *1 En.* 45:3; 61:8; 62:2.
45. *1 En.* 48:10: "For they have denied the Lord of Spirits and his Anointed"; Ps 2:1–2: "Why do the nations conspire and the peoples plot in vain? The kings of the earth set themselves and their rulers take counsel together against the LORD and his anointed."
46. Mowinckel states: "Later Judaism was familiar with the notion that there existed wicked, fallen angels, the protector deities of the heathen empires, and those who lured men into sin." Mowinckel, *He That Cometh*, 394.

As aspects of the Most High god, they may also be understood to represent the dual aspect of God (that is *Yahweh* and the *elohim*). In the later tradition of Enoch, a large number of the fallen angels have names ending with an *el* component (*el* means "god"), and their names appear to indicate either functions or aspects of God—thus *Kokabiel* (Star of God), *Tamiel* (Perfection of God), *Baraqijal* (Lightening of God). Referring to the *Hekhalot Zutarti* list of angels as names of God, Hannah states:

> On the basis of this and similar passages Grozinger has presented a good case for understanding the names of God and of angels as various hypostatic functions of the Deity. In other words, in *Hekhalot* texts a divine or angelic name is no longer simply an appellation, but a hypostasis of a particular divine power and function.[47]

Notably, not only in the Hekhalot texts but in the biblical literature itself the name of YHWH appears as a hypostasis. This is particularly evident in the *malakh YHWH* (Exod 23:20–22). Gieschen comments, "The need for some distinction between YHWH and his visible form arises from the paradox that YHWH appears in some form on many occasions, yet one cannot see YHWH and live (Exod 33:20)."[48] Nonetheless, Exod 23:20–22 makes clear that the possession of the Divine Name suggests some correspondence with Yahweh. Gieschen therefore states, "This text [Exod 23:20–22] testifies that a figure that has some independence from YHWH can still share in his being through the possession of the Divine Name (i.e., a divine hypostasis)."[49] Philo also used the Exodus angel, a figure "who possesses the Divine Name," as the foundation of his teaching about ὁ λόγος ("the Word").[50]

The Role of the Son of Man

In *1 En.* 46:3 and 48:6 we learn that the Lord of Spirits has chosen the Son of Man and kept him. The Son of Man is to carry out a work in the name of the Lord of Spirits. This work is yet to be revealed and throughout the text we are given clues about what that work will be: the Son of Man is to make the elect ones righteous (*1 En.* 38:3; 47:4); he is to dwell

---

47. Hannah, *Michael Traditions*, 117.
48. Gieschen, "The Name of the Son of Man," 243.
49. Ibid. For a fuller discussion of this phenomenon, see Fossum, *The Image of the Invisible God.*
50. Gieschen, "The Name of the Son of Man," 245.

among the elect ones (*1 En.* 57:4) who will one day be exalted with him (*1 En.* 62:80). Another aspect of the Son of Man's role is to reveal "all the treasures that are hidden" (*1 En.* 43:3), that is, he will reveal the heavenly mysteries (*1 En.* 46:1; 48:1–2). He is to be a light to the Gentiles, he will overthrow kings and their kingdoms (*1 En.* 46:5). He is also to carry out judgment (*1 En.* 49:4), judging the righteous from the wicked (*1 En.* 51:2) and judging "hidden things" (*1 En.* 59:4).

Collins states:

> It is not suggested that the Son of Man is a human descendant of David, but he is the Anointed, or Messiah, of the Lord, who takes over the functions of the Davidic King vis-à-vis the nations. He is also installed on a glorious throne, and takes over the function of eschatological judge (*1 En.* 51:3; 55:4; 61:8; 62:2; 69:29). The motif of enthronement is reminiscent of Psalm 110.[51]

The Son of Man is also to judge Azazel and the watchers (*1 En.* 55:4), which along with the following earlier passage of Enoch, throws further light on the scapegoat ritual of the Day of Atonement:

> And again the Lord said to Raphael: "Bind Azazel hand and foot, and cast him into the darkness; and make an opening in the desert, which is in Dudael, and cast him therein. And place upon him rough and jagged rocks and cover him with darkness, and let him abide there for ever and cover his face that he may not see light." (*1 En.* 10:4–5)

It is said that Behemoth, one of the two monsters mentioned in *1 En.* 60:7, is also banished to "a waste wilderness named Duidain"; the other, Leviathan, who we have encountered in the Hebrew Scriptures as a personification of the Chaos Waters, is to dwell in the abysses of the ocean over the fountains of the waters.

There is a correspondence between the role of the Son of Man figure in *1 Enoch* and that of Daniel, as well as the Servant, in Deutero-Isaiah. However, unlike the Servant figure, the Son of Man figure in both *1 Enoch* and Daniel[52] appears as an exalted being, with no suggestion that he has undergone any previous humiliation or suffering. That is not to say that the underlying concept is absent; it may represent the same phenomenon encountered in a number of Psalms, where only the triumphant part of the ritual is recorded. Why only this part should be represented can only be surmised. It is possible, however, that following

---

51. Collins and Collins, *King and Messiah as Son of God*, 90.
52. Unless we accept Barker's premise (quoted in Chapter 5 [p. 104 n. 44]) centring on the translation of the Hebrew *qrb*.

7. The Son of Man

the Hasmonean usurpation of the high priesthood, and the change in calendar, the earthly Anointed and the Temple were considered corrupt and the Day of Atonement ritual no longer effective.[53] The hope then became centred on an exalted heavenly redeemer.

Although *4 Ezra* is dated toward the end of the first century, nonetheless it also has clear allusions to Daniel. In the third of four visions, Ezra sees a wind bringing up from the depths of the sea "something resembling a man and that man was flying with the clouds of heaven." Whilst this is undoubtedly an allusion to Dan 7, a more explicit reference to Daniel is given in *4 Ezra* 12:11. Collins considers a number of allusions within the text to be messianic motifs in the Bible, and states that, "Taken together, these allusions suggest that the man from the sea has taken on the role traditionally ascribed to the messianic king."[54] Furthermore, he points out that in the Latin and Syriac versions of the text, the man is identified as "my son" (*4 Ezra* 13:32, 37), and that in *4 Ezra* 7:28–29 he is called "my son the messiah." Therefore, although both texts feature a Son of Man figure, in *4 Ezra* this is assimilated to the traditional, Davidic Messiah, nevertheless this messiah dies after a 400-year reign and the world reverts to primeval silence for seven days following which there is resurrection. Nonetheless, as John Collins points out, despite the differences the two texts share some common assumptions about the "Son of Man" figure in Daniel:

> Both assume that the figure in Daniel is an individual, not a collective symbol. Both identify him with the messiah, and describe his role in terms usually applied to the Davidic messiah, although they understand his role in different ways. Both the Enochic Son of Man and the man from the sea are pre-existent beings of heavenly origin. Both appropriate imagery that was traditionally reserved for God.[55]

Although *4 Ezra* is held to be later than the *Similitudes*, John Collins finds there to be no literary influence and concludes: "Precisely for that reason, they are independent witnesses to common assumptions about the meaning of Dan 7 in first-century Judaism."[56]

---

53. As we saw in Chapter 6, the temple rituals were understood to correspond with those of the heavenly sanctuary; the change in calendar therefore would mean that these no longer coincided and that the temple rituals would no longer be effective.

54. Collins and Collins, *King and Messiah as Son of God*, 96.

55. Ibid., 98.

56. Ibid.

The Outcome of the Son of Man's Role

The Son of Man will be seated on God's throne (*1 En.* 51:3; 69:27). He will judge and condemn the wicked, establish the New Jerusalem, convert the Gentiles and gather in the exiles (*1 En.* 90:28–38). The resurrection of the righteous dead and the setting-up of the Messianic kingdom will occur "on the appearance of the Messiah [a Lamb]."[57] "The day of the Elect One"[58] and the "day of the Son of Man" also appear to parallel "the day of Yahweh" in the Hebrew Scriptures.

Following judgment, the beast from the sea is destroyed and in *2 Bar.* 29:3 the two monsters (of the fifth day of Creation) Behemoth and Leviathan are also regarded as opponents of the Son of Man. His enthronement is the inauguration of his kingdom, which is universal[59] and everlasting. All the kings of the earth will be destroyed by him[60] and will bow down before him:[61] "All who dwell on earth shall fall down and worship before him, and will praise and bless and celebrate with song the Lord of Spirits."[62] Again, this replicates what is said of the Son of Man in Daniel (Dan 7:13).

As in the surrounding cultures and the Hebrew Scriptures, fertility is one of the expected outcomes of the role of the Anointed. In *1 En.* 10:17 there is a depiction of the Messianic Age, with children, trees, wine and oil in abundance, and, "in those days," after the great day of judgment (10:6), God will "open the store chambers of blessing" (11:1); all nations will offer adoration and praise and worship Yahweh the God of Israel (10:21; 38:5) and there will be peace and truth (11:1), as well as resurrection following the appearance and enthronement of the Son of Man (51:1–2). A similar picture is found in *2 Bar.* 29:5–8.

Conclusion

In the texts of this period, a pre-existent heavenly Son of Man figure, one who was also called the Anointed and understood as a messianic figure, appeared. Although there is nothing to suggest the suffering or humiliation of this figure, in many other ways his role and its outcome closely parallel that of the Anointed identified throughout: he is the agent of

---

57. W. O. E. Oesterley, "Introduction," in *The Book of Enoch* (trans. R. H. Charles; London: SPCK, 2006; first published 1917), 21.
58. *1 En.* 61:5; *2 Esd* 8:42; *2 Bar.* 62:2.
59. *1 En.* 46:4–6; 52:1, 4; 53:1; 62:1–2, 9; *2 Bar.* 39:7–8.
60. *1 En.* 45:4–5; 48:8–9.
61. *1 En.* 62:1–6, 9.
62. *1 En.* 70:1.

judgment and the one who will bring about the universal acknowledgment of the God of Israel. The Son of Man will be seated on God's throne and will be given dominion, glory and kingdom that will not pass away or be destroyed, and all nations will pay homage to him.

The Son of Man, then, is the title of a pre-existent heavenly messianic figure who is closely identified with the Lord of Spirits (that is, God). This figure appears in Jewish texts which either pre-date or are contemporary with the New Testament.

Having now examined the concept of Messiah in Jewish texts that for the most part pre-date the New Testament, we will now turn to the Christian New Testament in order to discover the kind of messiah presented therein and also to consider whether there is any evidence to suggest that this formed part of the natural development of the concept witnessed in the previous chapters, or whether, as the Jewish writers suggest, New Testament messianism is a radical departure from all that had gone before. It may be appropriate to consider Collins' summary before proceeding:

> In the Hellenistic period, when the Davidic line had been broken for centuries, hopes for deliverance often focused on supernatural, heavenly mediator figures. The rise of the Hasmonean dynasty brought a resurgence of hope for a messiah from the line of David, but messianic expectations were often fused with notions of a heavenly deliverer around the turn of the era. In this context the old idea of the king as son of God took on new overtones and it becomes more difficult to maintain a clear distinction between the messiah as a human king and the hope for a transcendent saviour.[63]

---

63. Collins and Collins, *King and Messiah as Son of God*, xi.

Chapter 8

THE MESSIAH IN THE NEW TESTAMENT

Introduction

It is important to be absolutely clear about what I am attempting to achieve in this present chapter. I am not trying to give a survey of current scholarship on the Christology of the New Testament, still less trace the development of early Christian views of Jesus, or offer fresh theological insights into the problems of Christology. My focus instead is on contemporary Jewish–Christian dialogue and the role that the question of Jesus' messiahship plays in this dialogue. In pursuit of this subject I need to establish what the fundamental Christian idea of the messiahship of Jesus is, as opposed to what the Jewish writers in dialogue have suggested. It is not that their version is necessarily incorrect, but if I am to answer their contentions I need to establish my own understanding of the New Testament portrayal of Jesus in order to be able to compare and contrast this with that of the Jewish writers. I will be considering the New Testament, therefore, not as a product of religious history but as a canonical text, held by the Church as authoritative Scripture. This means taking the New Testament synchronically as a whole and concentrating on how it has historically been understood by the Church. Academic scholarship cannot be entirely ignored, but its historical-critical, diachronic approach is of secondary importance to the plain sense of the New Testament, as well as the consensus Christian reading of its Christology, since it is that which is authoritative for the Church, and has featured and continues to feature in Jewish–Christian dialogue. Only in this way is it possible to establish some sort of statement of the Christian view of the Messiah from which to advance the argument.

The Person of the Messiah

Μεσσίας, the Greek transliteration of the Hebrew מָשִׁיחַ (Anointed One/ Messiah) is used in only two places in the New Testament—John 1:41 (τὸν Μεσσίαν) and 4:25—and only in the latter does Jesus directly associate himself with the title.¹ Nonetheless, elsewhere throughout the New Testament Jesus is spoken of as Χριστός (Christ), that is, the Greek translation of the Hebrew מָשִׁיחַ. It could be reasonably argued, therefore, that wherever Jesus is spoken of as Christ,² we have an allusion to his messiahship. On the other hand, Vermes³ understands Jesus' response not to tell anyone about him, which comes in response to Peter's declaration "You are the Christ" (Mark 8:29b), to be a refutation of his messiahship. However, in Matthew's version (Matt 16:17) Jesus calls Peter "blessed" "for flesh and blood has not revealed this to you, but my Father in heaven." This positive response is further confirmed in Matt 16:18.⁴ Further acceptance of Jesus as Messiah by the New Testament writers is found in Matt 27:22; Luke 2:26; 22:67; 24:26–27, 44–46; John 1:45; 10:24–25; Acts 3:18–20; 5:42, as well as at every point at which "Christ/Messiah" is applied to Jesus, if we accept the above premise.⁵

In Chapter 5 we saw the introduction of the idea that Elijah was to be the forerunner of the Messiah and in Matt 17:9–13 Jesus identifies John the Baptist as Elijah,⁶ further strengthening the suggestion that Jesus is understood to be the expected Messiah. Also in this passage, having accepted his identification as the Messiah, Jesus refers to himself as "the

---

1. This affirmation is disputed by some scholars. Williams comments: "A comparison of the use of ἐγώ εἰμι in 4:26 with other Johannine and non-Johannine examples of the bipartite phrase reveals that it forms an appropriate and natural expression of affirmation, serving either as a reply to a question introduced by σὺ εἶ (cf. LXX II Sam 2:20; Mark 14:62) or to a statement which does not necessary call for a direct form of response (cf. John 9:9)." Catrin H. Williams, *I am He: The Interpretation of Ani Hû in Jewish and Early Christian Literature* (Tübingen: Mohr Siebeck, 2000), 259.

2. Wright refutes the supposed misappropriation or "translation" of the title Messiah by the early Christians, and comments "Paul, in company with all other very early Christians actually known to us (as opposed to those invented by ingenious scholars), believed that Jesus was indeed the true Messiah, and held that belief as a central identifying mark." Wright, *Jesus*, 486.

3. Considered in Chapter 2.

4. "And I tell you, you are Peter, and on this rock I will build my church and the gates of Hades will not prevail against it."

5. "Messiah" is in fact the preferred translation in the English text used throughout this work, but only for the Gospels, Acts and Revelation. Elsewhere, although translating the same Greek word Χριστός (in whatever grammatical form), "Christ" is used instead.

6. The identification of John the Baptist and Elijah is further suggested in Matt 3:4: "Now John wore a garment of camel's hair, and a leather girdle around his waist." In 2 Kgs 1:8 it says of Elijah "He wore a haircloth with a girdle of leather about his loins." See also (Matt 11:11–15; Mark 9:11–13; John 1:19–20).

Son of Man," thus equating the two concepts. This scene forms part of a Mosaic typology identified by scholars in Matthew,[7] and later Rabbinic tradition also expected that the Messiah would be not a prophet,[8] but *the* prophet;[9] Jesus is therefore identified not just as a prophet,[10] but as *the* prophet "who is to come into the world,"[11] that is, the prophet like Moses.[12] This again would appear to underline Jesus' role as messianic,[13] as does the presence of both Moses *and* Elijah, representing the Law and the Prophets respectively at Jesus' transfiguration (Matt 17:1–7).[14]

I stated at the outset of this work that the origins of the concept of the Anointed were to be found in the role of the king, and this is indeed what was discovered in the preceding chapters. We should therefore expect to find Jesus' role as Anointed connected with that of the king, and in Matt 1:1–17/Luke 3:23–38[15] there is a genealogy which traces Jesus' ancestry back to King David, from whose line the Messiah is expected to come. Furthermore, when the kings from the East enquire where the "King of

---

7. The Moses typology of the infancy narratives in Matthew is widely recognized; see, for example, Dale C. Allison Jr., *The New Moses* (Edinburgh: T. & T. Clark, 1993), 140.

8. Ibid., 2.

9. "Rabbi Berekiah said in the name of Rabbi Isaac: 'As the first redeemer was, so shall the latter Redeemer be. What is stated of the former redeemer?' And Moses took his wife and his sons, and set them upon an ass (Exod 4:20). Similarly will it be with the latter Redeemer, as it is stated, 'Lowly and riding upon an ass' (Zech 9:9)" (*Eccl. Rab.* 1:28), cited in ibid., 85.

10. Luke 7:16; John 4:19. See ibid., 249.

11. John 6:14; Acts 3:22.

12. Deut 18:15.

13. In *Targum Yerushalmi* Moses and the Messiah are also linked. Levey comments: "The linking together of Moses and the Messiah is striking, carrying the force of historical determination, the final drama of Israel's history to be a re-enactment of the deliverance which marked the beginning of Israel's career as a nation." Levey then draws comparisons between Jesus' life and that of Moses. Levey, *The Messiah*, 13.

14. In *Targum Yerushalmi* there is an interesting parallel with this passage whereby the Messiah, Moses and the Memra of the Lord are together on the top of a cloud to bring about the final deliverance of the world. Ibid., 12–13.

15. Barnett has advanced two separate arguments to attempt to validate the statements in Luke (and Matthew) that Joseph was not Jesus' biological father and yet Jesus was considered to be descended from the line of David. He reasons: (1) that it is quite possible that Mary was also descended from the line of David, since Jewish ethnicity and tribal decent "were frequently reckoned through the mother," meaning that Jesus would be of that line; (2) that Joseph acted as legal father in the naming and registering of his son (Matt 1:20–21; Luke 2:1–5). Paul Barnett, *Jesus and the Rise of Early Christianity* (Downers Grove, Ill.: InterVarsity, 1999), 96.

the Jews" is to be born, Herod immediately asks where "the Christ" is to be born, thus making a king/Messiah equation. The scribes and chief priests, quoting from Mic 5:2,[16] then reply that the Messiah is to be born in Bethlehem of Judea (Matt 2:5–6), the place where we have been told earlier that Jesus was born (Matt 2:1) and which is also "the city of David" (Luke 2:4). In addition, the annunciation to Mary (Luke 1:32–33) takes the form of a divine kingship oracle, in which Mary is told Jesus will be given "the throne of his father David, and he will reign over the house of Jacob for ever; and of his kingdom there will be no end."[17] Mary's response (Luke 1:46–55) is resonant with that of Hannah (1 Sam 2:1–10) at the dedication of Samuel, a passage which is understood messianically in later Rabbinic tradition.[18] Hannah's "song" has also been identified as a "royal psalm" and the suggestion has been made that this narrative originally concerned Saul, the first king of Israel, rather than Samuel.[19]

Apart from the words spoken at Jesus' annunciation and baptism (Luke 3:22), the latter resonating with the words spoken to the newly enthroned king (Ps 2:7), there is little to indicate the kingship of Jesus between the infancy narratives and his final week, a factor that has led some scholars (as we saw in Chapter 2) to doubt the relevance of this aspect of Jesus' role.[20] On the other hand, not only is Jesus welcomed as king in his entry to Jerusalem, following his anointing,[21] but also this is

16. The paraphrase in *Targum Jonathan* reads: "…from you shall come forth before Me the Messiah to exercise dominion over Israel, he whose name was mentioned from before, from the days of creation." See Levey, *The Messiah*, 93.

17. The promise of an everlasting kingdom is also given to David in the Psalms (Ps 89:4) and to the Son of Man in Dan 7:14.

18. *Targum Jonathan*. Cf. Levey, *The Messiah*, 35.

19. "Hannah named her son Samuel. The name in the narrative is interpreted as meaning 'I have asked him of the Lord' but this interpretation belongs, etymologically, to the name Saul. It is almost impossible to connect the meaning 'asked' to the name Samuel except perhaps by assonance. It has therefore been suggested that the etymology, and probably the whole birth story with it, has been displaced from Saul to Samuel in the course of compilation or transmission." L. H. Brockington, "I and II Samuel," in Black, ed., *Peake's Commentary*, 319.

20. According to Collins, Jesus functions as a prophet rather than "a royal pretender" for most of his career. Collins comments: "The only episode in Jesus' career that fits a scriptural paradigm for a kingly messiah is the triumphal entry into Jerusalem." Collins, *The Scepter and the Star*, 206. Collins also quotes a number of scholars, including Hengel, Schweitzer, Mowinckel, Dunn and Juel, who see Jesus' messiahship as a departure from the expectations of a Davidic Messiah, the latter declaring that, in light of post-biblical Jewish tradition, "to claim Jesus is the Messiah is absurd." Collins, *The Scepter and the Star*, 204.

21. Matt 26:7; John 11:2; 12:3.

understood as fulfilment of Zech 9:9, which speaks of the triumphal entry of the king, further confirmed in the mention of both the ass and the colt in Zech 9:9 and in Matt 21:5–6.[22]

In addition, this takes place at Passover, the time when the King Messiah is traditionally expected to appear, coming over the Mount of Olives, as Jesus did, and entering into Jerusalem. The crowd gathered for Passover spread their clothes on the road for Jesus to ride over and proclaim, "Blessed is he who comes in the name of the LORD" (Matt 21:9), a direct quotation applied to the king from Ps 118:26.[23] Notably, in Matt 21:9, 15; Mark 11:9, 10 and John 12:13 the crowd shout "Hosanna," and in the latter we are told that the crowd cut palm branches and spread them across the road, a detail which is more suggestive of Sukkoth than Passover and may again evidence the post-exilic fragmentation of the original enthronement festival.[24] Luke's version reads "Blessed is the *king* who comes in the name of the Lord!" (Luke 19:38), and the succeeding line takes us back by allusion to the proclamation of Jesus' birth by the angels—"Peace in heaven and glory in the highest" (Luke 2:14)—confirming that, for Luke, Jesus' epiphany as a peaceful king and what that will entail is the consummation of the announcement at his birth.[25] A further phrase applied to the king in Ps 118:22, "the stone that the builders rejected has become the chief cornerstone," is applied

---

22. Allison, *The New Moses*, 251. Allison suggested that the plural version of the Zechariah quotation may have been used deliberately by Matthew to draw an association between this and the Septuagint version of Exod 4:20, which has Moses return to Egypt with *hypozugia* (beasts) again reflecting the idea that "the last things are as the first."

23. This takes us by allusion to 2 Kgs 9:13: "Then hurriedly they all took their cloaks and spread them for him on the bare steps; and they blew the trumpet, and proclaimed, 'Jehu is king'."

24. Morgenstern has advanced a comprehensive argument that this was also a feature of the festival of *Massoth* and that Jesus was in fact replicating the earlier practice carried out by kings of Israel and in particular David, as evidenced in 2 Sam 15:16–37. Morgenstern, *Some Significant Antecedents*, 16–40. Chilton suggests that Jesus' entry into Jerusalem was at Sukkoth, which therefore explains the use of "leafy branches" (Mark 11:8), that is, these were the *lulavim* which were used in the procession to the temple. In support of this he cites the crowd's cry of "Hosanna," meaning "save us" (Matt 21:9; Mark 11:9; John 12:13), which is a characteristic element of this festival. Chilton refers to *m. Suk.* 3:9 and 4:5, which cite Pss 18:25 and 118:25 as the source of the cry. Bruce Chilton, "Feast-Festival of Booths," *NIB* 1:493. In Chapter 4 I identified Pss 18 and 118 as enthronement psalms and observed that both form part of the Hallel, which, as noted, is sung at Sukkot.

25. Note that in Matt 21:9 Jesus is hailed as "Son of David" and that Mark 11:10 reads: "Blessed is the coming kingdom of our ancestor David!"

to Jesus (Luke 20:17; Acts 4:11), again suggesting Jesus' identification as king in the minds of the New Testament writers.

At his crucifixion Jesus is also mocked and saluted as "King of the Jews," having been clothed in a purple cloak and fitted with a crown of thorns. Furthermore, this title was fixed above his cross as his charge (Mark 15:26).[26] The absence of any political aspect to his kingship is understood by the Jewish writers to mitigate further against the importance of this title, whereas I would argue that the very lack of a political agenda,[27] coupled with the insistence on the title of kingship, leads to the supposition that what we are dealing with here is sacral kingship, as elicited from the earlier chapters where we saw that the Anointed's role as king was predominantly a cultic one. Jesus' role as king is further confirmed in the application of the term "shepherd."[28] In Mark 14:27 Jesus quotes Zech 13:7—"Strike the shepherd, that the sheep may be scattered"—and applies it to his betrayal and abandonment by his disciples. Shepherd imagery is also used in Matt 9:36; John 21:15–17; 1 Pet 5:2–4 and throughout John 10. In John 10:11 Jesus says, "I am the good shepherd" and in Heb 13:20 Jesus is called "that great Shepherd of the Sheep."

The identification of the king/god found in the preceding chapters is also evident here. The title Κύριος is used of Jesus in numerous places;[29] this is the Greek translation of the Hebrew יהוה (Yahweh) in the Septuagint; whereas אלהים (God) in the Hebrew Scriptures is translated

---

26. Each of the Synoptic Gospels records this; see Matt 27:37; Mark 15:26; Luke 23:38. In John's Gospel it is elaborated: "Pilate also wrote a title and put it on the cross; it read, 'Jesus of Nazareth, the King of the Jews'. Many of the Jews read this title, for the place where Jesus was crucified was near the city; and it was written in Hebrew, in Latin and in Greek. The chief priest of the Jews then said to Pilate, 'Do not write "The King of the Jews," but "This man said: 'I am King of the Jews'."' Pilate answered, 'What I have written I have written'" (John 19:19–22). The level of detail supplied here, as well as the repetition, suggests that John understood that he was dealing with a significant issue.

27. We saw in Chapter 2 that, despite his earlier work, Maccoby had rejected the idea that Jesus' messiahship was political. Also to be noted is John 18:36, in which Jesus states: "My kingdom is not from this world; if my kingdom were from this world, my followers would be fighting to keep me from being handed over to the Jews. But as it is my kingdom is not from here."

28. In the preceding chapters this term is applied to the king.

29. For example, in Luke 1:43 Elizabeth asks Mary "And why is this happened to me, that the mother of my Lord (τοῦ Κυρίου μου) comes to me?" In Luke 2:11 the angels announce, "for to you is born this day in the city of David, a Saviour who is Christ the Lord" (Χριστὸς Κύριος).

as θεός. In Col 3:13 Jesus is referred to as "the Lord" (ὁ Κύριος)[30] and 1 Cor 10:9 reads "we must not put the Lord to the test as some of them did and were destroyed by serpents." Although this alludes to the Exodus, "Lord" here translating יהוה of the Hebrew Scriptures, some manuscripts have "Christ" instead of Lord at this point, suggesting an identification between Jesus and Yahweh. Furthermore, in 1 Cor 5:5, "the Day of the Lord," that is, the Day of Yahweh, has become "the Day of the Lord Jesus."[31] In addition, the angel which led Israel through the desert had the name of Yahweh "in him,"[32] and again this has been identified with Yahweh in the Jewish tradition[33] and with Jesus in Christian tradition.[34] Additionally, what is said of the LORD in Isa 45:23 is applied to Jesus in Rom 14:11 and Phil 2:10–11. The declaration in Rom 10:9, "Jesus Christ is Lord," is understood as one of the earliest Christian confessions of faith, distinguishing "those who believed in Jesus from those who did not."[35] Again, it could be argued that it was the identification of Jesus as Yahweh that was at stake here, so that what was actually being said was "Jesus, the Messiah is Yahweh." Similarly, according to 1 Cor 12:3 no one can say "Jesus is Lord" except by the Holy spirit, again suggesting that the term "Lord" is more than an honorific title.

In Isa 41:4 and 44:6 Yahweh calls himself "the first and the last" and in Rev 1:8, 11; 21:6 and 22:13 Jesus is referred to as the Alpha and Omega. Furthermore, the term "stumbling block" applied to Yahweh in Isa 8:14 is applied to Jesus in 1 Cor 1:22 and 1 Pet 2:8, a further feature which may also suggest a Jesus–Yahweh identification. An additional

---

30. In Col 3:24 he is called "the Lord Christ" and in Col 1:3 "the Lord Jesus Christ." In Col 3:18–24 he is referred to as "Lord" five times.

31. It was noted in the previous chapter that at Qumran, in the 11QMelchizedek scroll (2.9), Melchizedek's name is substituted for that of "the Lord"—"in the year of the Lord's favour" (citing Isa 61:2, the text with which Jesus inaugurates his ministry). We will see below that Jesus is identified with the Melchizedek priesthood.

32. "This text [Exod 23:20–22] testifies that a figure that has some independence from YHWH can still share in his being through the possession of the Divine Name (i.e. a divine hypostasis). If this 'angel' has the name YHWH in him, he can be understood to be YHWH in a visible form." Gieschen, "The Name of the Son of Man," 243.

33. "Jewish tradition regarded also 'the Destroyer' in Exod 12:23 as an angel, even as the Angel of the Lord. This is only logical, because this verse bears witness to the same interchangeability of *Yahweh* and 'the Destroyer' as that of *Yahweh* and his Angel found in a good many theophanies related in Genesis, Exodus, and Judges." Fossum, *The Image*, 112.

34. This is understood as a Christophany by Justin, *Dialogue with Trypho* 120.3.

35. Alister E. McGrath, *Christian Theology* (Oxford: Blackwell, 1997), 328.

correspondence is found between Jesus and Yahweh in the ἐγώ εἰμι statements as this phrase in the Septuagint translates the אני הוא, the divine pronouncement of the Hebrew Scriptures:[36]

> In Greek, the phrase "I am" without a predicate is meaningless. Thus, there must be some esoterical significance of the use of ἐγώ εἰμι in these passages. It is commonly agreed that the absolute use of ἐγώ εἰμι in the Gospel of John reflects אני הוא (or אנכי הוא) as used in Deutero-Isaiah, where it occurs as a formula of self-revelation spoken by God, or even as a divine name.[37]

Further confirmation of this identification is given in the reaction to the pronouncements. In John 18:6, for example, at Jesus' arrest, as a consequence of the ἐγώ εἰμι pronouncement, the soldiers fall to the ground.[38] This has therefore been understood to suggest that Jesus was announcing himself as the LORD of the Hebrew Scriptures (Exod 3:14).[39] On the ἐγώ εἰμι statement of John 8:58, Fossum comments: "The reaction to Jesus' statement is noteworthy. The Jews want to stone him."[40] Stoning was the penalty for blasphemy, which required the utterance of the Divine Name.[41] This identification also occurs in Matt 14:27, where Jesus again declares ἐγώ εἰμι whilst walking on the water and then calms the storm. As a consequence, those who were in the boat worshiped him, saying, "Truly you are the Son of God" (Matt 14:33).[42] This appears to replicate Ps 89:9, where it is said of Yahweh, "You rule the raging of the sea; when its waves rise, you still them." Fossum comments: "The defeat and imprisonment of the Sea or Deep is of course the *sine qua non* for the creation of the cosmos. This was effected by the divine Word = Name."[43] The following line in the psalm—"You crushed Rahab like a carcass, you scattered your enemies with your mighty arm" (v. 10)—would

---

36. Deut 32:39; Isa 41:4; 43:10; 46:4. Williams also cites Isa 52:6. See Williams, *I am He*, 256.

37. Fossum, *The Image*, 127.

38. "When the high priest in the ritual of the Day of Atonement spoke the Name, the priests standing near him fell to the ground." Ibid., 129.

39. "Jews did not fall to the ground for a mere man. The utterance of the Divine Name, however, made people drop. The Jewish apologist Artapanus (ca. 100 B.C.E.), relates that Pharaoh fell as if dead when he heard Moses utter the Name of God." Ibid.

40. Ibid., 128.

41. Ibid.

42. "Some scholars have seen an allusion to the Exodus event when God led the people through the Sea, but a more plausible background is to be found in the myth that God in primordial times subdued the waters of Chaos." Ibid.

43. Ibid., 117.

appear to confirm this.⁴⁴ Fossum therefore concludes that when, for example, in John 6:20, Jesus utters "I am" while walking on the sea, he appears as the personified Divine Name.⁴⁵ This incident is also thought to replicate that which is said of Yahweh in the Septuagint version of Job 9:8.⁴⁶ Later tradition also associated "the Name" with the power to calm the sea.⁴⁷ Gieschen states:

> The Gospel of John, which identifies Jesus frequently as the Son of Man, also depicts him as the embodiment of the Divine Name of the Father to the extent that Jesus even prays πατερ δοξασον σου το ονομα ("Father, glorify your name," 12:28). This is not simply a pious prayer that God's name be glorified through Christ's sacrifice; it is the identification of Jesus as the one who possesses the Divine Name. This indicates that he can simply be identified as "the Name," much like the visible manifestations of YHWH of Deuteronomy and Jeremiah.⁴⁸

Although Jesus is identified with Yahweh himself, he is also called "Son of God" in numerous places throughout the New Testament, including not only John's Gospel but also the Synoptics.⁴⁹ The reaction to it, particularly at Jesus' trial,⁵⁰ suggests that it was understood as a claim to divinity. We saw in Chapter 4 that the king was understood to be "son of God" and that this title could refer to Jesus in his capacity as king.

---

44. It was demonstrated in Chapter 4 that Rahab was equated with the Chaos/Chaos Waters, which Yahweh conquered before his act of creation.

45. Fossum, *The Image*, 128–29.

46. Ibid., 128.

47. I noted in Chapter 6 the rabbinic understanding that a shard with the Divine Name written on it caused the waters of the deep, *Tehom*, that is, the Chaos Waters, to recede. This understanding lives on in popular mythology. Fossum cites a German tradition that John's Gospel, if cast into a troubled sea, would calm it. Fossum suggests that his tradition is based on the knowledge "that the Gospel according to John is *the* Gospel about the Name of God." Ibid. There is also a tradition that an Afikoman which is kept for seven years will also calm troubled waters. The Afikoman (the name is often taken to mean "the One who is to Come"—although this translation is disputed) is understood as a symbol of the Messiah. In light of the foregoing it could be argued therefore that it is also associated with the name of God. See Israel Jacob Yuval, *Two Nations in Your Womb: Perceptions of Jews and Christians in Late Antiquity and the Middle Ages* (London: University of California Press, 2006), 242.

48. Gieschen, "The Name of the Son of Man," 246.

49. Matt 4:3; 8:29; 14:33; 27:43; Mark 1:1; 3:11; Luke 1:35; 3:38; 4:41; 22:70; John 1:34, 49; 3:18; 5:25; 10:36; 11:27; 19:7; 20:31.

50. This is, in fact, the charge brought against him by "the Jews": "We have a law, and according to that law he ought to die because he has claimed to be the Son of God" (John 19:7).

However, in Heb 1:6 Jesus is said to be the "firstborn," and in John 1:3 and Heb 1:2 we are told that the world was created through him. Again, this replicates what is said of Yahweh (Isa 42:5). However, as I discussed, in Deut 32:8 Yahweh is also understood to be the pre-eminent son of the Most High. Thus, whilst Jesus' title "Son of God" *could* relate to his relationship as king/Anointed with Yahweh, equally it could be conjectured that in his identification with Yahweh he is "Son of (the Most High) God" and in Mark 5:7 and Luke 1:32 Jesus is in fact called "Son of the Most High God." Therefore, as I found in the surrounding cultures, the king/Anointed is identified with both the creator god and the high god. Furthermore, as the offspring of both Mary, (a virgin) to whom later Christian tradition attributed goddess status,[51] and the Most High,[52] like the kings in the surrounding cultures, Jesus could also be considered to be "offspring of the gods."

Further indications of the divinity of Jesus are found in Col 1:15–16a,[53] 19[54] and 2:9.[55] In Phil 2:5–7 we learn that Jesus "was in the form of God," but emptied himself, "taking the form of a servant being born in the likeness of men." Jesus' divinity is also attested in John 1:1, linked with his role as Anointed (John 1:41) and king (John 1:49) and in John 1:18, which also links Jesus with the Father: "No one has ever seen God, but the one and only Son, who is himself God and is in closest relationship with the Father, has made him known." This suggests that there is a hidden, unknowable God who is only made known through the manifestation of Jesus, a corollary of which must be that the God who is made manifest in the Hebrew Scriptures[56] is also Jesus—and this is in fact what was understood by the early Church Fathers.[57]

---

51. Mary's own conception becomes "immaculate"; she is declared *aiparthenos*, *theotokos*, and her bodily assumption represents the final stage in her "deification." She is also depicted in iconography as the woman of Rev 12 with twelve stars around her head and came to be associated with other goddess features and functions, particularly those connected with fertility. See Marina Warner, *Alone of All Her Sex* (London: Pan, 1985), 266.

52. Luke 1:35.

53. Col 1:15–16a: "He is the image of the invisible God, the first-born of all creation for in (or by) him all things in heaven and on earth were created."

54. Phil 2:5–7: "For in him all the fullness of God was pleased to dwell." It is interesting that it is also in Colossians that Jesus is referred to as "Lord," suggesting an identification with Yahweh, as noted above, and further confirming his divinity.

55. Col 2:9: "For in him the whole fullness of deity dwells bodily."

56. Gen 18:1, 13; Exod 24:10; 33:11; 34:29.

57. Irenaeus explains: "no doubt, because the Son of God is implanted everywhere throughout his writings: at one time, indeed, speaking with Abraham, when about to eat with him; at another with Noah, giving to him the dimensions [of the

In this light, Jesus, as Yahweh, may also be understood to represent an aspect of the high god, as we saw in the preceding chapters, and in Rabbinic thought Yahweh is equated with god's aspect of mercy. Interestingly, Jesus is similarly associated in the Christian tradition. Jesus' pre-existence is made clear in John 17:5[58] and 16:28, as is his heavenly status in 8:23. There is also a complete identification between Jesus the Son, and God the Father in John 14:7–9, which again is paralleled in the preceding chapters whereby not only are the gods spoken of in terms of a father/son relationship but also, whilst at times they are spoken of separately, at others there is a complete identification between them.

In Second Temple Judaism we saw that there was a development in the messianic concept whereby a pre-existent heavenly redeemer figure designated "Son of Man" emerged. In the Gospels Jesus is not only understood to be a pre-existent, heavenly redeemer (John 1:1, 29), but also "Son of Man" is in fact Jesus' preferred self-designation.[59] Indeed, in Heb 2:6 we see that "Son of Man" of Ps 8:4–6 is applied to Jesus. Furthermore, despite scholarly ambivalence about its meaning,[60] it was demonstrated in the previous chapter that "Son of Man" is not only a specific title,[61] it is, in fact, a title bearing divine and messianic connotations.[62] This was the understanding which seemingly prevailed in Jewish texts that pre-date the first century, texts which were extant at the

---

ark]; and another inquiring after Adam; at another bringing down judgment upon the Sodomites; and again, when He becomes visible, and directs Jacob on his journey and speaks with Moses from the bush." Irenaeus, *Against Heresies* 10.1.

58. John 17:5: "So now, Father, glorify me in your own presence with the glory that I had in your presence before the world existed."

59. Occurring here 82 times. According to Mowinckel, the phrase must have included "essential elements of what Jesus wanted to say about Himself; otherwise He would not have adopted it, and allowed it almost completely to supersede the title of Messiah." Mowinckel, *He That Cometh*, 348. Hurtado, however, states: "For 'the son of man' to be used so heavily by all three Synoptic authors and also by the author of the Gospel of John surely indicates that this feature of the Jesus tradition endeared itself early and wisely to a broad swath of Christians." Larry W. Hurtado, *Lord Jesus Christ: Devotion to Jesus in Earliest Christianity* (Grand Rapids: Eerdmans, 2005), 305.

60. See Wright for a discussion of the wide-ranging views and positions taken on the "Son of Man" phrase, including a useful bibliography. Wright, *Jesus*, 512.

61. As opposed to being a circumlocution, as is suggested by some scholars, including the Jewish writers examined in Chapter 2 (with the exception of Sandmel).

62. See also Chrys C. Caragounis, *The Son of Man* (WUNT 38; Tübingen: Mohr, 1986), 19–20. Caragounis surveys recent scholarship on the subject which discredits Vermes' circumlocution theory and attests the phrase as a designation of a pre-existent heavenly figure.

time of Jesus.⁶³ What is more, a correspondence is drawn between Jesus and the Son of Man figure of Dan 7:13–14, either through allusion or direct quotation in Matt 10:23; 13:41; 16:28; 19:28; 24:39; 25:31.

When Jesus says to the high priest at his trial (Matt 26:63–64; Mark 14:61–64), "From now on you will see the Son of Man seated at the right hand of Power and coming on the clouds of heaven" (an allusion to Dan 7:13), the high priest rends his garments. It is not possible to know whether the high priest's reaction was to Jesus acknowledging that he was "the Christ, the Son of God" or that he was the Son of Man.⁶⁴ However, in Acts 7:55 the charge of blasphemy and the title "the Son of Man" are directly connected, a fact which results in the crowd stoning Stephen. From the Mishnah we learn that blasphemy only takes place if the Divine Name is pronounced, upon which the judges are to stand on their feet and rend their garments.⁶⁵ This incidence in Acts 7:55–56 affords a direct identification of Jesus as the heavenly Son of Man. Other incidences also suggest an equation of the Son of Man title with God: in Matt 9:2–6, Jesus claims that the Son of Man "has authority on earth to forgive sins" and from the earlier reaction of the scribes we deduce that the forgiveness of sins is the sole prerogative of God (Matt 9:3).

---

63. Nonetheless, there are a number of scholars who think otherwise; these include: Barnabas Lindars, *Jesus Son of Man: A Fresh Examination of the Son of Man Sayings in the Gospels and in the Light of Recent Research* (Grand Rapids: Eerdmans, 1983), and Maurice Casey, *Son of Man: The Interpretation and Influence of Daniel 7* (London: SPCK, 1979). For a critique of Lindars' view, see Richard Bauckham, "The Son of Man: 'A Man in My Position' or 'Someone'?," in *The Jewish World Around the New Testament* (WUNT 233; Tübingen: Mohr Siebeck, 2008), 93–102.

64. "For the high priest/Sanhedrin it was blasphemy because in the words of Jesus he/they discerned Jesus' claim to be that Son of Man. Again, unless the designation SM was a current messianic title, loaded with the Danielic content—not to speak of the content which 1 En 37–71 (and later IV Ez 13) had added to the concept—there would seem to have been no reason for the high priest to be so upset or to condemn Jesus to death. Moreover, the equation of Son of Man with Son of God made by the Sanhedrin (Lk 22:69f) in drawing its conclusions from Jesus' words (vs. 69) shows that for the Jewish authorities Son of Man was actually equivalent to Son of God." Caragounis, *The Son of Man*, 141–42.

65. *M. Sanh.* 7:5. However, Williams states, "recent scholarship has shown that the narrow interpretation of blasphemy outlined in m.Sanh. 7:5 belongs to a date closer to 200 CE, whereas an earlier tradition attributed to Eliezer ben Yose ha-Gelili (T3) offers a considerably wider definition." Williams, *I am He*, 248. Nonetheless, Ford accepts the evidence of the Mishnah: "The charge of blasphemy must be due to using a substitute for the Divine Name. This substitute appears to be 'Son of Man'." Ford, cited in Caragounis, *Son of Man*, 141.

In Matt 12:8 Jesus says that the Son of Man is "Lord of the Sabbath." Also, in John 9:36–38, when Jesus announces himself as the Son of Man to the blind man that he has healed, we are told that the blind man worshiped Jesus. All of this would seem to indicate that the Son of Man title had divine connotations; we saw that was the case in the previous chapter. Collins states: "The 'one like a Son of Man' in Daniel's vision is described in imagery that normally is reserved for Yahweh in the Hebrew Bible."[66]

In the preceding chapters I noted an association of the sun with the Anointed/god/God, and that Isa 9:2 is quoted in Matt 4:16 and applied to Jesus. In John 8:12 Jesus says that those that follow him will have "the light of life" and in John 1:4, 8–9 he is referred to as "the light of the world."[67] Further allusions are found in 2 Cor 4:6 and Eph 5:14. He is also designated "the Morning Star" (Rev 22:16), and in later tradition "the sun of righteousness; risen with healing in its wings" (Mal 4:2) is also applied to Jesus.[68] Furthermore, Christianity took over the pagan sun festivals and celebrated its major events on the same dates.[69]

In the surrounding cultures and in the Hebrew Scriptures we have seen that the king (the Anointed) functioned as high priest, and that after the Exile the high priest in Israel became *the* Anointed. Although Jesus is not linked to the Aaronic priesthood[70] at his crucifixion, his robe is said to be seamless (John 19:23), which was a stipulation of Aaron's robe in Exod 28:32. By contrast, in the Letter to the Hebrews, Ps 110:4, which refers to the king as high priest "in the order of Melchizedek," is quoted and applied to Jesus,[71] and Jesus' role is set out as a recapitulation of that role effecting a final atonement.

In later tradition Jesus is associated with the tree of life[72] and he uses the imagery of himself as the vine who sustains his disciples, the

---

66. Collins, *The Scepter and the Star*, 208.

67. See also Eph 5:14 and 2 Cor 4:6, the latter being understood as an allusion to Gen 1:3.

68. See Melito of Sardis, *Bapt. Frg.* VIIB. This line also forms part of a traditional Christmas hymn by Charles Wesley dated 1739, suggesting this allusion had been passed down through tradition.

69. "Thus the Christian liturgical year commemorates the birth of its god after the winter solstice on the day when the sun has ended its long hibernation and… celebrates his rebirth from the dead on the day when the sun has finally triumphed over darkness…" Warner, *Alone of All Her Sex*, 256.

70. This formed one of the objections of the Jewish writers discussed in Chapter 2, above.

71. Heb 5:5–6; 7:17, 21.

72. See Origen, *Against Celsus* 6.4.34, where the cross is associated with the tree of life, as a counterpart of the tree of knowledge as the cause of the Fall. Also, in

branches.[73] He also identifies himself as the source of life-giving water,[74] which in turn is associated with the life-giving spirit (John 7:37–39), which he breathes onto his disciples (John 20:22). All of these are features identified with the king (the Anointed) in earlier chapters.

The Role of the Messiah

Throughout the New Testament, atonement and messiahship are equated: "he is the atoning sacrifice for our sins, and not for ours only but also for the sins of the whole world" (1 John 2:2); "for Christ also suffered for sins once for all, the righteous for the unrighteous" (1 Pet 3:18). Furthermore, this equation of the Messiah and his death as atonement is said to have been foretold in the Hebrew Scriptures and fulfilled in Jesus (1 Cor 15:3). In Acts 18:24–28 Apollos ("who was well versed in the scriptures") attested that it was possible to demonstrate from the scriptures that "the Messiah is Jesus," and in Acts 17:1–3 Paul argues from the Scriptures to the Jews in Thessalonica, "explaining and proving that it was necessary for the Messiah to suffer and to rise from the dead." Paul concludes: "This is the Messiah, Jesus whom I am proclaiming to you" (Acts 17:3). Again, this is confirmed in Luke 24:26–27[75] and Acts 3:18–22, as well as in Acts 7:52, where Jesus is referred to as "the Righteous One," which we saw in the previous chapter was a designation of the Son of Man in *1 Enoch*.

In Mark's Gospel the emphasis on suffering and atonement proceeds directly after Peter's messianic confession and is particularly associated with Jesus' "Son of Man" title.[76] Here Jesus explains that the "Son of Man" must suffer and be killed and will rise again on the third day (Mark 8:31). This is confirmed in Matt 17:22 and elaborated in Matt 20:18.[77] In

---

Recognitions of Clement 45 it is stated that Jesus is called "Christ" because he was anointed with oil from the wood of the tree of life.

73. John 15:1–8.
74. John 4:10–14; 6:35; 7:37–38.
75. Luke 24:26–27: "'…Was it not necessary that the Messiah should suffer these things and then enter into his glory?' Then beginning with Moses and all the Prophets, he interpreted to them the things about himself in all the scriptures."
76. James Dunn sees this as a natural progression: "Having at last got over to them the message that he is Messiah, he must now explain *what kind* of Messiah." Dunn, *The Christ*, 68 (original emphasis).
77. Matt 20:18: "See, we are going up to Jerusalem, and the Son of Man will be handed over to the chief priests and scribes and they will condemn him to death; then they will deliver him to the Gentiles to be mocked and flogged and crucified and on the third day he will be raised."

Matthew's Gospel the eschatological aspect of the Son of Man's role is more prominent,[78] with an emphasis on judgment (Matt 19:28; 25:31–46); in the latter, the Son of Man is seated as king and judges all nations, separating the sheep from the goats—a parallel of the passage in Ezek 34:17 where Yahweh as king judges "between the sheep and the goats." Jesus is given authority to judge by "the Father" *because* he is the Son of Man (John 5:27). This eschatological aspect of the Son of Man has also been held to relate directly to the "Son of Man" figure in Dan 7:13–14.[79] Further New Testament evidence of an eschatological aspect to the Son of Man is to be found in the Apocalypse: Rev 1:13 and 14:14 are understood to refer to the risen Jesus.[80]

On examination of the New Testament it becomes apparent that three distinct images are used to portray the one central event of the Gospels—the suffering, death and resurrection of the Anointed—involving three distinct figures. These are the Suffering Servant of Isaiah, the Passover lamb and the high priest on the Day of Atonement. I would argue that just as the festivals represent a fragmentation of the New Year festival and its enthronement ritual, these different images and roles are also part of that same phenomenon—not that each represents a different aspect, but that each complements the other, only together giving the full picture. Whilst the Passover and Day of Atonement images have obvious connections with the festivals and their expected outcomes, the Servant imagery also closely resembles features of the enthronement ceremony which we have elicited from the surrounding cultures and the Hebrew Scriptures. It becomes evident, however, that for the New Testament writers, this central event of Jesus' suffering, death and resurrection is not understood as a *recapitulation* of these other rituals, but their intentional fulfilment. This understanding of Jesus' role as fulfilment is particularly evident in the Letter to the Hebrews, which draws direct parallels with the high priest's actions on the Day of Atonement and Jesus' death and resurrection.

The Letter to the Hebrews portrays Jesus as the high priest[81] and identifies his role as the once-and-for-all intended fulfilment of what had been an annual requirement only partially and imperfectly fulfilled by the high priest. This priesthood, unlike the other earthly ones, is a priesthood

---

78. Although there are also eschatological aspects in the Markan Son of Man (Mark 8:38; 13:26–27; 14:62).

79. See Collins, *The Scepter and the Star*, 177–78.

80. There are, in effect, 19 direct references or allusions to ch. 7 of Daniel in the book of Revelation.

81. Heb 2:17; 3:1; 4:14; 5:5, 10; 6:20; 7:17, 26; 8:1; 9:11.

forever (Heb 7:17)—hence Jesus' sacrifice is also permanent and need not be repeated (Heb 7:27). Nonetheless, it is portrayed in exactly the same way as that of the high priest at the Day of Atonement (9:1–15), with Jesus' sacrifice and blood being paralleled with that of the animal sacrifice and blood, which instead of being presented in the Holy of Holies by the high priest, was presented by Jesus, the high priest into heaven (Heb 9:23–28). We saw in Chapter 6 that at Qumran in 11Q13,[82] the high priest Melchizedek was expected to make Atonement at the tenth jubilee:

> Throughout the Melchizedek text there is allusion to Isaiah 61, the one anointed by the Spirit "to proclaim liberty," the Jubilee prescription in Leviticus 25:10.
>
> Reckoning from Ezra's Jubilee in 424 BCE gives the date 66 CE for the end of the tenth Jubilee, and so the first week of that Jubilee would have fallen between 18 and 24 CE. Now if Jesus was born between 12 and 6 BCE (Herod the Great died in 4 BCE, when Jesus was a child, Matt. 2:19), then his baptism at the age of thirty (Luke 3:23) would have occurred, during the first week of the tenth Jubilee.[83]

Furthermore, Jesus announced his ministry with the opening words of Isa 61. In the heaven/Holy of Holies cosmology of the Letter to the Hebrews, therefore, Jesus' sacrifice as the great high priest in the order of Melchizedek and the offering of his blood in heaven to make atonement is understood as the final sacrifice, one that would bring to an end the annual act carried out by the high priest. Similarly, the Son of Man imagery of Dan 7:13, applied to Jesus' return from heaven on the clouds of glory,[84] is also understood as the fulfilment of the high priests' re-emergence from the Holy of Holies in clouds of incense on the Day of Atonement and at the great Jubilee.[85] As the high priest was set apart from the other priests, so Jesus, as high priest, was also understood to be "holy, blameless, unstained, separated from sinners" (Heb 7:26–27). He also underwent purification rituals before entering into his ministry (Luke 3:21–22) and before making atonement (John 12:1–7), as the high priest did in readiness for the Day of Atonement.

---

82. Cf. Vermes, *The Complete Dead Sea Scrolls*, 500.
83. Barker, *Revelation*, 49.
84. Matt 24:30; 26:64; Mark 13:26; 14:62; Luke 21:27; Rev 1:7; 14:14. In *Sanh.* 98a the Messiah is expected to come on the clouds of heaven.
85. "In the temple ritual which corresponded to its mythology, the incense which accompanied the high priest into the holy of holies was the clouds on which the Man entered heaven." Barker, *Revelation*, 169.

The veil in the temple was understood in later Jewish tradition[86] to contain heavenly knowledge of the past, present and future, and was accessible only to the high priest. At Jesus' death the veil was torn and in the New Testament it is said that Jesus will reveal heavenly secrets.[87] The identification of Jesus with Melchizedek in Hebrews is interesting, for not only does the name mean "righteous king," but also here we are told that Melchizedek is "without father or mother or genealogy and has neither beginning of days nor end of life, but resembling the Son of God he continues a priest for ever."[88] In addition, Melchizedek's appearance in Genesis was understood by the early Church Fathers to represent one of the Christophanies mentioned above. Therefore, rather than an attempt to circumvent the non-Aaronic descent of Jesus, this identification with Melchizedek strengthens Jesus' sacral kingship/high-priestly role, not only because of the meaning of the name and the role of this figure in Gen 14:18, but also because the king in Ps 110:4 is said to be a "priest forever according to the order of Melchizedek" and, as noted above, this psalm is applied directly to Jesus.[89] In fact, approximately 136 references, quotations or allusions from passages in the Hebrew Scriptures are quoted and applied directly to Jesus in the Letter to the Hebrews, suggesting that for this author, at least, a direct tangent could be drawn from the Hebrew Scriptures to the person and role of Jesus.

In John 11:49–50 Caiphas, the high priest, says to the people: "You know nothing at all! You do not understand that it is better for you to have one man die for the people than to have the whole nation destroyed." Rather than political expediency, which Vermes suggests, I would argue that, as high priest, Caiphas understood the sacral role of the Anointed. This would seem to be confirmed by John's comments: "He did not say this on his own, but *being high priest that year* he prophesied that Jesus was about to die for the nation, and not for the nation only, but to gather into one the dispersed children of God" (John 11:50–52). The fact that these words are repeated in John 18:14 further suggests it is an important notion. Finally, following his assumption, Jesus is understood to mediate as high priest in heaven (Heb 10:21).

In 1 Pet 1:18–20 Jesus is identified as the Passover lamb "without blemish or spot" whose blood served as a ransom. In John 1:29 Jesus is "the Lamb of God who takes away the sin of the world." In Rev 5:6 he is "the Lamb, as though it had been slain," and at his crucifixion Jesus is

---

86. *3 En.* 45.
87. Matt 13:35; Mark 4:11; Rom 16:25; 1 Cor 2:7.
88. In later tradition Melchizedek is said to be without a human father and emerges from his mother's body after her death (*2 En.* 71).
89. Matt 22:44; Mark 12:36; Luke 20:42, 43; Acts 2:34, 35; Heb 1:13; 5:5–6.

specifically identified with the Passover lamb, where, contrary to the usual custom, his legs were not broken (John 19:36). This reflects Ps 34:20, which was said of the king but which is also a stipulation applied to the Passover lamb in Exod 12:46/Num 9:12. Furthermore, the variant timing of the "Last Supper" in John's Gospel also serves the same purpose: in the Synoptics this takes place after the killing of the Passover lambs and as such constitutes a Passover supper;[90] however, in John's Gospel this takes place on the evening before, meaning that Jesus is killed (sacrificed) at the same time as the Passover lambs. Morgenstern takes this a step further when he suggests the timing of Jesus' "triumphal entry" was also chosen deliberately to coincide with the timing of the selection of the Passover lambs;[91] hence Jesus was identifying himself as both king and Passover lamb and consequently the one who would be sacrificed. The use of hyssop in John 19:29 also leads us by allusion to Exod 12:21–22.[92]

Despite the variant timing, this identification is still evident in the Synoptics when Jesus commands his disciples to eat his body and drink his blood. The conclusion has been drawn that Jesus has replaced the Passover lamb and therefore it is *his* body, represented by the unleavened bread which is now eaten as a fellowship meal,[93] and in commemoration of redemption and *his* blood, which affords both protection and eternal

---

90. Smalley, *John*, 27. Smalley discusses two alternative explanations, which attempt to account for the chronological difference. One suggestion is that John "theologized" the Synoptic tradition, and the other is Jaubert's suggestion that the Qumran calendar was being followed by Jesus and his disciples, which would give an alternative day for the Passover. See A. Jaubert, *The Date of the Last Supper* (New York: Alba, 1965). For a critique of Jaubert's position, see P. Benoit, *Jesus and the Gospel* (London: Darton, Longman & Todd, 1973), 87–93.

91. Morgenstern, *Some Significant Antecedents*, 36.

92. Exod 12:21–22: "Then Moses called all the elders of Israel and said to them, 'Go select lambs for your families and slaughter the Passover lamb. Take a bunch of hyssop, dip it in the blood that is in the basin and touch the lintel and the two doorposts with the blood in the basin.'"

93. *L.A.B.* 13:4 specifies that unleavened bread should be set before God (in the temple) as a memorial for the Exodus. Hayward comments that this was not the usual practice, the unleavened bread being eaten at home as part of the Passover activity. The dating of this text is a matter of continuing debate, although some posit a date after 70 C.E. If this is the case, it may be proposed that this was a way of legitimizing the substitution of the unleavened bread for the Passover lamb which took place following the demise of the temple, by suggesting that the bread already had a sacral nature as it was previously offered in the temple. In later rabbinic tradition the matzoth took on "sacrificial" qualities. The matzah has to be striped, pierced and scorched in such a way as to make it appear bruised. Thus it is pierced like the king in Zech 12:1, and bruised and striped like the Servant in Isa 53:5.

life.[94] Whilst the prohibition against ingesting blood has led scholars to suggest a symbolic understanding of Jesus' words at the "Last Supper," John's Gospel stresses that both Jesus' body *and* his blood must be consumed as a prerequisite of salvation,[95] indicating that whilst this *is* meant symbolically, nonetheless it refers back to an original underlying practice. The Passover sacrifice was understood, at least at one stage, as an atoning sacrifice (see Num 9:13). This would provide a partial explanation of Jesus' identification with the Passover lamb. The apotropaic nature of his blood would provide another, whilst the injunction to eat his body and blood, coupled with the stipulation mentioned above against breaking his bones, I propose, reflects the original understanding of Passover (as discussed in Chapter 6). Passover imagery is also evident in 1 Cor 5:7: "Clean out the old yeast so that you may be a new batch, as you really are unleavened.[96] For our Passover lamb, Christ, has been sacrificed." At the same time, an incident recorded only in John's Gospel may be indicative of a Sukkoth parallel. When the spear is thrust into Jesus' side, blood and water emerge, a detail which resonates with one of the Sukkoth rites in the temple.[97]

Intimately connected to Passover is the Exodus, and Jesus' suffering, death and resurrection are said to form a new Exodus[98] and a new redemption (John 12:47). Jesus is not only the Passover lamb whose blood affords protection, but also a new Moses,[99] as well as the miraculous "manna,"[100] which fed the Israelites in the wilderness, and the Rock

---

94. "The recitation of the story of the death of the Lord, in other words of the act of redemption in which the Christian Church originates and on which it depends, corresponds exactly to the *Haggadah* at the Jewish Pascal meal, the recitation of the act of redemption from Egypt on which the Jewish nation depended." Gray, *Sacrifice*, 252.

95. John 6:53–56: "Very truly, I tell you, unless you eat the flesh of the Son of Man and drink his blood, you have no life in you. Those who eat my flesh and drink my blood have eternal life and I will raise them up on the last day; for my flesh is true food and my blood is true drink. Those who eat my flesh and drink my blood abide in me, and I in them."

96. Unleavened bread is a feature of the Passover meal, and leaven is also associated with sin in rabbinic doctrine.

97. This rite, associated with fertility and therefore new life, was mentioned in Chapter 4, and involved the pouring of wine (traditionally symbolizing blood) and water into bowls with holes of different sizes so that the water and wine would empty out at the same time (*m. Suk.* 4:9).

98. Jesus' death is spoken of as τὴν ἔξοδον αὐτοῦ in Luke 9:31.

99. See Allison, *The New Moses*, 268, for a list of parallels and allusions.

100. In John 6:48–51 Jesus states: "I am the bread of life. Your ancestors ate the manna in the wilderness and they died. This is the bread that comes down from

8. The Messiah in the New Testament 177

which gave them water (1 Cor 10:4). In Matt 2:13–15 Joseph is told in a dream to go to Egypt with Jesus in order to fulfil the prophecy "out of Egypt I called my son." Notably, Jesus' role is seen as the fulfilment of the Exodus, *the* major redemption of Israel, just as his role of high priest fulfilled the annual Day of Atonement redemption. Furthermore, Jesus' resurrection took place on the feast of *Habbikurim*, the festival which commemorates the first harvest following the entry into the "Promised Land"; he is the "firstfruits" (1 Cor 15:20) of the new creation (2 Cor 5:17). According to Hengel, with his shout on the cross of τετέλεσται, "It is finished," Jesus "signifies the finishing of the work of new creation, at the eve of the sixth day; that is the day when the first creation was finished."[101] Hengel identifies the repetition of τετέλεσται (John 19:28, 30) with the repetition of ויכלו and ויכל in Gen 2:1–2 and suggests that John is here identifying Jesus' work of salvation as a prelude to the new creation with that of the original creation in Gen 1:1–2, which in turn corresponds with John 1:1–2, which also deals with things "in the beginning."[102] Therefore Jesus, "through whom all things were made" according to John, was also the one through whom all things were made new. He is the author of the new creation, and, as such, just as God breathed life[103] into Adam the first creation, so too Jesus breathes life into his disciples, the new creation.[104]

The third set of imagery used to describe Jesus' role as Messiah is that of the Servant figure of Isaiah. In Acts 8:26–27, Isa 53:7–8 is used as the starting point to explain "the goods news of Jesus." This is just one of the places where Servant passages of Isaiah[105] are applied to Jesus in the New Testament (cf. 1 Pet 2:22–25). This passage deals with the vicarious atonement achieved by the "Suffering Servant" and is applied directly to the suffering and death of Jesus. In Chapter 5 I considered the role of the servant and argued that he was a "type" of the king. When we compare Jesus' role with that of the servant, numerous parallels are evident. The Servant/Jesus is "chosen" (Isa 42:1/Luke 23:35), has Yahweh's spirit upon him (Isa 42:1/Mark 1:10), is called from the womb (Isa 49:1/Luke

---

heaven, so that one may eat of it and not die. I am the living bread that came down from heaven. Whoever eats of this bread will live for ever; and the bread that I will give for the life of the world is my flesh."

101. M. Hengel, "Christological Titles in Early Christianity," in Charlesworth, ed., *The Messiah*, 434.
102. Ibid.
103. Ibid., 435.
104. Ibid., 435 n. 33.
105. Isa 42:1–4; 49:1–6; 50:4–11; 52:13–53:12.

1:31) and is named by *Yahweh* (Isa 49:1/Luke 1:31). He is to bring "justice" to the nations/earth (Isa 42:1, 4/Matt 25:31–33), to raise up the tribes of Jacob and to restore the "preserved of Israel" (Isa 49:5–6/Matt 15:24). He is given as a covenant (Isa 42:6/Heb 9:15) and is also to be a light to the nations (Isa 42:6/Luke 2:32). He does not resist being humiliated (Isa 50:6/Mark 15:20), beaten (Isa 50:6/Mark 14:65) and being spat upon (Isa 50:6/Mark 14:65). He is despised and rejected (Isa 53:3/Mark 14:68); innocent himself (Isa 53:9/2 Cor 5:21), he suffers vicariously for the sins of the people (Isa 53:4[106]/Gal 1:4).[107] The suffering has been inflicted upon him by God (Isa 53:4, 10/Mark 14:36) and although oppressed and afflicted, he remains silent (Isa 53:3–7/Mark 15:5). He died and his grave was with the wicked (Isa 53:9/Mark 15:27) and his tomb with a rich man[108] (Isa 53:9/Matt 27:27–60). It is through his death that atonement is made for the people (Isa 53:5/Rom 5:11). Following his death, he will be exalted/lifted up (Isa 52:13/John 3:14).[109]

Not only does the role of the "Suffering Servant" of Isaiah match point for point Jesus' suffering, death and resurrection, but also direct quotations from,[110] or allusions to,[111] Isaiah are applied to Jesus, suggesting that this identification was not coincidental. Furthermore, Jesus also applies these scriptures to himself, demonstrating that he understood his own role in terms of that of the Servant.[112] At the "Last Supper," for example, Jesus (Luke 22:37) quotes Isa 53:9 and says that this scripture is fulfilled in him; further examples are found in John 12:38 (Isa 53:1) and John 12:39 (Isa 6:9–10). The healing that Jesus carries out in Matt 8:14–18 is also understood as fulfilment of the Servant's role (Isa 53:4). As the inaugural speech of his ministry (Luke 4:18–21) Jesus quotes Isa 61:1–2[113] and states: "Today this scripture has been fulfilled in your hearing."

106. See also Isa 53:5–6, 8–12.
107. See also 1 Cor 15:3; 1 John 2:2; 3:5; 4:10.
108. Morgenstern argues this is a corruption of the Hebrew. His proposal is that the reading "with evildoers" is to be preferred over "with the rich," thereby complementing the earlier phrase by way of parallelism. Morgenstern, *Some Significant Antecedents*, 55.
109. See also John 8:28; 12:32.
110. Matt 8:17; Luke 22:37; Acts 8:32–35; Rom 15:21.
111. Mark 9:12; Rom 5:19; Phil 2:7, 9; 1 Pet 2:24–25.
112. Nonetheless, I do not subscribe to Mowinckel's position that this identification first took place in the mind of Jesus. See Mowinckel, *He That Cometh*, 187–88.
113. As we saw in the previous chapter, this is incorporated in 4Q521, entitled "the Messianic Apocalypse," which speaks of "His Messiah." See Vermes, *The Complete Dead Sea Scrolls*, 391–92.

Also, at his baptism (understood as the starting point of his mission),[114] when Jesus is filled with the spirit of Yahweh, in addition to Ps 2:7, Isa 42:1 is understood to stand behind the announcement from God:[115] "Behold my servant, whom I uphold, my chosen in whom my soul delights; I have put my Spirit upon him, he will bring forth justice to the nations." Furthermore, when John the Baptist's disciples are sent to ask Jesus if he is the "One who is to Come," he answers "Go and tell John what you have seen and heard; the blind receive their sight, the lame walk, lepers are cleansed and the deaf hear, the dead are raised up, the poor have good news preached to them" (Luke 7:18–23). Although not directly from the "Servant Songs," nonetheless this is a quotation from Isa 35:5–6; Wright has argued that it is not only the "Servant Songs" in the Isaianic corpus that have messianic content.[116] Therefore, it would appear that Jesus, or at least the New Testament writers, viewed his role as the fulfilment of that of the Servant of Isaiah. The messianic content of Isaiah is also apparent in later Jewish tradition,[117] with an explicit identification of the Servant of Deutero-Isaiah with the Messiah.[118]

I proposed above that the Servant is a type of the king and the role of the Servant therefore is very close to that of the king identified in the preceding chapters. However, there are other elements within Jesus' role in the New Testament in the events leading up to his humiliation and death which also reflect the role of the king in the enthronement ceremony outlined in these chapters. Therefore, like the king in the Psalms, Jesus is betrayed by a friend with whom he shared his bread (Mark 14:20/Ps 41:9); he is "distressed and agitated" (Matt 26:37/Ps 86:7; 88:3; 102:2); he is "abandoned" by his disciples (Matt 26:56/Pss 69:8; 88:18);

---

114. And/or the point at which he became aware of who he was and what his mission would be. See Wright, *Jesus*, 537.

115. Ibid., 532.

116. Ibid., 602–4.

117. In *Targum Jonathan*, Isa 4:1–6; 9:5–6; 10:24–27; 11:1–16; 14:29–30; 16:1–5; 28:5–6; 42:1–9; 43:10; 52:13–53:12 are all understood messianically, the latter two also falling into the above-mentioned category of "Servant Songs." Nonetheless, the suffering as vicarious atonement aspect of the Servant in Isa 52:13–53:12 is completely changed at the hands of the Targumist. This leads Levey to comment that "This is an excellent example of Targumic paraphrase at its best…a reworking of the text to yield what the Targumist *desires it to give forth*." Levey, *The Messiah*, 67 (my emphasis). This is particularly interesting given that one of the charges brought against Christianity, not least by Christian writers, is that it has taken the Hebrew Scriptures and interpreted them to suit its own theology.

118. The phrase "Behold My servant" in Isa 42:1 is rendered "Behold My servant, the Messiah" in *Targum Jonathan*. See Levey, *The Messiah*, 59.

when questioned he remains silent (Mark 15:5/Pss 39:2, 9; 62:5). He is mocked and humiliated as king (Matt 27:28–31/Pss 69:10; 89:51), royal insignia are placed on him (Matt 27:28–29) and then stripped from him (Matt 27:31/Ps 89:39, 44). He is taunted about God's help (Matt 27:43/ Ps 22:8). At his crucifixion, lots are cast for his clothing (Mark 15:24/ Ps 22:18), he is given vinegar to drink (Mark 15:23/Ps 69:21), his hands and feet are pierced (Luke 23:33/Ps 22:16),[119] he is abandoned by God (Matt 27:46/Pss 43:2; 88:14; 89) and cries out to him: "My god, My God, why have you forsaken me?" (Matt 27:46/Ps 22:1–2). Subsequently he dies (Matt 27:50/Ps 18:5), is resurrected (Luke 24:1–2/Pss 3:3; 9:13; 27:6; 30:3; 71:20; 86:13) and is enthroned at the right hand side of God (Heb 1:3; 8:1; Col 3:1/Ps 110:1) who puts his enemies under his feet (Eph 1:22; Heb 10:12–13; 1 Cor 15:24/Ps 110:1). And yet, despite the close correspondence with the role of the king in the Psalms, Collins comments: "The Christian view of Jesus…departed decisively from the Jewish paradigms in many respects. One such respect was the development of the notion that the messiah should suffer and die." Referring to Ps 89:22, 31, 51, 69, he continues: "The Christian use of these psalms involved a new line of interpretation, however, for which there was no precedent in Judaism."[120]

The releasing of prisoners was also a feature of the enthronement ceremony in the surrounding cultures, and in Mark 15:6 we are told that it is the custom to release a prisoner at Passover.[121] Pilate offers to release "the King of the Jews," by which he means Jesus, but the crowd call for Jesus' crucifixion and instead choose Barabbas, an insurrectionist and murderer (Mark 15:8–15). It has been proposed that Barabbas is a

119. Though this is not explicit in the New Testament text. It is known that the normal practice in Roman crucifixions was for the nails to be driven through the ankles (one nail) and through the wrists. See Ben Witherington, III, *John's Wisdom: A Commentary on the Fourth Gospel* (Louisville, Ky.: Westminster John Knox, 1995), 304.

120. Collins, *The Scepter and the Star*, 208.

121. There is no evidence outside the Gospels to support this as a historical practice. This has led a number of scholars to reject this statement. Cf. John Dominic Crossan, *Who Killed Jesus?* (San Francisco: HarperSanFrancisco, 1995), 11; S. G. F. Brandon, *The Trial of Jesus of Nazareth* (New York: Dorset, 1968), 94–102; Paula Frediksen, cited in Ralph Martin Novak, *Christianity and the Roman Empire* (Harrisburg, Pa.: Trinity Press International, 2001), 305. However, there may be a suggestion of this in *m. Pes.* 8:6. Furthermore, Bond suggests this practice is consistent with Roman treatment of vassal states: "Mark's account implies that the amnesty is a custom which either Pilate had introduced himself or had inherited from his predecessors." Helen Katharine Bond, *Pontius Pilate in History and Interpretation* (Cambridge: Cambridge University Press, 1998), 109.

8. The Messiah in the New Testament

counterpart to Jesus (his name is suggestive of this).[122] If this were so, it would also cohere with the dual aspect of God represented by the identical goats of the Day of Atonement.

Closely connected to his role of king is Jesus' cleansing of the temple (which, apart from John's account, takes place immediately following his entry as king into Jerusalem)[123] and Jesus' claim that he will rebuild the temple (Matt 26:61; Mark 14:58). I have identified "temple"-building as part of the ritual that the king undertakes at the enthronement ceremony in the surrounding cultures, and temple-building and kingship are also connected in the Hebrew Scriptures.[124] Furthermore, throughout the preceding chapters I have identified a temple/cosmos correlation; therefore it could be concluded that cleansing the temple was a symbolic "foreshadowing" of Jesus cleansing of the cosmos, just as the blood of the animal sacrifices was understood to "unsin" and therefore cleanse the sanctuary and thereby (in the temple/cosmos identification) the world.

Although hierogamy was identified as a feature in the enthronement rituals of the surrounding cultures, there is no evidence in the New Testament of Jesus being connected with such a role; Jesus neither married, nor had offspring. Nonetheless, he is referred to (Rev 18:23) and refers to himself (Matt 9:15) as the "bridegroom," and in Eph 5:31–32 we are told that there is a "mystical significance" concerning the union of Jesus and his followers in the same way as there is between the "coming together in one flesh" of a man and his wife. Also, Rev 19:6–9 describes the marriage of the Lamb (Jesus) and his bride Jerusalem (Rev 21:1–2). Furthermore, in the parable of the sower (Matt 13:24–30) the "good seed" is understood to be Jesus' followers and the "sower" is the Son of Man, that is, Jesus' followers are in some respects understood as his "offspring."

---

122. This is Morgenstern's position. Morgenstern finds no record of prisoners being released at this period and suggests that Barabbas' name—"Son of god"—is significant, possibly related to the earlier practice of substitutes being made for the king's sacrifice: one who is indeed killed and one who is redeemed. Morgenstern, *Some Significant Antecedents*, 57–60.

123. In line with Chilton's suggestion (cited above) that Jesus' triumphal entry into Jerusalem took place at Sukkot, he proposes that this forms a further allusion to Zechariah (Jesus' entry is portrayed as fulfilment of Zech 9:9). Zech 14:1–2 speaks of the Day of the LORD, following which even the *goyim* will celebrate the Feast of Tabernacles in order that they may have rain. One of the prescriptions of that day is that "there will no longer be a trader in the house of the LORD Almighty." Chilton, in the *New Interpreter's Dictionary*, 492.

124. Starting with David, Wright lists a number of Israelite kings and demonstrates their association with the temple. For Wright, "Temple and kingship went hand in hand." Wright, *Jesus*, 483.

Outcome of the Messiah's Role

Jesus' central role in the New Testament involves his suffering, death, resurrection and enthronement at the right hand side of God in heaven (Eph 1:20). When examined, the outcomes of that role match closely those expected within the Prophets, that is, those expected "on the Day of the LORD." The major outcome was to be atonement,[125] the satisfaction of God's wrath, spoken of as his "cup of wrath,"[126] and consequently the overcoming of death.[127] As a result he is enthroned as king, not just of Israel but of all the earth,[128] on the throne of David[129] and he will reign forever.[130] He brings new life,[131] abundant life[132] and new creation.[133] Prior to his death, there was also the supernatural provision of food,[134] life-giving water[135] and the breath of life.[136] The deaf could hear and the blind see, the lame could walk and the dumb speak; the dead are resurrected and the poor have good news preached to them.[137]

As a result of Jesus' role as Messiah, the Kingdom of God has been inaugurated.[138] He has "avenged" his Father and overcome his enemy Satan,[139] the dragon/[140]Chaos Waters[141] and as a consequence he brings (supernatural)[142] peace[143] and the establishment of a new covenant.[144] The exiles will be gathered in, spoken of in terms of a new Exodus,[145] with Jesus as a new Moses[146] and the new manna.[147] Alternatively, a fishing

125. Rom 5:11; Heb 9:15/Isa 43:25; 53:5, 8, 11–12; Jer 31:34; 33:8; Ezek 36:25; Zech 13:1.
126. Luke 22:42/Jer 25:15; Hab 2:16; Zeph 2:3.
127. Rom 6:9; Rev 21:4/Isa 25:8.
128. Rev 17:14; 19:16/Zech 14:9.
129. Luke 1:32/Isa 9:7.
130. Luke 1:33; 1 Tim 6:16; Rev 11:15/Isa 9:7; Ezek 37:25; Dan 2:44; 7:14.
131. John 1:4; 3:36; 5:26; 11:25; 20:31/Ezek 18:31.
132. John 10:10/Isa 43:19; Ezek 34:26–29; Zech 10:1.
133. 2 Cor 5:17; Gal 6:15; Col 3:9, 10; 2 Pet 3:13; Rev 21:5/Isa 65:17.
134. Matt 16:9–10/Isa 55:1–2; Ezek 34:29.
135. John 4:10–14; 7:37–39/Ezek 47:1; Zech 14:8.
136. John 20:22; Rom 8:11/Isa 42:5; Joel 2:28–29.
137. Matt 11:4–5/Isa 26:19; 29:18–19; 35:5–6.
138. Mark 1:15/1 Chr 29:11; Dan 4:34; Obad 21.
139. Luke 10:18; Rev 20:7, 10/Zech 3:2.
140. Rev 12:7–8/Isa 27:1; 51:9.
141. Rev 21:1, "and the sea was no more"/Jon 1:15.
142. John 14:27/Isa 11:6–8.
143. Luke 19:38/Mic 4:3–4.
144. Luke 22:20; Heb 9:15; 10:16/Jer 31:31–34.
145. Luke 9:31/Isa 51:10–11; Jer 16:14; 23:7; Zech 10:11.
146. John 6:14; Acts 3:22/Deut 18:15.

metaphor is used.[148] A further consequence of Jesus' ministry will be the coming judgment.[149] This is not just forensic judgment, but divine justice, *mišpāṭ*, "the upholding of the universe by his word of power."[150]

During my examination of the prophets in Chapter 6 I discussed the elevation of Torah and the beginning of the democratization of the role of the Anointed, and this continuing democratization is the ultimate outcome of Jesus' role as the Anointed. Consequently, not just the king, nor just Israelites, nor just men but everyone is able to become "a child of God."[151] Through their own anointing[152] and recapitulation of his death and resurrection, that is, their baptism,[153] they are able to overcome death.[154] A "new and living way" has been opened up "through the curtain, that is, through his flesh."[155] His flesh being torn, as the veil in the temple was torn at his death,[156] enables everyone to enter into the Holy of Holies, that is, into the presence of God, which had been the privilege only of the high priest on the Day of Atonement.[157] Therefore, everyone can now draw near to God with "hearts sprinkled clean from an evil conscience" and "bodies washed with pure water,"[158] that is, spiritually pure as the high priest had been ritually pure. Thus, according to the writer of Hebrews, because of Jesus' sacrifice, believers are afforded the same privileges as the high priest;[159] they *are* "a royal priesthood," "a holy priesthood, to offer spiritual sacrifices acceptable to God through

---

147. John 6:48–51/Exod 16:4.
148. Matt 4:19/Jer 16:16.
149. John 12:31; Acts 17:31/Isa 42:3; Jer 23:5–6.
150. Heb 1:3/Gen 1:3. "A significant aspect of the understanding of the Divine Name in this literature is an emphasis on its power. This name is not another word among the myriad of words in the human language, but is the most powerful word of the world, even the very word that God spoke to bring the world into existence (Ps 124:8)." Gieschen, "The name of the Son of Man," 244.
151. Gal 3:28/Jer 31:34; Joel 2:28–29.
152. Acts 8:12/1 Kgs 1:33–34. "In these early rites [of baptism] the believer was anointed before being baptised and this was compared to the anointing of the ancient kings and priests." Barker, *The Risen Lord*, 35.
153. Rom 6:4: "Therefore we have been buried with him by baptism into death, so that, just as Christ was raised from the dead by the glory of the Father, we too might walk in newness of life."
154. Rom 6:8: "But if we have died with Christ, we believe that we will also live with him."
155. Heb 10:20/Exod 26:31–35; 28:5; Josephus, *Ant.* 3.138; *War* 5:212–213.
156. Luke 23:45/Exod 30:6–10.
157. Exod 30:10.
158. Heb 10:22/Exod 30:20–21; *m. Yoma* 2:3.
159. Heb 4:16/Exod 28:1.

Jesus Christ";[160] they are now kings[161] and priests,[162] crowned,[163] enthroned[164] and filled with the Spirit of Yahweh.[165] It is they who are the anointed[166] and who bear the Divine Name.[167] It is now through them that God rules,[168] through them that the exiles will be gathered in;[169] it is they who will be a light to the nations,[170] through whom all will come to worship the God of Israel.[171] It is through them that the healing will continue.[172] It is also through them that the temple will be rebuilt.[173]

Nonetheless, as the Jewish writers observed, this all forms part of a two-stage scenario whereby the atonement, once made, allows for these things to take place. However, according to the Gospel writers the ultimate consummation will only happen on Jesus' second coming.[174] Only then will there be a final judgment, when the sheep will be separated from the goats;[175] a final fixing of destinies.[176] All things will be "re-created" and, as promised in the Prophets, there will be a new heaven and a new earth;[177] there will be no more tears, death, mourning, crying or pain.[178] There will be a New Jerusalem[179] made with precious gems.[180] It is here that God will dwell with his people[181] and with the Messiah, and it is here that they will be enthroned.[182] All things will be made new,[183] in

160. 1 Pet 2:5/Exod 30:10.
161. Rev 22:5/Exod 15:18; Ps 89:4; Isa 9:7.
162. Rev 5:9–10/Exod 28:1.
163. Rev 2:10; 3:11/Isa 28:5.
164. Eph 2:4–6/Isa 9:7.
165. Acts 2:4, cited as fulfilment of Joel 2:28–32. See also Isa 44:3; Ezek 36:26–27.
166. 2 Cor 1:21–22; Phil 2:9.
167. Rev 3:12; 14:1; 22:3–4.
168. Luke 17:21/Isa 9:7: "For behold, the kingdom of God is within you."
169. Matt 28:19; Acts 9:15; 10:14; Rom 15:21/Ezek 34:12–13.
170. Matt 5:14/Isa 49:6.
171. Matt 28:19–20/Isa 11:9–10; 45:23; Zech 2:11.
172. John 14:12/Isa 26:19; 29:18–19; 35:5–6.
173. 1 Cor 6:19; Eph 2:14–15; 1 Pet 2:5.
174. Matt 25:31–33.
175. Matt 25:31–46/Ezek 34:17.
176. The names of those who are to dwell with God are written in the "Lamb's Book of Life" (Rev 21:27).
177. Rev 21:1/Isa 65:17; 66:22.
178. Rev 21:4/Isa 25:8; Hos 13:14.
179. Rev 3:12; 21:2/Isa 65:18.
180. Rev 21:18–19/Isa 54:11–12.
181. Rev 21:3/Ezek 48:35.
182. Rev 22:1.
183. Rev 21:5.

8. The Messiah in the New Testament

celebration of which there is a new song.[184] There will be life-giving water flowing from the throne of God,[185] and there will be a tree of life whose leaves are for healing.[186] Despite the contentions of the Jewish writers (discussed in Chapter 2), this two-stage scenario also became a feature of later Rabbinic messianism, with the Messianic age, according to Maimonides, containing no supernatural events. In contrast, the Age to Come, which follows, would witness those supernatural events prophesied in the Hebrew Scriptures themselves. Furthermore, later Rabbinic Judaism[187] also envisaged two Messiahs—the first who would be slain, the messiah ben Joseph,[188] and the second who would be triumphant, the Messiah ben David.[189]

Conclusion

In the foregoing I have attempted to collate what the New Testament writers said about Jesus under three main headings: his person, his role and the outcome of that role. There appear to be many inter-connecting threads, but the most obvious, and one which runs throughout, is that of Jesus' suffering and death as atonement. It would also appear from this survey that for the New Testament writers, Jesus *was* considered as the Anointed, the Messiah.[190] Although this was a complex issue, one which encompassed a number of other roles, these roles could in fact all be classified under the major role of Messiah, as they all constitute elements of Jesus' messianic role and elements of the role of the Anointed discovered in the preceding chapters.[191] Furthermore, certain elements within the Gospels, in particular the eschatological elements of the Son

---

184. Rev 14:3/Isa 42:10.
185. Rev 22:1/Ezek 47:1; Zech 14:8.
186. Rev 22:2/Ezek 47:12. The latter reads "all kinds of trees" rather than the tree of life.
187. *B. Suk.* 52a
188. Luke 4:22.
189. Matt 12:23.
190. "So why did his followers insist that he was, after all, the Messiah, the son of the living god? Because insist they did. From its very earliest days, the community of Jesus' followers regarded him as Messiah." Wright, *Jesus*, 486.
191. Wright discusses Charlesworth's "rigid differentiation" between "messianology" (Jewish beliefs) and "Christology" (Christian beliefs) and comments: "I find this unwarranted. Granted that the relation between Jewish and Christian beliefs is not straightforward, this does not justify us in categorizing them in advance as two automatically separate things—as Charlesworth himself seems to recognize. Certainly the earliest Christians thought their beliefs about Jesus still belonged on the Jewish map." Wright, *Jesus* 486 n. 30.

of Man, as well as the aspects of judgment, authority and equation with aspects of God's role, would seem to argue for a higher Christology than is usually associated with the Synoptic Gospels, a Christology which lies at the heart of even the earliest of the Gospels, rather than being a later product of the theologizing of the Church, which John's Gospel is thought to represent.[192] It is also apparent that in the minds of the New Testament writers the Son of Man figure, identified as Jesus, was connected both with the concept of Messiah and with the concept of vicarious atonement. The Messiah's role is clearly that of atonement, not a political role; and in Mark's Gospel, for example, there are three clear predictions of Jesus' suffering and death—Mark 8:31; 9:31; 10:33–34. His death is also presented as a necessity, one "which is written of him" (Mark 14:21), a conviction which Paul also held (1 Cor 15:3), as did the writer of Acts. The main suggestion for the source of this statement is Isa 52:13–53:12, and again this would seem to be confirmed in Acts 8:28–38.

Nonetheless, it could be argued that the evidence surveyed is apologetic, emanating from writers who considered that Jesus was the Messiah and set out to present him in such a way that it could not be disputed. But what would that mean? It would mean that for these writers, the type of person, his role and, in particular, his death and resurrection *as they had presented it*, all met the criteria, which *they* identified as messianic. The authors of these texts emanated from a group whose origins were not drawn from a particular cult or sect within Judaism[193] (although it later cohered into such), nor was it a separate identifiable group such as the society at Qumran, a group which had distanced itself from ordinary Jewish society; rather, this group, if we accept the evidence of the text,[194] comprised ordinary Jewish people, a cross-section of the diverse society of the time—fishermen,[195] tax collectors,[196] rich men,[197] learned men,[198] priests[199]—who were all Jewish, a number of whom, we must therefore assume, were also familiar with the Hebrew Scriptures.

---

192. Not only by the Jewish writers, as witnessed in Chapter 2, but according to Smalley, this understanding also formed part of critical orthodoxy of the first half of the twentieth century. Smalley, *John*, 8.
193. For an alternative view, see Morgenstern, *Some Significant Antecedents*, 24.
194. With the exception of John's Gospel, as noted in Chapter 2, it is the New Testament text with which the Jewish writers are engaging.
195. Matt 4:18.
196. Matt 9:9.
197. Matt 27:57.
198. John 3:1–10.
199. Acts 6:7.

If, on the other hand, we accept that the events detailed in the New Testament are factual, we can only draw the same conclusion as above—that is, that a number of first-century Jewish people from diverse backgrounds felt able to present the details of Jesus' life and claim that this fulfilled their messianic expectations. As we read, almost at the end of John's Gospel:

> Now Jesus did many other signs in the presence of the disciples, which are not written in this book; but these are written that you may believe that Jesus is the Christ, the Son of God, and that believing you may have life in his name. (John 20:30)

We have no means of proving the finer details of Jesus' life; that such a man lived and was crucified and had many followers from which the Christian faith eventually developed is attested in sources outside the New Testament—that much, then, must be accepted as fact. There are many more arguments that could be raised to support the view that the New Testament portrayal of Jesus is accurate: issues relating to the early transmission of the texts; the fact that eye-witnesses to events would still have been around to refute any false claims made within the newly circulating New Testament texts; the fact that many of the first disciples held so firmly to their beliefs that they submitted to martyrdom; and so on. But this is not relevant to my argument. What does matter is that, whether or not Jesus' life actually matched the details in the New Testament, nonetheless, the writers sought to portray Jesus as Messiah in the terms they did, and in many instances these were terms which, for them, were derived directly from the Hebrew Scriptures themselves. Therefore the type of Messiah portrayed in the New Testament, for them, is rooted in antecedent Jewish tradition.

Chapter 9

IMPLICATIONS FOR DIALOGUE

In Chapter 2 I considered the work of four Jewish writers "in dialogue" in order to understand what the Jewish contentions were concerning the messiahship of Jesus. In that chapter it was discovered that the contentions fell into three main categories: his person, his role and the outcome, or more particularly, the lack of outcome, of his role. In order to understand why two such seemingly different concepts of messiah[1] have emerged from a common source, it seemed pertinent to examine the source itself. I therefore went back to the origins of the concept *meshiah Yahweh* or *Ha-melekh ha-mashiah* in the Hebrew Scriptures. I also considered the role of the king in the cultures surrounding Israel, whose sacral kingship is understood to have influenced her. I then traced the concept through the Second Temple period and into the New Testament itself. I will now consider how those findings impact on the question of Jewish–Christian dialogue. Here, I will first consider whether these findings in any way answer the contentions of the Jewish writers and, if so, how this might lay the groundwork for future dialogue.

The Person of the Anointed

Contentions
The Jewish writers, with the exception of Vermes, acknowledge that Jesus understood himself to be Messiah, though a Messiah who was a purely human leader. This character, according to the writers, was the type of Messiah expected at this time. Furthermore, the writers proposed that the title "Messiah" carried no connotation of deity or divinity, meaning that, accordingly, Jesus never regarded himself as a divine being. The Jewish writers also rejected the title of "king" and thereby its corollary, "Son of David," which applied to Jesus in the New Testament. The

---

1. That is, the "Christian" and the "Jewish" concepts.

writers felt that Jesus' kingship was both marginal and ineffective,[2] that it achieved no political ends. Nor was Jesus' depiction as a peaceful king seen to be in line with "normative" messianic expectation. They also objected to the correlation of Jesus with the title of high priest and felt that his identification with Melchizedek was an attempt to legitimize this claim, as Jesus clearly was not descended from the line of Aaron and therefore could not be high priest. A further contention of the Jewish writers was that the "Son of Man" title attributed to Jesus had no particular connotation of divinity and, despite its connection with messianism, was considered (with one exception)[3] to be an Aramaic circumlocution and not a title—thus Christianity was wrong in ascribing to it a more profound meaning.

However, from my survey of the New Testament texts it became apparent that there was a disparity between how the Jewish writers perceive Jesus and the New Testament portrayal of him. The New Testament evidence clearly depicts Jesus as a divine, pre-existent figure; he is called "Son of God" and refers to God as his Father. There were also clear indications of his association both with Yahweh and with the Most High, and as a consequence of his association with Yahweh it was considered that he represented an aspect of the Most High (or Father God)—his aspect of mercy. Furthermore, Jesus' preferred self-designation was "Son of Man," and he was identified with the "Son of Man" figure in Daniel. Also, rather than being marginal, the kingship of Jesus was, in effect, central to his role as Messiah and his designation as king emerged at key moments of his life: the annunciation of his birth, his baptism, his triumphal entry into Jerusalem, as well as his trial and crucifixion. Closely connected with this was his title "Son of David"; the Messiah was (and still is[4]) expected to be king, a scion of the House of David. Jesus' connection with the title, far from being "random," was evident in the genealogies of Matthew and Luke, in his birthplace as well as featuring in specific miraculous healings.[5] The low Christology claimed for Jesus by the Jewish writers therefore did not tally with the evidence of the New Testament itself, nor was this evidence confined only to John's Gospel. And yet, that still leaves unanswered the Jewish

2. With the exception of Klausner.
3. Sandmel considered this figure to be fully consonant with the Judaism of that period.
4. Within Orthodox Judaism.
5. Space prohibited examination of this aspect of Jesus' Messiahship. Note, however, that Lidija Novaković discusses this in *Messiah the Healer of the Sick: A Study of Jesus as the Son of David in the Gospel of Matthew* (WUNT 2/170; Tübingen: Mohr–Siebeck, 2003).

contentions that the type of Messiah portrayed in the person of Jesus was un-Jewish and contrary to that expected within Judaism.

I proposed at the beginning of this work that the concept of Messiah found its roots in the ancient Israelite concept of king, a concept which was influenced by the cultures that surrounded Israel. When I examined the person of the king in the surrounding cultures, it was apparent that the king was in fact considered to be divine and as such was closely identified with both the creator god and the high god. It was also apparent that the various gods represented aspects of the high god, as did the king in his identification with them. Furthermore, the king was understood to be the offspring of the god(s); consequently, his relationship with the gods was spoken of in terms of that of a father and son. It emerged that a central part of the king's role was sacral, with the king functioning as high priest in the cult. Against this backdrop, it was interesting to note that in the Hebrew Scriptures there were indications of a very similar understanding, though here the Davidic monarchy was strongly featured. Whilst the king's cultic function was also evident, here it was linked with the line of Melchizedek, the priest-king of Salem/Jerusalem.[6] In addition, there was a development in the concept of the messiah in the Second Temple period whereby a heavenly, pre-existent messianic figure emerged, one entitled "Son of Man." Like the king, he is "Chosen," anointed,[7] enthroned and promised an everlasting dominion. It is through him that the righteous will be saved and it is said that all nations will worship him. In Daniel this figure comes "on clouds of glory" and in *1 Enoch* this figure has the Divine Name in him and is equated with God. Thus, a heavenly redeemer figure who stands in close relationship to the God of Israel is not a corruption of Jewish monotheism by Christianity, nor the invention of a Hellenistic or "Gentile" Paul, but an integral feature of Second Temple Judaism.[8] Consequently, this removes a number of objections to the type of Messiah portrayed in the New Testament.

---

6. Not all commentators agree with the identification of Salem as Jerusalem, but this is generally accepted.

7. *1 En.* 48:10; 52:4.

8. "The correspondence between Ezra and the Similitudes point to common assumptions about the interpretation of Daniel 7 in first-century Judaism. It is difficult to say how widespread these assumptions were… However, there is no evidence of influence between the Similitudes and 4 Ezra, and they were certainly not products of a single group. It is reasonable to suppose that their common assumptions were also shared by others in first-century Judaism." Collins, *The Scepter and the Star*, 188.

9. Implications for Dialogue

It would appear that rather than being a pagan import into Judaism, the New Testament portrayal of Jesus instead stems directly from antecedent Jewish messianic concepts and is therefore equally as valid as that of the "purely human leader" purported to be expected by Rabbinic and later Orthodox Judaism.[9] These two seemingly opposing concepts instead represent the crystallization of two of the major emphases of the pre-first-century concept of Messiah. Were the findings of this research accepted it would mean that the Jewish rejection out of hand of the "Christian" concept of Messiah is no longer tenable. At the same time, it would mean that, given the complexity of pre-first-century Judaism, the post-70 C.E. Rabbinic version of messiah was equally valid and that Judaism's rejection of Jesus' messiahship and contingent claim that the Messiah is still expected must also be taken seriously by Christianity.

Implications

This being demonstrated, what then are the implications of these findings for dialogue? Let us consider first the implications for Judaism. Although Judaism regards itself as fiercely monotheistic, so does Christianity. Whilst Rabbinic Judaism has defined and defended its monotheism over and against that of Christianity, nonetheless it not only shares the same background as Christianity but also took forward much of the same understanding of God. The understanding in question is that God can be both hidden and manifest, that different aspects of God are spoken of, and to a great extent understood as, separate personalities/hypostases; this much is visible in the Hebrew Scriptures themselves.[10] We have also surveyed evidence from non-canonical texts which further suggest the identification of Yahweh with an individual—whether human, as in the case of the high priest, or such transcendent figures as Melchizedek at Qumran and the Son of Man of *1 Enoch*. Referring to the latter, Gieschen asks: "If the Divine Name cannot be separated from the reality of YHWH, then how could Jews who confessed the Shema identify a second figure

---

9. Nonetheless, as Lacocque has pointed out, "Jewish Messianic thought is hardly monolithic. A study of biblical, rabbinic, medieval and modern texts will reveal a wide variety of opinions and attitudes concerning the Messiah." André Lacocque, "Messiah," in *A Dictionary of the Jewish–Christian Dialogue* (ed. Leon Klenicki and Geoffrey Wigoder; exp. ed.; New Jersey: Paulist, 1995), 133.

10. Gen 1:26; 18:1–15; Exod 3:1–22; Deut 32:8; Judg 13:1–23, amongst others. Gieschen comments: "The need for some distinction between YHWH and his visible form arises from the paradox that YHWH appears in some form on many occasions, yet one cannot see YHWH and live (Exod 33:20)." Gieschen, "The Name of the Son of Man," 243.

with this name?" For him, the solution lies in the significant antecedents in the Pentateuch; he concludes: "the possession of the Divine Name was a theological category that became vital to faithful depictions of YHWH; by it clear—and complex—monotheism is confessed."[11] Therefore, although not raised specifically by the writers examined in Chapter 2, the Shema is raised as an objection to the Trinity in dialogue.[12] This objection rests on one understanding of *ehad* and does not allow for a more nuanced understanding that is evident in the Hebrew Scriptures and other Jewish texts, as well as that understood within the Hasidic element of Judaism. Nor does it take into consideration the existence of the midrashim generated precisely to overcome the "anomalies" of passages such as Gen 1:26.[13]

Judaism already acknowledges that the spirit of God has a particular function and operates "independently" from God,[14] and whilst space prohibits an examination of the mystical tradition there is, within this tradition, the same idea of a hidden unknowable God and his self-revelation through the *Sefirot*.[15] Similarly, Philo introduced the idea of the Logos figure as an intermediary, whilst the *Memra* of the *Targumim* provides another example. This is also acknowledged by Idel:

> In some instances, the Messiah has been conceived also as the representative of the divine in this world. The very fact that the phrase *meshiah Yhwh* recurs in the sources shows that special connection between him and God. This nexus could sometimes be stronger and richer, as it later became in Christian theology and in the ecstatic Kabbalah and Sabbateanism, or less evidently, in some other cases in Jewish sources, though such a view is found also in the Rabbinic literature, where the Messiah is described as one of the three entities designated by the *Tetragrammaton*.[16]

---

11. Ibid., 249.
12. Although this is implicit in the other objections raised to Jesus' identity as God.
13. That is, the midrashim witness to the fact that the strict monotheism claimed by Rabbinic Judaism is not always evident in the Hebrew Scriptures themselves. Therefore, if there had been no such "anomalies" there would have been no need to have provided a midrash on them to "bring them in line with Rabbinic thought" *as it had developed*.
14. Whilst I am aware of the controversy concerning the identification of the Holy Spirit (in Christian terms), the Spirit of God in the Hebrew Scriptures and the Shekhinah, space prohibits entering into this debate here. Nonetheless, both the Spirit of God and the Shekhinah operate independently from God even though understood to emanate from him.
15. See Scholem, *Major Trends in Jewish Mysticism*, 213.
16. Idel, *Messianic Mystics*, 41.

9. Implications for Dialogue

If this more nuanced understanding of the Godhead was "allowed" within Orthodox Judaism, particularly in light of its more recent accommodation of Kabbalistic thought, what would that mean? It would mean that Judaism may then be able to accept that Christianity *is* strictly monotheistic—as it contends—and that the two faiths *are* worshipping the same God, even though Christianity chooses at times to worship the different persons, as it understands it, of the godhead.

If the same understanding were to prevail in Christianity, how would that affect *its* self-understanding? The suggestion that Jesus is Yahweh, although ancient in itself, is beginning to be rediscovered and reprised. For Christianity, it presents no conflict of interest, even though it may initially cause surprise. What may be more problematic for Christianity, if this premise is accepted, is the suggestion that the Jewish people who acknowledge and worship Yahweh as their god have therefore known and worshipped Jesus (in his manifestation as Yahweh in the Hebrew Scriptures), even though they have not accepted his definitive manifestation as the incarnated Jesus; consequently, it could be argued, contrary to Christian tradition, that they are not in need of evangelization. Undoubtedly this would not satisfy the Evangelical strand of Christianity, which may argue that worshipping the God of Israel is not the same as acknowledging Jesus as saviour and thereby acknowledging his atoning sacrifice.[17] The same may be true of those Christian organizations which specifically target Jews for conversion to Christianity. However, the challenge to them both would be to accept that other forms of Judaism that are not Christianity are also valid means of relationship with the God of Israel, and that, consequently, "conversion" to Christianity is not necessary.

Jesus himself said that he had come to point the way to the Father. At the same time, Jesus' statement in John 14:6[18] that he is the *only* way to the Father has formed the basis of Christianity's exclusivism. However, as Rosenzweig has pointed out, the Jewish people already have a way to the Father through the Torah.[19] This position is shared by Neusner, who states:

---

17. The traditional Christian position has been that Christianity has superseded Judaism and now provides the only means of relationship with the God of Israel. Therefore, according to this way of thinking, Jews, as much as anyone else, need to acknowledge Jesus as saviour in order to gain eternal life.

18. John 14:6: "I am the way the truth and the life. No-one comes to the Father except through me."

19. "What Christ and his Church means within the world—on this point we are agreed. No one comes to the Father—but the situation is different when one need no

> The word [*halakhah*] is normally translated as "law," for the *halakhah* is full of normative, prescriptive rules about what one must do and refrain from doing in every situation of life and at every moment of the day. But *halakhah* derives from the root *halakh*, which means "go," and a better translation would be "the way." The *halakhah* is "the way"; *the way* man lives his life; *the way* man shapes his daily routine into a pattern of sanctity, *the way* man follows the revelation of the Torah and attains redemption.[20]

According to Wyschogrod, Acts 15 represents the early Church's attempt to address the mirror image of this same problem, with Paul obtaining the agreement of the Jerusalem Church that Gentile Christians need only obey the Noachide laws, whereas Jewish believers in the Messiah should continue worshipping as Jews, following Torah and being circumcised.[21] Therefore, it was decided that there was no need to convert "Christians" to Judaism. Nonetheless, the question remains: If, as Christianity claims, messianism is so central a concept to Judaism,[22] and if it forms the basis of Christianity's existence, what purpose has the messiahship of Jesus served to that form of Judaism which did *not* accept him as Messiah 2000 years ago and has managed without it ever since?

Wyschogrod has attempted to address this question too and, ironically,[23] he suggests that Paul provides the answer. As central as the Christ event is to Paul, Wyschogrod believes that Paul was clear that this did not produce the same effect for Gentiles as it did for Jews.[24] Accordingly,

---

longer come to the Father because he is already with him. That is the case with the nation of Israel (not the individual Jew)." Rosenzweig in Fry ed. *Christian–Jewish Dialogue*, 188.

20. Jacob Neusner, *The Way of Torah: An Introduction to Judaism* (Belmont, Calif.: Dickenson, 1970), 25.

21. Michael Wyschogrod, "A Jewish Reading of St. Thomas Aquinas on the Old Law," in *Understanding Scripture: Explorations of Jewish and Christian Traditions of Interpretation* (ed. Clemens Thoma and Michael Wyschogrod; New York: Paulist, 1987), 137.

22. Despite Jewish ambivalence to this suggestion, the belief in the messiah is one of the thirteen principles of Judaism drawn up by Maimonides. See Barry Freundel, *Contemporary Orthodox Judaism's Response to Modernity* (New Jersey: Ktav, 2004), 98–109.

23. In Chapter 2 we saw that the Jewish writers were unanimous in their belief that it was Paul who had caused the final split between Jewish believers and non-believers in the Messiah by developing the completely new and alien faith of "Christianity."

24. Michael Wyschogrod and R. Kendall Soulen, *Abraham's Promise: Judaism and Jewish–Christian Relations* (Grand Rapids: Eerdmans, 2004), 192.

9. *Implications for Dialogue*

he suggests that Paul's understanding of what Jesus had done for Jews was to bring them out of the curse of the law. In the preceding chapters I identified two aspects of God associated with the two major designations in the Hebrew Scriptures of Yahweh and *Elohim*: one representing his aspect of mercy, and one his aspect of justice. Wyschogrod also refers to this and associates *elohim* with law and Yahweh with mercy.[25] It is this latter aspect which, for Wyschogrod, is represented by Jesus.[26] He proposes that these two aspects have been in conflict throughout the Hebrew Scriptures. With the coming of Jesus, Wyschogrod argues, God's aspect of mercy has triumphed:

> This then is the significance of the Christ event for Jews, in Paul's theology. Gentiles are brought into the house of Israel by Christ, which previously they could only achieve by circumcision. Jews are freed from the danger of punishment if they disobey Torah because God is all mercy now. It must be added that in one respect God's justice remains operative. Those who are outside Christ (however "outside" is to be defined) are not assured of God's mercy (Rom 8:1).[27]

According to Wyschogrod, Jesus was the "lightening rod" that drew all punishment to himself (Gal 3:13) and thereby altered the relationship with God for both Jew and Gentile.[28]

Although still based on an interpretation of Paul, Räisänen offers a different explanation. In his exposition of Rom 7:7–8, he states:

> The special thing about the passage is that nothing really happens to the Law! There is no discussion there of its abolition or new interpretation. The power of sin over a person is relieved by the rule of the Spirit. This change of regime has the consequence that the person who used not to be able to fulfil what the law required can now do so charismatically. It is the position of the person that has changed. The position of the law stays the same as it was before.[29]

Therefore the change that the Christ event has wrought, according to Räisänen, is the gift of the Spirit (as prophesied in Joel 2:28) which has enabled both Jew and Gentile to live according to the law. Consequently, Jesus has not come to do away with the law (as he makes clear in Matt 5:17); instead, through his messiahship he made the Holy Spirit available

---

25. Ibid., 196.
26. This was also my conclusion.
27. Wyschogrod and Soulen, *Abraham's Promise*, 197.
28. Ibid.
29. Heikki Räisänen, *Jesus, Paul and Torah* (trans. David E. Orton; Sheffield: JSOT, 1992), 97.

to everyone, a development that made possible the means whereby the law can be kept.[30] Should this fail, Jesus has also provided the means of forgiveness, according to Wyschogrod. Jesus therefore has removed the curse of the law, not the law itself, meaning that God's aspect of justice is now always tempered with his aspect of mercy.

The Role of the Messiah

Contentions
The Jewish writers of Chapter 2 make contentions concerning Jesus that focus not only on the claims made about his person, but also about the type of Messiahship—that is, the role he played. Although ambivalent about any political aspect to Jesus' kingship, nonetheless each of the writers argued that Jesus never considered himself to be divine; rather, he considered himself to be a messiah "in the normal sense of the word," by which is meant a purely human leader. The death as atonement aspect of Jesus' messiahship was considered to be "un-Jewish," a later construct of the Church (in particular of Paul) occasioned by the failure of Jesus' (political?)[31] messiahship. Therefore, although several of the writers acknowledge the parallels between the Passion narrative in the Gospels and Ps 22, as well as the Suffering Servant passages of Isaiah, nonetheless it was thought that these were read back into the life of Jesus.[32]

Again, the New Testament evidence suggested otherwise. Coupled with the complete absence of any political agenda in the Gospels, Jesus' frequent references to his suffering, death and resurrection suggest that

---

30. It is stated in the Mishnah that where two sit together "and the words of the Law are spoken between them" the Shekhinah will be with them (*m. Abot.* 3:20). Compare Matt 18:20.

31. With the exception of Klausner, the writers under consideration fail to identify any political aspect to Jesus' messiahship. Nevertheless, they do all consider that the crucifixion represents a failure of that messiahship which occasioned a revaluation of it by the disciples. This view, however, fails to explain just what was expected by the disciples and what Jesus himself (according to the Jewish writers) thought he was trying to achieve. This is because the writers reject both the New Testament evidence that Jesus' mission was to effect atonement through his death *and* any political motivation.

32. The resurrection of the messiah is understood, even by Jewish theologians, to have been an expectation of first-century Judaism. As Novak states: "It appears that in this period Pharisaic Jews (out of whose Judaism subsequently came both Christianity and Rabbinic Judaism) believed that when the Messiah comes, he will either be resurrected or resurrect the dead himself in order for the living and the dead to live forever in communion with God their king." Novak, *Talking with Christians*, 48.

he did not view himself as "a purely human leader." Furthermore, whilst Jesus' teaching does feature in the Gospels, nonetheless the central theme of the New Testament is atonement as a consequence of Jesus' role.[33] It became apparent in the foregoing that both Isa 52:13–53:12 and Ps 22 *do* reflect the role of the king/Anointed in the Hebrew Scriptures, the Servant figure of Isaiah being a "type" of the king whose role closely resembled that of the king, a role which, in turn, was found to reflect that of the surrounding cultures, the practice of *sacral* kingship and the central role played out in the New Year festival. It was also demonstrated from the Psalms that at this festival the king was "abandoned" by Yahweh and his followers, that he underwent a form of cultic humiliation, followed by a ritual in which he battled with Yahweh/ Israel's enemies (physical and spiritual) in the form of the Chaos Waters. He subsequently "descended to the underworld," was rescued by Yahweh (resurrected) and was enthroned, whereupon he became "Son of God"/ Yahweh.

A comparison with the New Testament revealed that each of these points is reflected in Jesus' suffering, death and resurrection. Furthermore, Jesus' role is referred to frequently in terms of the Servant's role in Isaiah. It was also demonstrated in the foregoing that the role of high priest on the Day of Atonement was a post-exilic translation of the former role of the king in the cult. Therefore, the identification of Jesus with the Melchizedek priesthood not only associates him with the enthronement of the king in the Psalms (see Ps 110:4) and the role of the high priest on the Day of Atonement, but also with the Melchizedek figure who in the Qumran scrolls was expected to effect atonement at the tenth Jubilee. A further paradigm used for Jesus' role was that of the Passover lamb with his death understood as a new exodus and his body as the new bread from heaven that brought eternal life. I also proposed that both the Day of Atonement and Passover represented a fragmentation of the original Enthronement ritual at the New Year festival; both, containing blood sacrifices, the underlying mythology of which concerns vicarious sacrifice as atonement. Each of these paradigms is rooted in the Hebrew Scriptures, all of which suggests that the New Testament portrayal of Jesus' messiahship can in fact be grounded in antecedent Jewish tradition rather than being a hasty post-Easter reconstruction of the Church, or a pagan import. Furthermore, any pagan influences that were discovered to lie behind some of this tradition had been absorbed by Judaism long before the time of Jesus and was therefore the result of early Jewish,

---

33. Mark's Gospel has been called "a Passion narrative" with a short introduction and conclusion.

rather than later "Christian" syncretism. Whilst the expectation of a militant messiah was also inherent in the original concept,[34] there is no evidence that this was the dominant form of messianic expectation at the time. "There was not a uniform belief or a unilinear development of beliefs, though the main source of such beliefs in all their variety appears to have been the anointed ruler and the anointed priest of pre-exilic times."[35] Therefore, whilst it may be claimed that Rabbinic Judaism jettisoned the idea of a suffering messiah (although that fails to account for the *Messiah ben Joseph* and the Rabbinic doctrine of vicarious suffering as atonement,[36] as well as the messianic interpretation of the Suffering Servant passage of Isa 52:13–53:12), it is no longer possible to claim that the messiahship of Jesus is "un-Jewish" because he suffered, died and was resurrected.

Nonetheless, according to Vermes the messiahship of Jesus would be unpalatable to first-century Palestinian Aramaic-speaking Jews:

> Jews in Judea and Galilee must have found this new kind of Messiah alien, untraditional and unappealing, and it can cause no surprise that apart from cosmopolitan Jerusalem, with its substantial immigrant populations from the Diaspora, the New Testament is silent on any progress on the new movement in the Palestinian Homeland.[37]

In Acts 2:5 we read that rather than being comprised of the native population of Jerusalem, it was "devout men from every nation under heaven" who had come to Jerusalem for Shavuot—in other words, Jewish pilgrims from outside of Jerusalem—who believed Peter's message about Jesus. This was not relayed as an innovation but as fulfilment of prophecy: "what God foretold by the mouth of the prophets that his Christ should suffer he thus fulfilled" (Acts 3:18). Jesus was also said to be the prophet that Moses promised (Acts 3:22). "Indeed, all the prophets

---

34. "The idea of a future earthly king also had its Old Testament roots since a number of passages refer to David *redivivus*, an ideal king on the model of David, who would rule a restored Israel." Grabbe, *Judaic Religion*, 289.

35. Ibid.

36. See Solomon Schechter, *Some Aspects of Rabbinic Theology* (New York: Macmillan, 1909), 294–95, for suffering as atonement. See also p. 310 where suffering and death is said not only to be effective for the person, but for "all the generation." See also the "Confession on a Death Bed": "May my death be an atonement for all the sins, iniquities and transgressions which I have committed before you." *Authorised Daily Prayer Book*, 812. Note, however, that this is not atonement on behalf of others, unless the following line implies that "protect my dear family, with whose soul my own soul is bound." Nonetheless, death is linked with atonement.

37. Vermes, *The Religion of Jesus*, 211.

9. Implications for Dialogue

from Samuel on, as many as have spoken, have foretold these days" (Acts 3:24). Following this declaration "the number of men grew to 5000" (Acts 4:4). This message was not just accepted by unlearned Jewish people; rather, according to Acts 6:7, a great many of the priests "became obedient to the faith." Furthermore this message was not just accepted in "cosmopolitan Jerusalem," but in "all Judea and Galilee and Samaria" (Acts 9:31). Wherever the disciples travelled, the synagogue was the first place used for teaching.[38] Here they demonstrated "from the scriptures" that it was "necessary for the messiah to suffer and die." Nonetheless, only some of those who heard believed. Whilst the reluctance to believe could be attributed to the fact that those in Diaspora had not witnessed the events for themselves, undoubtedly the diversity of expectation would also account for why others rejected the message. The important thing here is that the Jewish disciples were demonstrating from the Hebrew scriptures to other Jews that Jesus was the Messiah, and that it was necessary for him to suffer, die and rise from the dead (Acts 17:1). Furthermore, although the Church in subsequent years became increasingly Gentile, the inclusion of the Gentiles into the messianic redemption was not originally envisaged, gauging by the reaction of the Jewish believers in Acts 10:45 as well as Peter's reaction in Acts 10:34 despite Jesus' final command to the disciples to "go and make disciples of all nations" (Matt 28:19). Therefore, the modern Jewish writers' contention that Jesus' messianic role was un-Jewish and unpalatable to mainstream Judaism does not fit with the New Testament picture. It could, of course, be argued that the figures in the New Testament are exaggerated, yet this would not account for the rapid spread of Christianity recorded elsewhere.[39] Nor would it account for its present status as the world's largest religion,[40] nor the fact that despite their own initial antagonism, many contemporary messianic Jews acknowledge the fact that it was the "demonstration from the Hebrew Scriptures" that convinced them that Jesus was the Messiah.[41]

---

38. Acts 3:13; 14:1; 17:1, 10; 19:8.

39. See Marianne Dacy, "The Dissemination of Early Christianity beyond the Jewish Diaspora," in *Encyclopedia of the Jewish Diaspora: Origins, Experiences and Cultures* (ed. Mark Avram Ehrlich; Santa Barbara, Calif.: BAC-CLIO, 2009), 3:123–24.

40. "Today roughly one-third of the people on earth are Christians. Not only is Christianity the largest religion in the world but it embraces a huge variety of forms…" Dana Lee Robert, *Christian Mission: How Christianity became a World Religion* (Chichester: Wiley-Blackwell, 2009), 1.

41. See, for example, Stan Telchin, *Betrayed* (rev. ed.; Grand Rapids: Chosen, 2007).

Implications

None of the foregoing removes the problem (for Christianity) that Judaism does not acknowledge the saving sacrifice, as it perceives it, of Jesus, and that Judaism still looks to the reinstatement of the very sacrificial system that Christ made obsolete by his once-for-all sacrifice. However, I would argue that the reinstatement of the sacrificial system is in fact an anomaly, for if atonement is made without sacrifice, through *Avodat-ha-lev* and the Day of Atonement, what further atonement can then be made with the reinstatement of that system? In other words, the question arises: What purpose is served by the Day of Atonement? According to the Talmud, the temple sacrifice had proven to be ineffective 40 years prior to the temple's destruction,[42] and empirically Judaism without sacrifice has existed for almost 2000 years. Furthermore, even before the destruction of the temple, the community at Qumran had developed a theology in which they saw themselves as the Temple and their service as sacrifice.[43] This would suggest that for Judaism the belief that the sacrificial system would not be reinstated (as Christians believe, because of Jesus' messiahship) would not be insurmountable.[44]

Even if this was to be accepted, and the type of Messiahship portrayed in the New Testament understood to be authentically Jewish, the Jewish contentions concerning the Eucharist would surely remain. However, I have shown above that in fact the origins of the Passover meal, which in turn is the origin for the Eucharist,[45] lie in the pagan understanding that the animal represented the god and that by partaking in its "living" flesh and blood the *nephesh* or life/spirit of the god is imbibed. I suggested that this concept was taken over by Judaism and given the etiological explanation attached to the Passover in the Exodus narrative. Again, if this original understanding of Passover is acknowledged as underlying

---

42. "Originally they used to fasten the thread of scarlet on the door of the [Temple] court on the outside. If it turned white the people used to rejoice, and if it did not turn white they were sad…for forty years before the destruction of the Temple the thread of scarlet never turned white but it remained red." *B. Rosh Hashanah* 31b; cf. *b. Yoma* 39b.

43. VanderKam, *The Dead Sea Scrolls Today*, 116. See also Philip S. Alexander, *The Mystical Texts* (London: T&T Clark International, 2006).

44. This is already the case within Reform Judaism.

45. Although the words of institution of the Eucharist are said by Jesus at the "last supper" (Matt 26:26–29), if John's dating of Jesus' death is accepted this could not have constituted a Passover meal. Despite the objections that have been raised against the identification of the "last supper" as a Passover meal, the evidence of the Synoptic Gospels suggests otherwise; see Matt 26:17–30; Mark 14:12–26; Luke 22:7–20.

the Eucharist, the injunction to eat Jesus' body and drink his blood, an injunction which is considered so alien by the Jewish writers, becomes once again a Judaic concept—albeit one originating as a pagan concept which Judaism took over, rather than representing a contortion of an originally Jewish concept by a predominantly Gentile Christianity. Consequently, whilst the pagan origin of this rite may be repugnant to both Jews *and* Christians,[46] nonetheless, it forces anyone who wishes to enter into dialogue seriously to face up to the issue and excludes the possibility of it being dismissed out of hand as a Christian misappropriation of a Jewish symbol.

The Outcome of the Messiah's Role

Contentions

One of the major contentions of the Jewish writers examined in this study, and Jewish writers in dialogue in general, concerns the non-occurrence of the expected messianic era. If Jesus was Messiah as Christianity claims, why are none of the messianic conditions apparent? According to Maccoby, the Messiah was expected to "restore the Jewish monarchy, drive out the Roman invaders, set up an independent Jewish state and inaugurate an era of peace, justice and prosperity (known as the Kingdom of God) for the whole world."[47] Accordingly, he concludes, "When the Kingdom of God prophesied by Jesus did not materialise this was considered to be the refutation of his messianic claims. Jesus was rejected not by Jews, but by events."[48] This is confirmed by Falk, who states: "It is important to recognise that the disagreement about Jesus as Christ is not over what Jesus taught or did, but rather about what did not occur during his lifetime."[49] Similarly Novak comments: "In Jewish belief… Jesus was not the Messiah precisely because he did not bring about the full restoration of the Jewish people in the Land of Israel and God's universal reign of peace."[50]

A corollary of this, and therefore a further contention, surrounds Christianity's "solution" (as the Jewish writers perceive it) of the "innovation" of a two-stage system, whereby the kingdom of God is inaugurated by Jesus' death but will only come to full fruition when Jesus returns:

---

46. Even so, it is interesting to speculate how Christians over the centuries have understood Jesus' words in John 6:53–56.
47. Maccoby, *The Mythmaker*, 15.
48. Maccoby, cited in Fry, ed., *Jewish–Christian Dialogue*, 146.
49. Randall Falk, cited in ibid., 144.
50. Novak, *Talking with Christians*, 222.

> Those Jews who had accepted Jesus as the Messiah, despite his death on the cross, made an initial significant alteration in the messianic pattern, changing it, as it were, from one single event, ushering in the great climax, into two parts, preparation first, and after an interval, the climax.[51]

From my examination of the surrounding cultures and the Hebrew Scriptures it became apparent that fertility and new creation (and its prerequisite rain)—that is, salvation in its most prosaic sense—was the major outcome expected from the cultic role of the king. Nonetheless, this also involved atonement for sins. At times this was spoken of in mundane terms, at others in supramundane terms, suggesting that there was not only a temporal but also an eschatological aspect to the king's function. It was through him that the well-being of the people was maintained, and indeed the whole cosmos and all else was a corollary of that: peace, fertility, freedom from illness, food, clothing, shelter, protection from enemies—all, as I have suggested, implied in the term *mišpāṭ* (divine justice, right order), so that rain, just as equally as forensic judgment, could be said to be "the king's justice."[52] The two aspects therefore were held in tension: a this-worldly immediate outcome and an otherworldly future outcome. This two-stage system therefore was not an innovation of the early followers of Jesus, but an integral part of the concepts surrounding the Messiah as emerged in the later Rabbinic doctrine of the Messianic Age and the Age to Come.

Implications

Consequently, contrary to the Jewish writers' contentions, both Orthodox Judaism and Christianity expect a two-stage scenario and both expect the Messiah to play a part in both eras. In addition, both faiths expect very similar conditions to prevail. According to Maimonides, the messianic era will contain nothing supernatural, and will constitute a period between the arrival of the Messiah and the Age to Come. By contrast, the Age to Come is understood as an apocalyptic end to life as it is now known, and the consequent beginning of a "supernatural" new life. This expectation is shared by Christianity and its vision of the Age to Come. Indeed, the book of Revelation contains 217 direct references or allusions to the "Day of the Lord" in the Hebrew Scriptures.[53]

---

51. Sandmel, *We Jews*, 33.
52. Engnell, *Studies*, 36; cf. Ps 72:1–7.
53. For an alternative view, see Barker, *Revelation*. Barker considers the events recorded here to relate to the first century and the events surrounding the destruction of the Temple.

In the Age to Come, Christianity expects that the God of Israel will reign as king in a New Jerusalem (Rev 21:5), with the whole earth acknowledging him. The expected conditions include superabundant fertility, everlasting life, freedom from pain and tears (Rev 21:4)—in effect, conditions which were also allocated to the Age to Come[54] in later Rabbinic documents.[55] As may be expected, therefore, the two "faiths," having derived from a shared antecedent tradition, also share an almost identical expectation for the future. Unfortunately for dialogue, however, this difference between the two ages is either forgotten or ignored. Consequently, the modern Jewish writers examined made no reference to this "two-stage" Jewish understanding and therefore used the "two-stage" Christian ideology as proof *against* Jesus' messiahship. In order to get dialogue back on track, this difference needs to be acknowledged and explored

Christianity bases its very existence on the belief that the Messiah has *already* come once and inaugurated the Messianic era. If it were acknowledged that the two-stage system outlined above forms a legitimate part of the Jewish messianic scenario, then this would remove the Jewish contention that it was a construct of the "Church" to cover over the failed messianic mission of Jesus. Furthermore, were this difference recognized and accepted, then it would mean that Jews and Christians could anticipate *together* the Age to Come. Together they could continue expecting the arrival of the Messiah; the only difference for Judaism would be the perception of the present era. If the messiahship of Jesus was accepted as one that *could* have legitimately been expected in the Judaism of that time, as I have attempted to demonstrate in the foregoing, this would make the present period, between his resurrection and the Age to Come, the Messianic Age. This would be an in-between period, as Maimonides suggested, whereby the kingdom of God has been set in motion but will only be fully realised in the Age to Come:

---

54. Davies found it difficult to distinguish between the two ages and "had constant difficulty in deciding to which Age a particular passage referred." Davies, *Torah in the Messianic Age/Age to Come*, 91.

55. According to Klausner: "Throughout the post-Biblical literature the Messianic age, the life after death, and the New World that is to follow the resurrection of the dead are constantly interchanged. For the two latter conceptions (the life after death and the New World) the Talmudic and Rabbinic literature has only one phrase, 'the World to Come' (*'Olam Ha-Bah*)... '[T]he World to Come' is frequently interchanged or confused with 'the Days of the Messiah.'" Klausner, *The Messianic Idea*, 408–9.

> The ultimate and perfect reward, the final bliss, which will suffer neither interruption nor diminution, is the life in the world to come. The messianic era, on the other hand, will be realised in this world, which will continue in its normal course except that independent sovereignty will be restored to Israel. The ancient sages already said: "The only difference between the present and the messianic era is that political oppression will then cease."[56]

Consequently the argument that this is not an era of "peace, justice and prosperity," and therefore that Jesus could not have been the Messiah, would also be annulled. Such a two-stage theory would also cohere with the Rabbinic doctrine of the two-stage messiahship of Messiah *ben Joseph* who would be slain[57] (as Jesus was) and the Messiah *ben David*, who would be a triumphant Messiah[58] (as Jesus, according to Christianity will be on his return); "He is the 'Lamb of God,' not yet the Lion of Judah," as Moltmann has suggested.[59]

This would mean that Judaism as well as Christianity could understand this period as a time to begin the in-gathering of the exiles. Traditionally, God was understood to dwell in the temple in Jerusalem and one of the prayers of the *Amidah* is a plea for God to return (to Zion). Christianity also expects a permanent return of God to earth, but this will be in the Age to Come. Whilst exile from Jerusalem is now only self-imposed (albeit the Temple Mount remains out of bounds), if the exile is understood spiritually (as it is in Christianity) then the in-gathering of the exiles would relate to those Jews (and non-Jews) who are distanced spiritually from the God of Israel. Rosenzweig suggested over half a century ago that Judaism is the intense core of the star of redemption and Christianity the missionary rays.[60] That is, Judaism, maintaining its

---

56. Maimonides, trans. Moses Hyamson, *Misneh Torah: The Book of Knowledge* (New York: Block, 1938), 922.

57. B. *Suk.* 52a (top): "Here we find the Messiah descended from Joseph, who will be slain, with Zech 12:10 applied to him with a causal link understood between his slaying and the end of the evil inclination." See David C. Mitchell, "Rabbi Dosa and the Rabbis Differ: Messiah ben Joseph in the Babylonian Talmud," *Review of Rabbinic Judaism* 8 (2005): 77–90.

58. Commenting on *b. Suk.* 52a, Mitchell comments, "Here Messiah *ben Joseph* appears in the same scene as the Messiah from David. Therefore the two figures are not part of rival eschatological schemas, but part of the same drama." Ibid. 83.

59. Jurgen Moltmann, *The Way of Christ: Christology in Messianic Dimensions* (trans. Margaret Kohl; Minneapolis: Fortress, 1993), 32.

60. Rosenzweig stated that God had set "enmity between the two for all time." Franz Rosenzweig, *Star of Redemption* (trans. William W. Hallo; London: University of Notre Dame Press, 1985), 415.

intimacy with God, and in its role as a "light to the nations" in its ethics, mode of life and relationship with God, intensifies the core of the star whereas Christianity takes the light of the star out into the world.

Related to this is the fact that, as the Lubavitch and others have recognized, there are many within Judaism itself who have fallen away. The aim of the Lubavitch and others is actively to bring those who have fallen away back into Judaism. Christianity, too, is engaged in a mission of in-gatherings, one directed to "the nations" (Matt 28:19). Therefore, if Jews and Christians were to acknowledge one another's role in the "in-gathering of the exiles," bringing the knowledge of the God of Israel to the whole earth (Isa 49:6), recognizing that this is the messianic era and the appropriate time for in-gathering before the final judgment, they could work in partnership to fulfil that aim—Jews gathering in Jews through Judaism and Christians gathering in "the nations." The legitimacy of such a concept has been acknowledged by Lapide:

> If the conversion of humanity to Israel's God is the penultimate goal of world history, the Christianisation of a billion people—which happened in Jesus' name—is a significant step forward in the direction of this salvation.[61]

Furthermore, the awaited "Second Coming" of Jesus (for Christianity) would then be the first arrival of the Messiah for the Jewish people; again, Lapide has already considered this:

> That Jesus had a central role to fulfil in the divine plan of salvation (which is largely unknown to me) through which the West has been led to faith in the one God in his name is beyond every doubt as far as I am concerned. If Paul is right (in the quotation from Isaiah 59:20 that he transforms into a reference to the parousia of Christ in Romans 11:26) and the coming redeemer turns out to be Jesus, then all of Israel will surely welcome him as the anointed of the Lord.[62]

But what of the other messianic expectations which, according to the Jewish writers, have also failed to emerge as a consequence of Jesus' messiahship? One of the conditions expected within the Messianic era by the Jewish writers was the establishment of the kingdom of God. When Jesus began his ministry he declared that the kingdom of God was at hand (Mark 1:15), and as a consequence various changes were set in motion—healings were carried out,[63] people were brought back into the

---

61. Lapide, cited in Fry, ed., *Christian–Jewish Dialogue*, 220.
62. Lapide, cited in ibid., 219.
63. Matt 4:24; 9:35; 12:15; 14:14; Luke 7:21; 9:6; 22:51.

covenant,[64] the power of Satan was challenged and demons were exorcised and returned to the Chaos Waters (Luke 8:26–33). At Pentecost Jesus' followers were filled with the Holy Spirit (understood as fulfilment of Joel 2:28–29) in order to continue establishing the kingdom of God and gather in those exiled from God. All of these consequences are still understood to be part of the ministry of the Church—healing, exorcism, in-gathering of exiles, feeding the poor, housing the homeless, in short, establishing *mišpāṭ*, God's justice on earth—an aim it quite naturally shares with the other form of Judaism to emerge from the first century.[65]

Nonetheless, Rome was not defeated during Jesus' lifetime, and in fact the "man-made" attempt to overthrow the Romans ended in catastrophe, with the destruction of large parts of Jerusalem, the dispersion of a large proportion of the Jewish people and, most importantly of all, the destruction of the temple, which has never been replaced. Empirically, however, the Jewish people, because of their marginalization and persecution, have been enabled, in the majority of host countries, to live under their own sovereignty, "as if" they were living in the land of Israel,[66] albeit often at a price. Furthermore, almost 2000 years later, the State of Israel itself is again sovereign, although secular, with the return of the exiles having taken place on a massive scale and remaining open to all Orthodox Jews who wish to avail themselves of the opportunity. Thus, a number of the messianic conditions *have* come about, albeit over a long period of time.

Although it is difficult to obtain a clear statement on what messianic expectation involves within contemporary Orthodox Judaism, nonetheless the rebuilding of the temple and the restoration of the temple service and consequent return of God to Zion referred to in the *Amidah* usually constitute part of it (Benediction 14). Whilst the contemporary writers consider the rebuilding of the temple to be a physical phenomenon, an alternative reading is possible. It could be argued that the rebuilding of the temple could be understood as a spiritual phenomenon; certainly the

---

64. That is, people were healed whose infirmities put them outside the community of Israel and excluded them from entry into the temple.

65. The Jewish concept of *Tzedakah*, "Justice," incorporates a similar understanding.

66. This was certainly true in the early period: "There is little hint till late in the Amoraic period that Jewish existence outside of the land of Israel is somehow impaired or deficient.... [T]he Babylonian communities, surely, felt no inferiority towards the land of Israel: quite the reverse. Talmudic Judaism, then, it can be argued, was largely anti-nationalistic, and showed little interest in the re-establishment of a Jewish state." Alexander, "The King Messiah," 471.

Jewish sect which developed into Christianity understood it to be so. Believers themselves are understood to constitute the temple, in which case it could be argued that the rebuilding of the temple has been in process since the inauguration of the Messianic Age with Jesus:

> As you come to him, the living stone—rejected by men but chosen by God and precious to him—you also, like living stones are being built into a spiritual house to be a holy priesthood, offering spiritual sacrifices acceptable to God through Jesus Christ. (1 Pet 2:4–5)

It is interesting to speculate whether the stipulation concerning a *minyan* is indicative of a similar spiritualization of the temple within Orthodox Judaism. Certainly, since the demise of the temple, the symbolism and elements of the service[67] have been translated into that of the synagogue and its service,[68] as well as to the home, a process begun even before the destruction of the temple by the Pharisaic movement. As noted above, the community at Qumran had already recognized and distanced themselves from what they considered to be the corruption of the temple, following the usurpation of the high priest's position by the Hasmoneans and the subsequent change in calendar.[69] Consequently, they considered themselves to be a temple. Also, as noted above, on the Rabbinic side, the Talmud records that for approximately the last forty years of the temple's existence, the sacrifice of the Day of Atonement had ceased to be effective. The timing of this inefficacy coincides with the final, "once-for-all" sacrifice of Jesus, as Christianity understands it. Within the Mystical Tradition ascents into the presence of God continued to be made without the physical presence of the temple.[70] All of this

---

67. The synagogue services taking place at the same time of day as the sacrifices were made in the temple.

68. The Torah is now the mediator between the people and God, the position previously held by the king and subsequently the high priest. As a consequence, the Torah scroll now bears the accoutrements of both (the crown of the king and the breastplate of the high priest). It is the Torah scroll that is hidden behind the veil in the *Aron haKodesh*, from whence it emerges, which mediates the presence of God. Thus, it is to the Torah scroll and not to the temple that the Jewish believer now makes *aliyah*. It is the Torah scroll that is now subject to the taboos previously accorded the king (1 Sam 24:5)—it cannot be touched (hence the use of the *yad*), and if it is dropped the congregation has to fast.

69. The change of calendar meant that the Temple services would no longer be in line with those of the heavenly cult. The synchronization of the earthly worship and that of the heavenly cult was an important feature of the Qumran community. See Alexander, *The Mystical Texts*, 84.

70. Scholem, *Major Trends in Jewish Mysticism*, 42.

suggests that, despite its centrality in the theology of Orthodox Judaism, the Jewish faith has been able to function without the physical presence of the temple, much in the same way that Christianity has been able to function without the physical presence of Jesus—even though both are expected to be present in the Age to Come; the temple in Judaism and Jesus in Christianity.

Furthermore, the new temple envisioned in Ezekiel accords very closely with the New Jerusalem of Revelation (Rev 21:12–13/Ezek 48:31–34) and also the Jerusalem in Isa 54:11–12 (cf. Rev 21:19); 60:11, 20 (Rev 21:25); Ezek 47:1, 12 and 48:35 (Rev 22:1–3). That is, in the age to come, both Christianity and Judaism have almost identical expectations for the temple and the names of the gates of the heavenly Jerusalem, which come down to earth, are the names of the twelve tribes of Israel. Nonetheless, according to Revelation, 24 thrones have been established, which might suggest that twelve are for the heads of the tribes and twelve for the disciples as heads of the nations.[71]

Conclusion

If, then, the oscillation between what was expected in the messianic era and what was expected in the Age to Come is acknowledged, coupled with the fact that not only physical but spiritual consequences were expected with the arrival of the messiah, along with the fact that these expectations are paralleled in both "faiths," then the contention of the Jewish writers that the messiahship of Jesus is invalid because of the non-occurrence of these events becomes more problematical. The fact that a two-stage messianic expectation is to be found in both "faiths" further admits of the possibility that the differences in messianic expectation are more semantic than real, and are in fact the result of mutual polemic and misunderstanding as those Jews who accepted the messiahship of Jesus distanced themselves and sought to define themselves over and against those Jews who did not.[72] Such redefinition and misunderstanding,

---

71. Despite being Jewish, and therefore being primarily concerned for spreading the word among the Jewish people (as we saw above), the disciples were nonetheless commissioned by Jesus himself to go out to all nations (Matt 28:19; Mattathias replaced Judas in Acts 1:26, bringing the number of apostles back up to twelve). Furthermore, both Paul (Acts 9:15) and Peter (Acts 15:7) were commissioned to bring the teaching about Jesus to the Gentiles.

72. "The doctrinal intersection of Judaism and Christianity has not been a once-for-all matter but, rather, something that began in Christianity's self-differentiation from Judaism. One can see this ongoing intersection as dialectical: a constant back and forth, forth and back." Novak, *Talking with Christians*, 47.

exacerbated by continuing persecution, has hardened into the positions which now prevail, positions which have been maintained at all odds and have cost so dearly.

If Jesus' first coming is accepted as the inauguration of the messianic era (based on the acceptance that his messiahship was authentically Jewish, as I have attempted to demonstrate), and if at his second coming all of the expected conditions of the Age to Come were to prevail, then there is nothing in this proposition that would jeopardize the integrity of Judaism as it now stands. Effectively, therefore, this invalid-dates the statement made in the quotation with which the present work began,[73] thus allowing a move away from assertion and denial that has plagued dialogue from the "parting of the ways" (ca. 70 C.E.), opening up fresh possibilities and a new foundation on which dialogue can be built.

Admittedly, however plausible this may be, it cannot wipe out 2000 years of persecution, mistrust and hatred. Even so, if the premise of this work is accepted—namely, that the messiahship of Jesus as portrayed in the New Testament can be rooted in antecedent Jewish tradition—then I believe that, contrary to Neusner's claim,[74] this will provide a bridge to dialogue that has hitherto not existed. If in a spirit of openness both sides recognize that each has emphasized different strands within the rich historic mix of early Judaism, then further dialogue could be directed at exploring what is to be gained and what is to be lost by emphasizing one strand to the exclusion of the other.

For example, the political, this-worldly messianism of classic Judaism could provide for Christians a basis for re-engaging with political processes, and also a means for recognizing the nationhood and the statehood of the Jewish people. Conversely, Christian messianism could lead Jews to rediscover the transcendent and the cosmic, to connect more intimately with the divine. That is not to say that this is not already a feature inherent in Judaism; but, as Greenberg has stated, "Increasingly I realised the heavy price Jews had paid in defining Christianity as the totally other. In impoverishing their own religious thought to stay clear of Christian concepts, Jews were rejecting an important part of their own psyche and tradition."[75]

---

73. "Is Jesus the Christ? If so, then Judaism falls. If not, then Christianity fails." Neusner, *Jews and Christians*, 49.

74. Contrary to Neusner's assertion (quoted in Chapter 2), that there is no bridge back to Judaism from Christianity and that there should be none. Ibid., 120.

75. Greenberg, *For the Sake of Heaven and Earth*, 25–26.

Both faiths could continue to worship in the same way, but the pressure that had previously prevailed would be alleviated; there would be no need to evangelize and no need to suspect that evangelization would take place. Instead, Christians and Jews could both engage in gathering in the exiles to their own faith. Both faiths could start to build up mutual trust and be further enriched by the different ways each has developed for worshipping "the one true God, the Holy One of Israel."

BIBLIOGRAPHY

Ackerman, Robert. *The Myth and Ritual School: J. G. Frazer and the Cambridge Ritualists*. Cambridge: Routledge, 2002.
Alexander, Philip S. "The King Messiah in Rabbinic Judaism." Pages 456–73 in Day, ed., *King and Messiah*.
———. *The Mystical Texts*. London: T&T Clark International, 2006.
———. ed. and trans. *Textual Sources for the Study of Judaism*. Manchester: Manchester University Press, 1984.
Allison, Dale C., Jr. *The New Moses*. Edinburgh: T. & T. Clark, 1993.
Baines, John. "Ancient Egyptian Kingship: Official Forms, Rhetoric, Context." Pages 16–53 in Day, ed., *King and Messiah*.
Barker, Margaret. *The Revelation of Jesus Christ*. Edinburgh: T. & T. Clark, 2000.
———. *The Risen Lord*. Edinburgh: T. & T. Clark, 1996.
Barnett, Paul. *Jesus and the Rise of Early Christianity*. Downers Grove: Inter-Varsity, 1999.
Bauckham, Richard. "The Son of Man: 'A Man in my Position' or 'Someone'?" Pages 93–102 in *The Jewish World Around the New Testament*. WUNT 233. Tübingen: Mohr Siebeck, 2008.
Benoit, P. *Jesus and the Gospel*. London: Darton, Longman & Todd, 1973.
Bentzen, Aage. *King and Messiah*. Oxford: Blackwell, 1970.
Bidmead, Julye. *The Akitu Festival: Religious Continuity and Royal Legitimation in Mesopotamia*. New Jersey: Gorgias, 2002.
Black, Matthew, ed. *Peake's Commentary on the Bible*. 3d repr. London: Thomas Nelson & Sons, 1964.
Blackman, Aylward Manley. "Myth and Ritual in Ancient Egypt." Pages 15–39 in Hooke, ed., *Myth and Ritual*.
Blenkinsopp, Joseph. "The Servant and the Servants in Isaiah and the Formation of the Book." Pages 155–73 in vol. 1 of Broyles and Evans, eds., *Writing and Reading the Scroll of Isaiah*.
Boccaccini, Gabriele, ed. *Enoch and the Messiah Son of Man: Revisiting the Book of Parables*. Grand Rapids: Eerdmans, 2007.
———. *Roots of Rabbinic Judaism*. Grand Rapids: Eerdmans, 2002.
Boda, Mark J. "Figuring the Future: The Prophets and Messiah." Pages 35–74 in Porter, ed., *The Messiah in the Old and New Testaments*.
Bond, Helen Katharine. *Pontius Pilate in History and Interpretation*. Cambridge: Cambridge University Press, 1998.
Borowitz, Eugene B. *Contemporary Christologies: A Jewish Response*. New York: Paulist, 1980.

Bottéro, Jean. *Mesopotamia: Writing, Reasoning and the Gods*. Translated by Zainab Bahrani and Marc Van de Mieroop. Chicago: University of Chicago Press, 1995.
Brandon, S. G. F. "The Myth and Ritual Position Critically Considered." Pages 12–43 in *Ritual and Myth: Robertson Smith, Frazer, Hooke, and Harrison*. Theories of Myth 5. Edited by Robert Segal. London: Garland, 1996.
———. *The Trial of Jesus of Nazareth*. New York: Dorset, 1968.
Brockington, L. H. "I and II Samuel." Pages 318–37 in Black, ed., *Peake's Commentary on the Bible*.
Brooke, George J. "Kingship and Messianism in the Dead Sea Scrolls." Pages 434–55 in Day, ed., *King and Messiah*.
Brown, Raymond E. *The Birth of the Messiah*. New York: Doubleday, 1993.
Broyles, Craig C., and Craig A. Evans, eds. *Writing and Reading the Scroll of Isaiah*: *Studies of an Interpretive Tradition*. 2 vols. Leiden: Brill, 1997.
Bruce, F. F. *The Gospel of John*. Grand Rapids: Eerdmans, 1983.
Bryce, Trevor, *The Kingdom of the Hittites*. Oxford: Oxford University Press, 2005.
———. *Life and Society in the Hittite World*. Oxford: Oxford University Press, 2002.
Caragounis, Chrys C. *The Son of Man: Vision and Interpretation*. WUNT 38. Tübingen: Mohr Siebeck, 1986.
Carson, D. A. *The Gospel According to John*. Grand Rapids: Eerdmans, 1991.
Casey, Maurice. *Son of Man: The Interpretation and Influence of Daniel 7*. London: SPCK, 1979.
Charles, R. H., trans. *The Book of Enoch*. London: SPCK, 2006. First published 1917.
Charlesworth, James H. "Can We Discern the Composition Date of the Parables of Enoch?," in Boccaccini, ed., *Enoch and the Messiah Son of Man*.
———, ed. *The Messiah: Developments in Earliest Judaism and Christianity*. Minneapolis: Fortress, 1992.
Chester, Andrew. *Messiah and Exaltation*. Tübingen: Mohr Siebeck, 2007.
Chialà, Sabino. "The Son of Man: The Evolution of an Expression." Pages 153–78 in Boccaccini, ed., *Enoch and the Messiah Son of Man*.
Childs, Brevard S. *Isaiah*. Louisville, Ky.: Westminster John Knox, 2001.
Chilton, Bruce. "Feast-Festival of Booths." Page 493 in *New Interpreter's Dictionary of the Bible*. Vol. 1, *A–C*. Edited by Katherine Doob Sakenfeld. Nashville: Abingdon, 2007.
Clines, David J. A. *On the Way to the Postmodern: Old Testament Essays, 1967–1998*, vol. 2. Sheffield: Sheffield Academic, 1998.
Cohen, Andrew C. *Death Rituals, Ideology and the Development of Early Mesopotamian Kingship*. Leiden: Brill, 2005.
Collins, Adela Yarbro, and John J. Collins. *King and Messiah as Son of God*. Grand Rapids: Eerdmans, 2008.
Collins, John J. "Enoch and the Son of Man: A Response to Sabino Chialà and Helge Kvanvig." Pages 216–27 in Boccaccini, ed., *Enoch and the Messiah Son of Man*.
———. *The Scepter and the Star: The Messiahs of the Dead Sea Scrolls*. New York: Doubleday, 1995.
Collins, John J., Peter W. Flint and Cameron VanEpps, eds. *The Book of Daniel: Composition and Reception*, vol. 1. Boston: Brill, 2002.
Coogan, M. D. *Stories from Ancient Canaan*. Philadelphia: Westminster, 1978.
Croner, Helga, ed. *More Stepping Stones to Jewish–Christian Relations. An Unabridged Collection of Christian Documents 1975–1983*. New York: Paulist, 1985.

―――. *Stepping Stones to Further Jewish–Christian Relations*. New York: Stimulus, 1977.
Cross, Frank Moore. *Canaanite Myth and Hebrew Epic*. Cambridge, Mass.: Harvard University Press, 1997.
Crossan, John Dominic. *Who Killed Jesus?* San Francisco: HarperSanFrancisco, 1995.
Dacy, Marianne. "The Dissemination of Early Christianity beyond the Jewish Diaspora." Pages 123–25 in *Encyclopedia of the Jewish Diaspora: Origins, Experiences and Cultures*, vol. 3. Edited by Mark Avram Ehrlich. Santa Barbara, Calif.: BAC-CLIO, 2009.
Danby, Herbert, trans. *The Mishnah*. London: Oxford University Press, 1933.
Davies, W. D. *Torah in the Messianic Age/Age to Come*. Philadelphia: Society of Biblical Literature, 1952.
Day, John. "The Canaanite Inheritance of the Israelite Monarchy." Pages 72–90 in Day, ed., *King and Messiah*.
―――. ed. *King and Messiah in Israel and the Ancient Near East*. JSOTSup 270. Sheffield: Sheffield Academic, 1998.
―――. *Psalms*. T&T Clark Study Guides. London: T&T Clark International, 2003.
―――. *Yahweh and the Gods and Goddesses of Canaan*. London: Sheffield Academic, 2002.
De Vaux, Roland. *Ancient Israel, Its Life and Institution*. Translated by John McHugh. 2d ed. London: Darton, Longman & Todd, 1968.
Dell, Katherine J. "The King in the Wisdom Literature." Pages 163–86 in Day, ed., *King and Messiah*.
Dempsey, Carol J. *Jeremiah: Preacher of Grace, Poet of Truth*. Interfaces. Minnesota: Liturgical, 2007.
Drower, Margaret S. "Canaanite Religion and Literature." Pages 148–60 in *The Cambridge Ancient History*. Vol. 2, Part 2, *The Middle East and the Aegean Region c. 1380–1000 B.C.* Edited by I. E. S. Edwards, C. J. Gadd and N. G. L. Hammond. Cambridge: Cambridge University Press, 1980.
Dunn, James D. G. *The Christ and the Spirit*. Cambridge: Eerdmans, 1998.
Eaton, John. *The Psalms*. London: T&T Clark International, 2005.
Edersheim, Alfred. *The Temple*. London: James Clarke & Co., 1959.
Emerton, John Adney. *Studies in the Pentateuch*. Leiden: Brill, 1990.
Engnell, Ivan. *Studies in Divine Kingship in the Ancient Near East*. 2d ed. Oxford: Blackwell, 1967.
Falk, Daniel K. *Daily, Sabbath, and Festival Prayers in the Dead Sea Scrolls*. Leiden: Brill, 1998.
Falk, Randall. "Understanding Our Relationship to Jesus: A Jewish Outlook." Pages 101–44 in Harrelson and Falk, *Jews and Christians*.
Finlay, Timothy D. *The Birth Report Genre in the Hebrew Bible*. FAT 2/12. Tübingen : Mohr Siebeck, 2005.
Fisher, Eugene J., ed. *Visions of the Other: Jewish and Christian Theologians Assess the Dialogue*. New Jersey: Paulist, 1994.
Fletcher-Louis, Crispin H. T. *All the Glory of Adam: Liturgical Anthropology in the Dead Sea Scrolls*. Leiden: Brill, 2002.
Fossum, Jarl E. *The Image of the Invisible God*. Göttingen: Vandenhoeck & Ruprecht, 1995.
Frankfort, Henri. *Kingship and the Gods*. London: University of Chicago Press, 1978.

Freedman, Rabbi Dr. H., trans. *Midrash Rabbah*. London: Soncino, 1939.
Freundel, Barry. *Contemporary Orthodox Judaism's Response to Modernity*. New Jersey: Ktav, 2004.
Fry, Helen, comp. and ed. *Christian–Jewish Dialogue, a Reader*. Devon: University of Exeter Press, 1996.
Gaster, T. H. *Thespis: Ritual, Myth and Drama in the Ancient Near East*. New York: Norton, 1977.
Gerbrandt, Gerald Eddie. *Kingship According to the Deuteronomistic History*. Atlanta: Scholars Press, 1986.
Gieschen, Charles A. "The Name of the Son of Man in the Parables of Enoch." Pages 238–49 in Boccaccini, ed., *Enoch and the Messiah Son of Man*.
Gillingham, S. E. "The Messiah in the Psalms: A Question of Reception History and the Psalter." Pages 209–37 in Day, ed., *King and Messiah*.
Goldingay, John. *The Message of Isaiah 40–55: A Literary-theological Commentary*. London: T&T Clark International, 2005.
———. *Psalms*. Vol. 1, *Psalms 1–41*. Baker Commentary on the Old Testament Wisdom: and Psalms. Grand Rapids: Baker Academic, 2006.
———. *Psalms*. Vol. 2, *Psalms 42–89*. Baker Commentary on the Old Testament: Wisdom and Psalms. Grand Rapids: Baker Academic, 2006.
———. *Psalms*. Vol. 3, *Psalms 90–150*. Baker Commentary on the Old Testament: Wisdom and Psalms. Grand Rapids: Baker Academic, 2006.
Gordon, Cyrus H. "Canaanite Mythology," in Kramer, ed., *Mythologies of the Ancient World*, 181–218.
Grabbe, Lester, L. *Ancient Israel: What Do We Know and How Do We Know It?* London: T&T Clark International, 2007.
———. *Judaic Religion in the Second Temple Period*. London: Routledge, 2000.
———. *Priests, Prophets, Diviners, Sages*. Valley Forge, Pa.: Trinity Press International, 1995.
Gray, G. Buchanan. *Sacrifice in the Old Testament*. Oxford: Clarendon, 1925.
Gray, John. *The Legacy of Canaan the Ras Shamra Texts and Their Relevance to the Old Testament*. Leiden: Brill, 1957.
Green, Alberto Ravinell Whitney. *The Storm God in the Ancient Near East*. Biblical and Judaic Studies 8. Winona Lake: Eisenbrauns, 2003.
Greenberg, Irving. *For the Sake of Heaven and Earth: The New Encounter between Judaism and Christianity*. Philadelphia: The Jewish Publication Society of America, 2004.
Greenstone, Julius H. *The Messiah Idea in Jewish History*. Philadelphia: The Jewish Publication Society of America, 1943.
Gurney, O. R. *The Hittites*. London: Book Club Associates, 1975.
Güterbock, Hans G. "Hittite Mythology." Pages 139–79 in *Mythologies of the Ancient World*. Edited by Samuel Noah Kramer. New York: Doubleday, 1961.
Hagner, Donald. *The Jewish Reclamation of Jesus*. Grand Rapids: Zondervan, 1993.
Hannah, Darrel D. *Michael Traditions and Angel Christology in Early Christianity*. Tübingen: Mohr–Siebeck, 1999.
Hanson, Paul D. *Isaiah 40–66*. Louisville: John Knox, 1995.
———. "Messianic Figures in Proto-Apocalypticism." Pages 67–75 in Charlesworth, ed., *The Messiah*.
Harrelson, Walter, and Randall Falk. *Jews and Christians: A Troubled Family*. Nashville: Abingdon, 1990.

Harries, Richard. "Judaism and Christianity." In *The Blackwell Encyclopaedia of Modern Christian Thought*. Edited by Alister E. McGrath. Oxford: Blackwell, 1996.
Hayward, C. T. R. *The Jewish Temple: A Non-Biblical Sourcebook*. London: Routledge, 1996.
Hengel, M. "Christological Titles in Early Christianity." Pages 425–48 in Charlesworth, ed., *The Messiah*.
Hick, John, ed. *The Myth of God Incarnate*. London: SCM, 1956.
Hollis, F. J. "The Sun Cult and the Temple at Jerusalem." Pages 87–110 in Hooke, ed., *Myth and Ritual*.
Hooke, Samuel Henry, ed. *Myth and Ritual*. London: Oxford University Press, 1933.
———. *The Siege Perilous: Essays in Biblical Anthropology and Myth and Ritual Reconsidered*. London: SCM, 1956.
Horbury, William. *Jewish Messianism and the Cult of Christ*. London: SCM, 1998.
———. *Jews and Christians in Conflict and Controversy*. Edinburgh: T. & T. Clark, 1998.
———. 'Messianism in the Old Testament Apocrypha." Pages 402–33 in Day, ed., *King and Messiah*.
Hurtado, Larry W. *Lord Jesus Christ: Devotion to Jesus in Earliest Christianity*. Grand Rapids: Eerdmans, 2005.
Hyamson, Moses, trans. *Misneh Torah: The Book of Knowledge*. New York: Block, 1938.
Idel, Moshe. *Messianic Mystics*. London: Yale University Press, 1998.
James, Edwin Oliver. "Initiatory Rituals." Pages 147–77 in Hooke, ed., *Myth and Ritual*.
———. *The Tree of Life*. Leiden: Brill, 1966.
Janowski, Bernd, and Peter Stuhlmacher, eds. *The Suffering Servant: Isaiah 53 in Jewish and Christian Sources*. Translated by Daniel P. Bailey. Grand Rapids: Eerdmans, 2004.
Jaubert, A. *The Date of the Last Supper*. New York: Alba, 1964.
Johnson, A. R. *Sacral Kingship in Ancient Israel*. Cardiff: University of Wales Press, 1967.
Jones, Douglas R. "Isaiah II and III." Pages 516–36 in Black, ed., *Peake's Commentary on the Bible*.
Joyce, Paul M. "King and Messiah in Ezekiel." Pages 323–37 in Day, ed., *King and Messiah*.
Kaiser, Walter C. *Messiah in the Old Testament*. Grand Rapids: Zondervan, 1995.
Karasu, Cem. "Why Did the Hittites have a Thousand Deities?" Pages 221–35 in *Hittite Studies in Honour of Harry A. Hoffner, Jr*. Edited by Gary Beckman, Richard Beal and Gregory McMahon. Winona Lake: Eisenbrauns, 2003.
Kemp, Barry J. "Old Kingdom, Middle Kingdom and Second Intermediate Period c. 2686–1552 BC." Pages 71–182 in *Ancient Egypt: A Social History*. Edited by B. G. Trigger, B. J. Kemp, D. O'Connor and A. B. Lloyd. Cambridge: Cambridge University Press, 2001.
Kessler, Edward, and Neil Wenborn, eds. *A Dictionary of Jewish–Christian Relations*. Cambridge: Cambridge University Press, 2005.
Klausner, Joseph. *From Jesus to Paul*. Translated by William F. Stinespring. London: George Allen & Unwin, 1947.
———. *The Messianic Idea in Israel: From Its Beginning to the Completion of the Mishnah*. Translated by William F. Stinespring from the 3d Hebrew ed. London: Bradford & Dickens, 1956.

Klein, George L. *Zechariah*. The New American Commentary. Nashville: B. & H. Publishing, 2008.
Klenicki, Leon, and Geoffrey Wigoder, eds. *A Dictionary of the Jewish–Christian Dialogue*. Exp. ed. New York: Paulist, 1995.
Knohl, Israel. *The Divine Symphony: The Bible's Many Voices*. Philadelphia: The Jewish Publication Society of America, 2003.
Knoppers, Gary N. 'David's Relation to Moses: The Contexts, Content and Conditions of the Davidic Promises." Pages 91–118 in Day, ed., *King and Messiah*.
Kramer, Samuel Noah, ed. *Mythologies of the Ancient World*. New York: Doubleday, 1961.
Kraus, Hans Joachim. *Worship in Israel: A Cultic History of the Old Testament*. Translated by Geoffrey Buswell. Oxford: Blackwell, 1966.
Kuhrt, Amélie. *The Ancient Near East C3000–330 BC*, vol. 1. London: Routledge, 2003.
———. "Usurpation, Conquest and Ceremonial: From Babylon to Persia." Pages 20–55 in *Rituals of Royalty: Power and Ceremonial in Traditional Societies*. Edited by David Cannadine and Simon Price. New York: Past & Present, 1987.
Kutzko, John F. *Between Heaven and Earth: Divine Presence and Absence in the Book of Ezekiel*. Biblical and Judaic Studies 7. Winona Lake: Eisenbrauns, 2007.
Kvanvig, Helge S. "The Son of Man in the Parables of Enoch." Pages 179–215 in Boccaccini, ed., *Enoch and the Messiah Son of Man*.
Laato, Antti. *A Star is Rising: The Historical Development of the Old Testament Royal Ideology and the Rise of the Jewish Messianic Expectations*. Atlanta: Scholars Press, 1997.
Lacocque, André. "Allusions to Creation in Daniel 7." Pages 114–31 in vol. 1 of Collins, Flint and VanEpps, eds., *The Book of Daniel*.
———. "Messiah." Pages 133–38 in Klenicki and Wigoder, eds., *A Dictionary of the Jewish–Christian Dialogue*.
Lambert, W. G. "Kingship in Ancient Mesopotamia." Pages 54–70 in Day, ed., *King and Messiah*.
Lapide, Pinchas, and Ulrich Luz. *Jesus in Two Perspectives: A Jewish–Christian Dialogue*. Minneapolis: Augsburg, 1985.
Lauderville, Dale. *Piety and Politics*. Grand Rapids: Eerdmans, 2003.
Levey, Samson H. *The Messiah: An Aramaic Interpretation*. New York: Hebrew Union College—Jewish Institute of Religion, 1974.
Lindars, Barnabas. *Jesus Son of Man: A Fresh Examination of the Son of Man Sayings in the Gospels and in the Light of Recent Research*. Grand Rapids: Eerdmans, 1984.
Longman III, Tremper. "The Messiah." Pages 35–74 in Porter, ed., *The Messiah in the Old and New Testaments*.
Maccoby, Hyam. *Judaism in the First Christian Century*. London: Sheldon, 1989.
———. *Judaism on Trial*. London: Associated University Presses Inc., 1982.
———. *The Mythmaker: Paul and the Invention of Christianity*. London: Weidenfield & Nicholson, 1986.
———. *Revolution in Judea: Jesus and the Jewish Resistance*. London: Ocean Books, 1973.
Maimonides. *Misneh Torah: The Book of Knowledge*. Translated by Moses Hyamson. New York: Block, 1938.
Mason, Rex. "The Messiah in the Postexilic Old Testament Literature." Pages 338–64 in Day, ed., *King and Messiah*.

McGrath, Alister E. *Christian Theology an Introduction.* Oxford: Blackwell, 1997.
McWhirter, Jocelyn. *The Bridegroom Messiah and the People of God: Marriage in the Fourth Gospel.* Cambridge: Cambridge University Press, 2006.
Merrill, Eugene H. *Haggai, Zechariah, Malachi: An Exegetical Commentary.* Washington: Biblical Studies, 2003.
Mettinger, Tryggve N. D. *A Farewell to the Servant Songs: A Critical Examination of an Exegetical Axiom.* Scriptora Minora 13. Lund: Gleerup, 1983.
———. "In Search of the Hidden Structure: Yhwh as King in Isaiah 40–55." Pages 143–54 in vol. 1 of Broyles and Evans, eds., *Writing and Reading the Scroll of Isaiah.*
Meyboom, P. G. P. *The Nile Mosaic of Palestrina.* Leiden: Brill, 1995.
Miller, Patrick D., *The Religion of Ancient Israel.* Library of Ancient Israel. Louisville, Ky.: Westminster John Knox, 2000.
Mitchell, David C. "Rabbi Dosa and the Rabbis Differ: Messiah ben Joseph in the Babylonian Talmud." *Review of Rabbinic Judaism* 8 (2005): 74–90.
Moltmann, Jurgen. *The Way of Christ: Christology in Messianic Dimensions.* Translated by Margaret Kohl. Minneapolis: Fortress, 1993.
Moody Smith, D. "Judaism and the Gospel of John." Pages 76–96 in *Jews and Christians: Exploring the Past, Present and Future.* Edited by James H. Charlesworth, Frank X. Blisard and Jeffrey S. Siker. New York: Crossroad, 1990.
Morgenstern, Julian. *Some Significant Antecedents of Christianity.* Leiden: Brill, 1966.
Mowinckel, Sigmund. *He That Cometh.* Translated by G. W. Anderson. Oxford: Blackwell, 1959.
———. *The Psalms in Israel's Worship.* Grand Rapids: Eerdmans, 2004. First published Oxford: Blackwell, 1962.
Neusner, Jacob. *Jews and Christians: The Myth of a Common Tradition.* London: SPCK, 1991.
———. *The Way of Torah: An Introduction to Judaism.* Belmont, Calif.: Dickenson, 1970.
Neusner, Jacob, William J. Green and Ernest Frerichs, eds. *Judaisms and Their Messiahs at the Turn of the Christian Era.* New York: Cambridge University Press, 1987.
Nicklesburg, George W. E. "Discerning the Structure(s) of the Enochic Book of Parables." Pages 23–47 in Boccaccini, ed., *Enoch and the Messiah Son of Man.*
Niehaus, Jeffrey Jay. *Ancient Near Eastern Themes in Biblical Theology*. Grand Rapids: Kregel, 2008.
Novak, David. *Talking with Christians: Musings of a Jewish Theologian.* Grand Rapids: Eerdmans, 2005.
Novak, Ralph Martin. *Christianity and the Roman Empire.* Harrisburg, Pa.: Trinity Press International, 2001.
Novaković, Lidija. *Messiah the Healer of the Sick: a Study of Jesus as the Son of David in the Gospel of Matthew.* WUNT 2/170. Tübingen: Mohr–Siebeck, 2003.
Oakley, Francis. *Kingship: The Politics of Enchantment.* Oxford: Blackwell, 2006.
Ochs, Peter. "Judaism and Christian Theology." Pages 607–25 in *The Modern Theologians.* Edited by David F. Ford. 2d ed. Oxford: Blackwell, 1998.
O'Connor, David B. "Beloved of Maat, the Horizon of Re: The Royal Palace in new Kingdom Egypt." Pages 263–300 in O'Connor and Silverman, eds., *Ancient Egyptian Kingship.*
O'Connor, David, and David P. Silverman, eds. *Ancient Egyptian Kingship.* Leiden: Brill, 1995.

Oesterley, W. O. E. "Early Hebrew Festival Rituals." Pages 111–46 in Hooke, ed., *Myth and Ritual*.
———. "Introduction." Pages 2–25 in Charles, trans., *The Book of Enoch*.
Oswalt, John N. *The Book of Isaiah Chapters 40–66*. The New International Commentary on the Old Testament. Grand Rapids: Eerdmans, 1998.
Parpola, Simo. *Letters from Assyrian Scholars to the Kings Esarhaddon and Assurbanipal*. Part 2, *Commentary and Appendices*. Winona Lake: Eisenbrauns, 2007.
Patai, Raphael. *Man and Temple in Ancient Jewish Myth and Ritual*. Edinburgh: Thomas Nelson & Sons, 1947.
Peterson, David. *Zechariah 9–14 and Malachi*. Louisville, Ky.: Westminster John Knox, 1993.
Porter, Stanley E., ed. *The Messiah in the Old and New Testaments*. Grand Rapids: Eerdmans, 2007.
Prosic, Tamara. *The Development and Symbolism of Passover Until 70 CE*. London: T&T Clark International, 2004.
Räisänen, Heikki. *Jesus, Paul and Torah*. Translated by David E. Orton. Sheffield: JSOT, 1992.
Redford, Donald B. "The Concept of Kingship during the Eighteenth Dynasty." Pages 157–84 in O'Connor and Silverman, eds., *Ancient Egyptian Kingship*.
Riegner, Gerhart M., and Franz von Hammerstein, eds. *Jewish Christian Dialogue*. Geneva: International Jewish Committee on Inter-Religious Consultations and the World Council of Churches' Sub-unit on Dialogue with the People of Living Faiths and Ideologies, 1975.
Ringgren, Helmer. *The Messiah in the Old Testament*. London: SCM, 1956.
Robert, Dana Lee. *Christian Mission: How Christianity Became a World Religion*. Chichester: Wiley-Blackwell, 2009.
Robinson, T. H. "Hebrew Myths." Pages 172–96 in Hooke, ed., *Myth and Ritual*.
Rooke, Deborah W. "Kingship as Priesthood: The Relationship between the High Priesthood and the Monarchy." Pages 187–208 in Day, ed., *King and Messiah*.
———. *Zadok's Heirs: The Role and Development of the High Priesthood in Ancient Israel*. OTM. Oxford: Oxford University Press, 2000.
Rose, Wolter H. *Zemah and Zerubbabel: Messianic Expectations in the Early Postexilic Period*. Sheffield: Sheffield Academic, 2000.
Rosenberg, Stuart. *The Christian Problem: A Jewish View*. New York: Hippocrene, 1986.
Rosenzweig, Franz. *The Star of Redemption*. Translated by William W. Hallo. London: University of Notre Dame Press, 1985.
Ruether, Rosemary Radford. *Faith or Fratricide: The Theological Roots of Anti-Semitism*. New York: Seabury, 1974.
Russell, David Syme. *The Method and Message of Jewish Apocalyptic, 200 BC–AD 100*. London: SCM, 1964.
Sandmel, Samuel. *Antisemitism in the New Testament*. Philadelphia: Fortress, 1978.
———. *A Jewish Understanding of the New Testament*. Cincinnati: Alumni Association of the Hebrew Union College—Jewish Institute of Religion, 1956.
———. *We Jews and Jesus*. London: Gallancz, 1965.
Schechter, Solomon. *Some Aspects of Rabbinic Theology*. New York: Macmillan, 1909.
Scholem, Gershom. *Major Trends in Jewish Mysticism*. New York: Schocken, 1961.
———. *The Messianic Idea in Judaism, and Other Essays on Jewish Spirituality*. London: Allen & Unwin, 1971.

Segal, J. B. *The Hebrew Passover*. London: Oxford University Press, 1963.
Segal, Robert A., ed. *The Myth and Ritual Theory: An Anthology*. Oxford: Blackwell, 1998.
Silverman, David P. "The Nature of Egyptian Kingship." Pages 49–92 in O'Connor and Silverman, eds., *Ancient Egyptian Kingship*.
Smalley, Stephen. *John—Evangelist and Interpreter*. Rev. ed. Carlisle: Paternoster, 1998.
Smith, Carol. "Queenship in Israel? The Cases of Bathsheba, Jezebel and Athaliah." Pages 142–62 in Day, ed., *King and Messiah*.
Smith, Mark S. *The Origins of Biblical Monotheism*. New York: Oxford University Press, 2001.
Stannard, Brendan. *The Cosmic Contest*. Southport: CARIB, 1992.
Tasker, David R. *Ancient Near Eastern Literature and the Hebrew Scriptures About the Fatherhood of God*. Studies in Biblical Literature 69. New York: Lang, 2004.
Telchin, Stan. *Betrayed*. Rev. ed. Grand Rapids: Chosen, 2007.
Tollington, Janet E. *Tradition and Innovation in Haggai and Zechariah 1–8*. Sheffield: Sheffield Academic, 1993.
VanderKam, James C. *The Dead Sea Scrolls Today*. Grand Rapids: Eerdmans, 1994.
Vanderkam, James C., and Peter W. Flint, eds. *The Meaning of the Dead Sea Scrolls: Their Significance for Understanding the Bible, Judaism, Jesus and Christianity*. London: T&T Clark International, 2002.
Van der Toorn, Karel. "The Babylonian New Year Festival: New Insights From the Cuneiform Texts and Their Bearing on Old Testament Study." Pages 331–44 in *Congress Volume: Leuven 1989*. Edited by J. A. Emerton. Leiden: Brill, 1991.
Vermes, Geza. *The Complete Dead Sea Scrolls in English*. London: Penguin, 1997.
———. *Jesus the Jew: An Historian's Reading of the New Testament*. London: Collins, 1973.
———. *The Religion of Jesus the Jew*. London: SCM, 1993.
Von Soden, Wolfram. *The Ancient Orient*. Grand Rapids: Eerdmans, 1994.
Walton, John H. *Ancient Israelite Literature in its Cultural Context*. 2d printing 1990 with corrections and additions. Grand Rapids, Regency Reference Library, 1990.
———. "The Anzu Myth as Relevant Background for Daniel 7?" Pages 69–89 in Collins, Flint and VanEpps, eds., *The Book of Daniel*.
Warner, Marina. *Alone of All Her Sex*. London: Pan, 1985.
Wegner, Paul D. *An Examination of Kingship and Messianic Expectation in Isaiah 1–35*. New York: Mellen Biblical, 1992.
Weisinger, Herbert. *Tragedy and the Paradox of the Fortunate Fall*. London: Routledge & Kegan Paul, 1953.
Whiston, William, trans. *The Works of Josephus*. Peabody, Mass.: Hendrickson, 1998.
Williams, Catrin H. *I am He: The Interpretation of Ani Hû in Jewish and Early Christian Literature*. Tübingen: Mohr Siebeck, 2000.
Williamson, H. G. M. "The Messianic Texts in Isaiah 1–39." Pages 239–70 in Day, ed., *King and Messiah*.
Winter, Paul. *On the Trial of Jesus*. 2d ed. Rev. and ed. T. A. Burkill and Geza Vermes. Berlin: de Gruyter, 1974.
Witherington III, Ben. *John's Wisdom: A Commentary on the Fourth Gospel*. Louisville, Ky.: Westminster John Knox, 1995.
Wright, Christopher J. H. *The Message of Ezekiel: A New Heart and a New Spirit*. Leicester: Intervarsity Pres, 2001.

Wright, David Pearson. "Anatolia: Hittites." Pages 189–96 in *Religions of the Ancient World*. Edited by Sarah Iles Johnston. Cambridge: The Belknap Press of Harvard University Press, 2004.
———. *Ritual in Narrative*. Winona Lake: Eisenbrauns, 2001.
Wright, N. T. *Jesus, the Victory of God*. London: SPCK, 1996.
Wyatt, N. "Epic in Ugaritic Literature." Pages 246–54 in *A Companion to Ancient Epic*. Edited by John Miles Foley. Oxford: Blackwell, 2005.
———. "The Religious Role of the King in Ugarit." Pages 41–74 in *Ugarit at Seventy-Five*. Edited by K Lawson Younger Jr. Winona Lake: Eisenbrauns, 2007.
———. *Religious Texts from Ugarit*. London: Continuum International, 2006.
———. *"There's such Divinity doth Hedge a King": Selected Essays of Nicolas Wyatt on Royal Ideology in Ugaritic and Old Testament Literature*. SOTSMS. Aldershot: Ashgate, 2005.
Wyschogrod, Michael. "A Jewish Postscript." Pages 179–87 in *Encountering Jesus: A Debate on Christology*. Edited by Stephen T. Davis. Atlanta: John Knox, 1988.
———. "A Jewish Reading of St. Thomas Aquinas on the Old Law." Pages 125–38 in *Understanding Scripture: Explorations of Jewish and Christian Traditions of Interpretation*. Edited by Clemens Thoma and Michael Wyschogrod. New York: Paulist, 1987.
Wyschogrod, Michael, and R. Kendall Soulen, eds. *Abraham's Promise: Judaism and Jewish–Christian Relations*. Grand Rapids: Eerdmans, 2004.
Yonge, C. D., trans. *The Works of Philo*. Peabody, Mass.: Hendrickson, 1997.
Yuval, Israel Jacob. *Two Nations in Your Womb: Perceptions of Jews and Christians in Late Antiquity and the Middle Ages*. London: University of California Press, 2006.

INDEXES

INDEX OF REFERENCES

HEBREW BIBLE/ OLD TESTAMENT

Genesis
1	131
1:1–2	177
1:2	141
1:3	183
1:20–25	115
1:26	191, 192
2:1–2	177
5:21–24	146
6	152
12:3	112
14:8	125
14:18–24	124
14:18	73, 174
18:1–15	191
18:1	167
18:13	167
19:24	100
19:29	100
26:24	109

Exodus
2:10	90
3:1–22	191
3:1–4	120
3:8	91
3:14	165
3:17	131
4:20	160
12	136
12:2	136
12:5–6	137
12:9	138
12:15	137
12:19	141
12:21–22	175
12:23	137, 164
12:46	85, 138, 175
14:31	109
15:18	184
16:4	183
16:15	91
17:6	91
23:20–22	153, 164
24:10	167
25–31	131
25:1–2	90
25:9	130
25:40	130
26:30	130
26:31–35	183
28:1	183, 184
28:5	134, 183
28:30	134
28:31	134
28:32	170
28:36–38	108, 134
28:36	134
29:7	124
29:21	124
30:6–10	183
30:10	183, 184
30:20–21	183
32:30–32	90
33:11	167
33:20	153, 191
34:10	90
34:29–35	90
34:29	90, 167
35–44	131
40:17–32	131

Leviticus
6:4	134
8:12	124
8:30	124
15:25–26	136
16	132
16:4	134
16:7–10	112
16:15–22	135
16:33–34	141
17:11	138
21:14	124
23:24–25	133
23:36–41	89
23:40	89
25:9	133
25:10	173
25:13	138

Numbers
6:22–27	134
6:24–27	71
9:12	85, 175
9:13	141, 176
35:28	123

Deuteronomy
11:13–15	94
15:2	138
16	137
16:1	136
16:3	137
17	99

Index of References

Deuteronomy (cont.)		18:4–5	16, 71	10:18	91
18:15	160, 182	23:4–5	16, 71	11:4	73, 134
28	120			14:6	91
32:8	69, 71,	*1 Chronicles*		17:8–12	76
	152, 167,	16:8–36	86	18	73–77, 80,
	191	17:14	67		82, 162
32:39	165	28:5	67, 68	18:4–6	77
		28:6	68	18:4	78
Judges		29:11	67, 182	18:5	180
13:1–23	191	29:20	68	18:6	76
21:19–21	136	29:23	67, 68	18:16–19	110
				18:16–17	79
1 Samuel		*2 Chronicles*		18:16	90
2:1–10	161	4:2–5	81	18:20–21	110
9:17	109	4:6	81	18:20	79
10:6	67	9:8	67	18:25	162
16:13	67	13:8	67	18:33	79
24:5	207			18:36	79
		Job		18:50	67
2 Samuel		1:6	70	20	73
2:20 LXX	159	9:8	166	20:1	76
3:18	109			20:6	67
6	86	*Psalms*		20:7–10	69
7:12–16	68	2	72–76, 93,	21	73–75
7:12	129		99, 104,	21:4	69
7:13	129		152	21:7	69
7:14	129	2:1–3	77	22	32, 79, 84,
14:17	68	2:1–2	152		196, 197
15:10	85	2:2	67	22:1–18	76
15:16–37	162	2:3	78	22:1–2	78, 180
22	82	2:6–7	67	22:6–7	78, 110
		2:7	161, 179	22:7–8	78
1 Kings		3:1–3	76	22:8	79, 180
1:32–40	82	3:3	80, 180	22:14	84
1:33–34	183	4:6	71	22:16–18	84
1:39	82	5:2	73	22:16	180
7:23–25	81	6:1–5	76	22:18	112, 180
8	130	6:6–8	78	22:27–29	91
8:2	130	7:1–2	76	23:1–4	71
8:31–53	140	7:8	91	23:5	67
15:9–13	16, 71	7:17	69	24:7–10	73, 86
22:19	70	8:4–6	168	25:7	79
		9	180	25:11	79
2 Kings		9:1–2	69	25:21	79
1:8	159	9:7	73	26:1–7	79, 110
9:13	85, 162	9:13	80, 180	26:1	80
11:12	109	10:16	73	26:12	79

27:5–6	80	47:7–8	91	72:12–14	92
27:5	80	47:7	73	72:16–17	92
27:6	180	47:8	73	72:16	92
27:11	80	48:9	76	72:17	68
28:8	67	51:1–5	79	73:2	78
28:9	71	54:1	72	73:13	79
29:3	80	56:13	79	74	83
29:10	73, 80, 82	59:3–4	79	74:3–7	83
30:3	80, 180	59:16	76	74:12–17	80, 84
31:16	71	62:5	78, 110, 180	74:12–14	82
32:4	78			74:12	73
32:5	79	65	83	74:15–17	82
32:6	78	65:5–7	83	74:21	91
33:3	91	65:9–13	83	77:2	76
33:6	72	65:9–10	92	77:10–11	69
34:20	85, 175	65:11–13	92	77:15–20	89
35:15	78	67:1	71	77:16	82
37:24	78	67:4	91	78:70–71	72
38:2	78, 110	67:6	92	80	71, 88
38:3–4	79	68:1	91	80:1	71, 73
38:16–17	78	68:6	92	80:3	71
39:2	78, 180	68:7–9	92	80:7	71
39:9–10	78	68:24–27	86	80:19	71
39:9	78	68:24	73	81	85
39:12	78	69:1–2	76	81:3	85
40:2–3	110	69:2	78	82	70, 125
40:2	79	69:7	78	82:1–2	138
40:3	91	69:8	78, 179	82:1	125
41:4	79	69:10	180	82:3–4	70
41:9	78, 179	69:12–17	84	82:5	71
41:10	80	69:12	78	83:18	69
42:3	78	69:14–15	77	84:3	73
42:5–7	78	69:19	78	84:6	92
43:2	78, 180	69:21	84, 180	84:9–10	69
44:4	73	69:26	78	86:7	76, 179
44:5	72	70:1–2	76	86:9	91
44:15	78	71:2	76	86:13	80, 180
45	68, 73, 85, 89	71:4	76	88:3–7	78
		71:6	68	88:3	76, 179
45:6–7	68	71:20	80, 180	88:6–7	78
45:6	68	72	73, 74	88:7	78
45:7	68	72:1–7	202	88:14	78, 180
46:2–4	83	72:1–2	109	88:16–17	78
47	74, 75	72:1	92	88:18	78, 179
47:2	91	72:4	92	89	73–76, 86, 180
47:3	91	72:5	68		
47:5–7	85	72:6	92	89:3–4	67

Psalms (cont.)		96:1	91	113–18	75		
89:4	91, 161, 184	96:10	73, 85, 91	113–118	87		
		96:13	91	116:3	78		
89:6–7	86	97:1–5	71	116:8	78		
89:8–18	83	97:1–2	91	116:16	78		
89:9–10	82, 112	97:1	73, 85	118	74, 76, 81, 86, 88, 162		
89:9	82, 86, 165	98	85				
		98:1–2	86, 113				
89:10	82, 86, 165	98:1	91	118:5	82		
		98:6	68, 73, 86	118:10–11	82		
89:11–12	82	99:1	71, 73, 85	118:13	82		
89:18	73	100	86	118:18	78		
89:20–22	91	100:1	91	118:19	87		
89:20	67	100:3	71	118:20	87		
89:22–23	86	101	73, 74, 76	118:21–22	72		
89:22	180	102:2	76, 78, 179	118:21	82, 87		
89:24	67, 72			118:22	162		
89:25	86, 112	102:9	78	118:25	162		
89:26–27	68	104	76	118:26	87, 162		
89:27	86	104:1–4	71	118:27	87		
89:29	104	104:5	82	119:75	78		
89:31	180	104:6–9	82	119:81–88	78		
89:36–37	91	104:6–7	82	120–34	88		
89:38	67, 78	104:9	82	121:3	79		
89:39	67, 84, 180	104:10–30	82	123:1	73		
		104:10–28	92	124	77		
89:44	84, 180	104:26	82	124:2–5	78, 79		
89:45	78	104:30	72	124:8	183		
89:46	78	105:1–15	86	126:6	92		
89:50	67	105:1	72	130:1	78		
89:51	67, 78, 180	105:44	90	132	73, 74		
		106:1	86	132:1–2	86		
89:69	180	106:47–48	86	132:3–5	86		
91:11–12	79	107:33–34	92	132:6–10	86		
91:14	72	107:35–36	92	132:8–9	86		
92:1–4	69	107:41	91	132:10	67		
93	74, 75, 77	108:6	86	132:11–12	67		
93:1–2	82	109:31	91	132:11	67		
93:1	73, 85	110	73–76, 93, 99, 104, 141, 154	132:15	91		
93:2	73			132:17	67		
93:3–4	82			140:5	78		
93:3	78	110:1	68, 72, 91, 135, 180	140:12	91		
95–99	74			144	74, 76		
95–100	75	110:3	72, 82	144:1–11	73		
95:7	71	110:4–5	73	144:7	79		
96	85	110:4	170, 174, 197	144:9	91		
96:1–13	86			144:12–15	92		

Index of References

145:5–10	91	11:12	117	42:3	117, 183
146	139	13:9–13	116	42:4	109, 120, 178
146:7	91	14	114		
146:8	91	14:14	100	42:5	101, 167, 182
146:10	73	14:29–30	179		
147:8	92	16:1–5	179	42:6	109, 120, 148, 150, 178
149:1	91	16:14	119		
		17:13	119		
Proverbs		24:21	119	42:7	117
16	68	24:22	119	42:10	119, 185
16:15	71	25:8	120, 182, 184	43:5–6	119
22	68			43:10	165, 179
24:21–22	68	26:16	120	43:15	98
30:19	96	26:19	101, 116, 120, 182, 184	43:19	119, 182
				43:25	118, 182
Isaiah				44:3	120, 184
1–39	96, 97	27:1	119, 182	44:6	98, 164
4:1–6	179	28:5–6	179	44:23	119
4:2	99	28:5	184	44:28	106, 117
4:28	148	28:16	101	45:1–4	148
5	114	29:18–19	120, 182, 184	45:1	106
6:1–13	134			45:5	106
6:1	110, 123	30:7	90	45:6	106
6:2–3	139	30:9	120	45:8	116
6:5	98	30:11	208	45:17	119
6:7–9	106	30:20	208	45:23	118, 164, 184
7–9	97	33:10	110		
7:14	96, 97	34:2	119	46:3	150
9	99	35:5–6	179, 182, 184	46:4	165
9:2–7	99, 106			48:2–5	150
9:2	100, 170	35:5	120	48:2–3	150
9:5–6	179	35:6	120	48:3	150
9:6–7	96, 97	35:8–10	119	48:4	150
9:6	68	35:10	120	48:5	150
9:7	95, 116, 119, 182, 184	40–55	96, 108, 119, 140	48:14	148
				49–55	105
		40–48	107	49–54	105
10:24–27	179	40:11	106	49:1–6	108, 177
11:1–16	179	41:1–42:9	105	49:1	105, 150, 177, 178
11:1–6	97	41:4	164, 165		
11:1	99, 106	41:8	105	49:2	105
11:4	106, 116	42–48	105	49:5–6	109, 178
11:6–8	182	42:1–9	110, 179	49:6	109, 117, 150, 184, 205
11:6–7	117	42:1–4	108, 177		
11:9–10	118, 184	42:1	105, 148, 150, 177–79		
11:9	117			49:7	105
11:11	119			49:8	120

Isaiah (cont.)		55:1–2	182	16:16	119, 183
50:4–11	177	56–66	96, 105	17:8	101
50:4–9	108	56:6–8	118	17:13	101
50:6	109, 178	56:11	99	17:25	106
50:7	110	57:15	101, 110	20:7–10	111
50:9	110	57:20	82	20:7	106
51:9	182	58:4	150	20:11–13	111
51:10–11	182	59:20	205	22:22	99
51:11	113	60:1	100	23:1–7	119
52–53	76	60:19	100	23:1–2	98
52:6	165	61	173	23:4	99
52:7	83, 139	61:1–4	110	23:5–6	99, 119, 183
52:13–53:12	108, 111, 177, 179, 186, 197, 198	61:1–3	110	23:5	99
		61:1–2	117, 139, 178	23:7	182
		61:1	117, 138	23:10	114
52:13	105, 110, 178	61:2	125, 164	25:15	119, 182
		62:7	150	25:34–36	99
52:15	110	62:10	115	30:9	99
52:53	111	65:17	116, 119, 182, 184	31:10	106
53	30, 33, 34, 140			31:31–34	182
		65:18	184	31:31	120
53:1	150, 178	66:22	119, 184	31:34	118, 182, 183
53:2	100	70:1	150		
53:3–7	110	71:14–16	150	33:8	118, 182
53:3	110, 178			33:14–15	99
53:4–6	110	*Jeremiah*		46:18	98
53:4	110, 178	1:5–10	105	48:15	98
53:5–12	110	1:5	105	50:6	98
53:5–6	178	1:7	106	51:57	98
53:5	117, 175, 178, 182	1:10	106	52:17	107
		2:2	114		
53:7–8	177	2:13	101	*Lamentations*	
53:7	111	3:2–3	118	3:35	100
53:8–12	178	3:3	114	3:38	100
53:8	110, 117, 182	3:15	99	4:20	101
		3:20	114		
53:9	110, 178	5:22	82	*Ezekiel*	
53:10–12	110	6:3	99	1:4–3:12	134
53:10	110, 178	8:19	98	1:26–28	150
53:11–12	117, 182	10:21	99	1:28	131
53:11	118	11:18–20	111	2:1	106
54:5	118	11:19	111	2:3	106
54:10	120	12:10	99	4:4	111
54:11–12	184, 208	14:1–9	114	11:22–25	107
54:11	119	14:22	118	12	208
55–66	105	16:14	119, 182	17	100

17:3	100	7	28, 102,	Obadiah	
18:31	182		103, 128,	21	182
28:1–10	114		129, 152,		
34:1–10	98		155, 172	Jonah	
34:2	99	7:2–3	102	1–2	112
34:7–10	99	7:9–14	108, 151	1:15	182
34:11–17	106	7:9–10	151	2:2–3	112
34:12–13	184	7:9	151	2:2	112
34:12	117	7:13–14	151, 169,	2:3	112
34:15	98		172	2:4	112
34:16	117	7:13	29, 104,	2:6	112
34:17	117, 172,		119, 156,	4:5	113
	184		169, 173		
34:23–24	107	7:14	103, 104,	Micah	
34:23	98, 99,		161, 182	2:12–13	99
	104, 106,	7:27	100, 103	4:3–4	119, 182
	117	8–12	103	4:6–7	119
34:25	117	8:15	29	4:9	106
34:26–29	182	9:2	29	5:2	97, 161
34:26–27	117	9:25	139	5:4	99
34:29	117, 182	10	71		
34:31	117	10:5	29	Nahum	
36:25	118, 182			2:11	83
36:26–27	120, 184	Hosea		3:18	99
37:1–10	120	1:10	115		
37:25	119, 182	2:1–13	118	Habakkuk	
40–48	120	2:8–9	114	2:16	182
43:1–9	107	2:16–17	115	3:3–4	101
43:1–5	101	3:4–5	106		
44:1–3	101	4:1–3	120	Zephaniah	
47:1	182, 185,	9:2	115	2:3	119, 182
	208	13:14	120, 184	3:8	119
47:12	185			3:19	119, 120
48:31–34	208	Joel		3:20	119
48:35	107, 184,	2:28–32	184	14:3	119
	208	2:28–29	182, 183,		
			206	Haggai	
		2:28	120, 195	1:9–10	107
Daniel					
2:44	119, 182			Zechariah	
3:26	100	Amos		2:11	118, 184
4:12	100	3:2	115	3	108
4:17	100	4:1	118	3:2	182
4:34	100, 182	4:6–9	118	3:6–8	108
5:14	106	4:11	100	3:8	99
5:18	100	9:11–15	107	3:9	108
6:26	104				

Zechariah (cont.)		NEW TESTAMENT		20:18	171		
6:11	102	*Matthew*		21:5–6	162		
8:12	118, 119	1:1–17	160	21:9	162		
9:9	24, 115, 118, 160, 162, 181	1:20–21	160	21:15	162		
		2:1	161	22:44	174		
		2:5–6	161	24:30	173		
10:1	118, 182	2:6	97	24:39	169		
10:4	101	2:13–15	177	25:31–46	172, 184		
10:8–9	113	2:19	173	25:31–33	178, 184		
10:11	113, 182	3:4	159	25:31	169		
11:7–8	99	4:3	166	26:7	161		
12:1	175	4:16	170	26:17–30	200		
12:10–11	118	4:18	186	26:26–29	200		
12:10	114, 204	4:19	183	26:26	136		
12:11	114	4:24	205	26:37	179		
13:1	118, 182	5:14	184	26:56	179		
13:7–9	114	5:17	195	26:61	181		
13:7	163	8:14–18	178	26:63–64	169		
13:9	101	8:17	178	26:64	173		
14:1–3	106	8:29	166	27:22	159		
14:1–2	181	9:2–6	169	27:27–60	178		
14:8	117, 182, 185	9:3	169	27:28–31	180		
		9:9	186	27:28–29	180		
14:9	117, 119, 182	9:15	181	27:31	180		
		9:35	205	27:37	163		
14:16–19	115	9:36	163	27:43	166, 180		
14:17	118	10:23	169	27:46	180		
		11:4–5	182	27:50	180		
Malachi		11:11–15	159	27:57	186		
1:14	98	12:8	170	28:19–20	184		
4:2	101, 170	12:15	205	28:19	184, 199, 205, 208		
4:5	101	12:23	185				
		13:24–30	181				
2 Esdras		13:35	174	*Mark*			
8:42	156	13:41	169	1:1	166		
		14:14	205	1:10	177		
APOCRYPHA/DEUTERO-CANONICAL WORKS		14:33	165, 166	1:15	182, 205		
		15:24	178	3:11	166		
Ecclesiasticus		16:9–10	182	4:11	174		
50	131	16:17	159	5:7	167		
50:1–21	127	16:18	159	8:29	159		
50:5–7	126, 127	16:28	169	8:31	171, 186		
50:6	135	17:1–7	160	8:38	172		
50:7	131	17:9–13	159	9:11–13	159		
50:8–10	127	17:22	171	9:12	178		
50:19	132	18:20	196	9:31	186		
		19:28	169, 172	10:33–34	186		

Index of References

11:8	162	7:18–23	179	4:19	160
11:9	162	7:21	205	4:25	158
11:10	162	8:26–33	206	4:26	21, 159
12:36	174	9:6	205	5:25	166
13:26–27	172	9:31	176, 182	5:26	182
13:26	173	10:18	114, 182	5:27	172
14:12–26	200	17:21	184	6:14	160, 182
14:20	179	19:38	162, 182	6:20	166
14:21	186	20:17	163	6:35	171
14:27	163	20:42	174	6:48–51	176, 183
14:36	178	20:43	174	6:53–56	176, 201
14:58	181	21:27	173	7:37–39	171, 182
14:61–64	169	22:7–20	200	7:37–38	171
14:62	159, 172, 173	22:20	182	8:12	170
		22:37	178	8:23	168
14:65	178	22:42	182	8:28	178
14:68	178	22:51	205	8:58	165
15:5	178, 180	22:67	159	9:9	159
15:8–15	180	22:69	169	9:36–38	170
15:20	178	22:70	166	10	163
15:23	180	23:19	25	10:10	182
15:24	180	23:33	180	10:11	163
15:26	163	23:35	177	10:24–25	159
		23:38	163	10:36	166
Luke		23:45	183	11:2	161
1:31	178	24:1–2	180	11:25	182
1:32–33	161	24:26–27	159, 171	11:27	166
1:32	167, 182	24:44–46	159	11:49–50	174
1:33	182			11:50–52	174
1:35	166, 167	*John*		12:1–17	173
1:43	163	1:1–2	177	12:3	161
1:46–55	161	1:1	167, 168	12:13	162
2:1–5	160	1:3	126, 167	12:28	166
2:4	161	1:4	170, 182	12:31	183
2:11	163	1:8–9	170	12:32	178
2:14	162	1:18	167	12:38	178
2:26	159	1:19–20	159	12:39	178
2:32	178	1:29	168	12:47	176
3:21–22	173	1:34	166	14:6	193
3:22	161	1:41	158, 167	14:7–9	168
3:23–38	160	1:45	159	14:12	184
3:23	173	1:49	166, 167	14:27	182
3:38	166	3:1–10	186	15:1–8	171
4:18–21	178	3:14	178	16:28	168
4:22	185	3:18	166	17:5	168
4:41	166	3:36	182	18:6	165
7:16	160	4:10–14	171, 182	18:14	174

John (cont.)		17:3	171	3:13	195
18:36	163	17:10	199	3:28	183
19:7	166	17:31	183	6:15	182
19:19–22	163	18:24–28	171		
19:23	170	19:8	199	*Ephesians*	
19:29	175	19:9	12	1:20	182
19:36	175	19:23	12	1:22	180
20:22	171, 182	22:4	12	2:4–6	184
20:30	187	24:14	12	2:14–15	184
20:31	166, 182			5:14	170
21:15–17	163	*Romans*			
		5:11	178, 182	*Philippians*	
Acts		5:19	178	2:5–7	167
1:26	208	6:4	183	2:7	178
2:4	184	6:8	183	2:9	184
2:5	198	6:9	182	2:10–11	164
2:34	174	7:7–8	195	9	178
2:35	174	8:1	195		
3:13	199	8:11	182	*Colossians*	
3:18–22	171	10:9	164	1:3	164
3:18–20	159	11:26	205	1:15–16	167
3:18	198	14:11	164	1:19	167
3:22	160, 182, 198	15:21	178, 184	2:9	167
		16:25	174	3:1	180
3:24	199			3:9	182
4:4	199	*1 Corinthians*		3:10	182
4:11	163	1:22	164	3:13	164
5:42	159	2:7	174	3:18–24	164
6:7	186	5:5	164	3:24	164
7:52	171	5:7	176		
7:55–56	169	6:19	184	*1 Timothy*	
7:55	169	10:4	177	6:16	182
8:12	183	10:9	164		
8:26–27	177	12:3	164	*Hebrews*	
8:28–38	186	15:3	171, 178, 186	1:2	167
8:32–35	178			1:3	180, 183
9:2	12	15:20	177	1:6	167
9:15	184, 208	15:24	180	1:13	174
9:31	199			2:6	168
10:14	184	*2 Corinthians*		2:17	172
10:34	199	1:21–22	184	3:1	172
10:45	199	4:6	170	4:14	172
14:1	199	5:17	177, 182	4:16	183
15	194	5:21	178	5:5–6	170, 174
15:7	208			5:5	172
17:1–3	171	*Galatians*		5:10	172
17:1	199	1:4	178	6:20	172

7:17	170, 172, 173	3:12	184	37–71	29, 144, 145, 169
7:21	170	5:9–10	184	37	144
7:26–27	173	11:15	182	38–44	144
7:26	172	12:7–8	182	38:2	148
7:27	173	13:8	126	38:3	153
8:1	172, 180	14:1	184	38:5	156
9:1–15	173	14:3	185	40:5	148
9:11	172	14:14	172, 173	40:6	149
9:15	178, 182	17:14	182	41:2	149
9:23–28	173	18:23	181	41:61	149
10:12–13	180	19:6–9	181	43:3	154
10:16	182	19:16	182	45–57	144
10:20	183	20:7	182	45:3	148, 152
10:21	174	20:10	182	45:4–5	156
10:22	183	21:1–2	181	46:1–7	150
13:20	163	21:1	182, 184	46:1–6	148
		21:3	184	46:1	148, 154
		21:4	182, 184, 203	46:3	153
1 Peter				46:4–6	156
1:18–20	174	21:5	182, 184, 203	46:4–5	149
2:4–5	207			46:5	154
2:5	184	21:6	164	47:3	151
2:8	164	21:12–13	208	47:4	153
2:22–25	177	21:18–19	184	48:1–2	150, 154
2:24–25	178	21:19	208	48:2–7	148
3:18	171	21:25	208	48:2–3	68, 148
5:2–4	163	21:27	184	48:3	149
		22:1–3	208	48:5	148, 149
2 Peter		22:1	184, 185	48:6	146, 153
1:19	114	22:2	185	48:8–9	156
3:13	182	22:3–4	184	48:10	148, 152, 190
		22:5	184		
1 John		22:13	164	49:2	148
2:2	171, 178	22:16	170	50:2–3	149
3:5	178			51:1–2	156
4:10	178	PSEUDEPIGRAPHA		51:2	154
		1 Enoch		51:3–4	149
Jude		6	152	51:3	148, 154, 156
1:6	119	10:4–5	154		
		10:6	156	52:1	156
Revelation		10:17	156	52:4	148, 156, 190
1:7	173	10:21	156		
1:8	164	11:1	156	53:1	156
1:11	164	12:1	146	55:4	154
1:13	172	12:18–22	151	56:1	151
2:10	184	26:26–29	148	57:3	149
2:110	184				

232 Index of References

1 Enoch (cont.)			*2 Enoch*			*11QT*	
57:4	154		71	174		29:9	131
58–69	144						
59:4	154		*3 Enoch*			MISHNAH	
60:7	154		12:5	147		*Pesahim*	
61:5	156		45	174		5:7	75
61:8	148, 152, 154					8:6	180
			4 Ezra				
62:1–6	156		7:28–29	155		*Yoma*	
62:1–2	156		12:11	155		2:3	183
62:2	152, 154		13	169		6:4	135
62:5–9	148		13:32	155		6:8	135
62:5	152		13:37	155			
62:6–7	149					*Sukkah*	
62:7	148, 152		*Jubilees*			3:1–2	88
62:9	148, 156		2:1–3	131		3:9	162
62:10–11	149					4:5	162
62:10	149		*Liber antiquitatum*			4:7	75
62:14	148, 149		*biblicarum*			4:9	88, 176
62:80	154		13:4	175		5:2–4	87
63:1	149		13:7	130		5:4	88
63:4	152						
63:11	148, 149		*Testament of Levi*			*Rosh HaShanah*	
66–70	152		13:2–50	128		1:1	142
67	119					1:2	142
69:16–26	149		QUMRAN				
69:27	149, 152, 156		*1QS*			*Ta'anit*	
			9:11	123		4:8	136
69:29	154						
70:1–4	144		*4Q246*			*Sotah*	
70:1	148, 156		2	128		9:12	140
71	147		2:1	128			
71:1–17	144		2:7–8	128		*Sanhedrin*	
71:14	146, 147		2:7	128		7:5	169
71:17	148		5–10	141		98a	173
89:59	152						
90:28–38	156		*4Q521*			*Abot*	
			2 ii	139		3:20	196
2 Baruch							
29–30	129		*4Q541*			BABYLONIAN TALMUD	
29:3	156		9	139		*Yoma*	
29:5–8	156		24	139		39b	200
39:7–40:3	129						
39:7–8	156		*11QMelchizedek*			*Sukkah*	
62:2	156		2:9	124, 164		52	114
70:9	129					52a	185, 204
72–74	129						

Rosh HaShanah		2.103	132	*Against Apion*	
31b	200	2.117–126	132	1.183	124
		2.133–135	132		
Baba Batra				CLASSICAL SOURCES	
73a	112	*On the Special Laws*		Diodorus Siculus	
		1.16.84	126	*Biblotheca Historica*	
JERUSALEM TALMUD		1.16.86	126	XL, 3.5	124
Yoma		1.17.97	126, 141		
7:3	125			Irenaeus	
		Questions and Answers		*Against Heresies*	
MIDRASH		*in Exodus*		10.1	168
Genesis Rabbah		2.85	132		
12:15	70			Justin	
38:8	125	JOSEPHUS		*Dialogue with Trypho*	
		Jewish Antiquities		120.3	164
Leviticus Rabbah		2.143	132		
21.11	125	3.7.7	134	Melito of Sardis	
		3.7.7 §185	126	*Bapt. Frg.*	
Ecclesiastes Rabbah		3.7.7 §186	126	VIIB	170
1:28	160	3.8.9	134		
		3.123	132	Origen	
PHILO		3.138	183	*Contra Celsus*	
On Dreams		3.179–187	132	6.4.34	170
1.216–17	134	3.180	132		
2.18.188	126	3.183–187	132	UGARITIC TEXTS	
				KTU	
On the Life of Moses		*Jewish War*		1.10	58
2.26.134	126	5.146, 217	132	1.12	58
2.71–145	132	5.212–213	132	1.23	58
		5.212–213	183	1.113	47

INDEX OF AUTHORS

Ackerman, R. 39
Alexander, P. S. 14, 200, 206, 207
Allison, D. C., Jr. 160, 162, 176

Baines, J. 40–43, 47, 48, 60, 61
Barker, M. 98, 104, 129–31, 135, 136, 139, 173, 183, 202
Barnett, P. 160
Bauckham, R. 169
Benoit, P. 175
Bentzen, A. 15, 16
Bidmead, J. 52, 53
Blackman, A. M. 51
Blenkinsopp, J. 105
Boccaccini, G. 15, 145
Boda, M. 13, 116
Bond, H. K. 180
Borowitz, E. B. 8
Bottéro, J. 54
Brandon, S. G. F. 39, 180
Brockington, L. H. 161
Brooke, G. J. 128
Brown, R. E. 96
Bruce, F. F. 12
Bryce, T. 45, 55, 56, 63

Caragounis, C. C. 168, 169
Carson, D. A. 22
Carson, M. 22
Casey, D. A. 169
Charlesworth, J. H. 13, 122, 145
Chester, A. 97
Chialà, S. 145, 147, 152
Childs, B. S. 96, 97
Chilton, B. 162, 181
Clines, D. J. A. 74, 75
Cohen, A. C. 44, 61
Collins, A. Y. 2, 17, 68, 69, 72, 73, 75, 77, 95–97, 125, 129, 145–49, 154, 155, 157

Collins, J. J. 2, 17, 44, 67–70, 72, 73, 75, 77, 95–97, 99, 102, 104, 111, 118, 122, 124, 125, 127–29, 139, 140, 145–49, 151, 152, 154, 155, 157, 161, 170, 172, 180, 190
Coogan, M. D. 56
Croner, H. 7
Cross, F. M. 64
Crossan, J. D. 180

Dacy, M. 199
Davies, W. D. 14, 18, 203
Day, J. 16, 37, 41, 46, 47, 58, 64, 68, 69, 72–74, 80, 85, 96
De Vaux, R. 15, 81, 123
Dell, K. J. 68, 91
Dempsey, C. J. 101, 114
Drower, M. S. 47
Dunn, J. D. G. 7, 171

Eaton, J. 67, 72, 74–77, 79, 80, 82, 84, 85
Edersheim, A. 81, 123, 136, 141
Emerton, J. A. 69
Engnell, I. 16, 37, 44, 46, 52, 54, 56–58, 61–63, 202

Falk, D. K. 133
Falk, R. 6, 18
Finlay, T. D. 96
Fisher, E. J. 6
Fletcher-Louis, C. H. T. 124, 125, 127, 131, 132
Flint, P. W. 125, 141
Ford, D. F. 7
Fossum, J. E. 112, 153, 164–66
Frankfort, H. 38–40, 42–44, 49–54, 59, 61, 62
Freedman, H. 70
Frerichs, E. 17, 122

Index of Authors

Freundel, B. 194
Fry, H. 6, 201, 205

Gaster, T. H. 57
Gerbrandt, G. E. 37, 38
Gieschen, C. A. 147, 149, 150, 153, 164, 166, 183
Gillingham, S. E. 68, 69, 74, 75, 77, 86
Goldingay, J. 67, 70–72, 77, 79, 80, 86, 90, 105
Gordon, C. H. 64
Grabbe, L. L. 40, 43, 46, 51, 66, 73, 103, 123–25, 127, 129, 133, 136, 140, 145, 198
Gray, G. 132, 137, 138, 176
Gray, J. 48, 57, 82, 83, 93
Green, A. R. W. 63
Green, W. J. 17, 122
Greenberg, I. 7, 209
Greenstone, J. H. 14
Gurney, O. R. 45, 55, 56, 63
Güterbock, H. G. 45

Hagner, D. 10, 19, 20
Hammerstein, F. von 5
Hannah, D. D. 146, 153
Hanson, P. D. 12, 70, 71, 120
Harrelson, W. 6
Harries, R. 7
Hayward, C. T. R. 124, 125, 127, 132, 135, 140
Hengel, M. 177
Hick, J. 7, 8
Hollis, F. J. 81, 87
Hooke, S. H. 39, 74
Horbury, W. 6, 13, 127
Hurtado, L. W. 168
Hyamson, M. 204

Idel, M. 2, 14–16, 39, 192

James, E. O. 42, 45, 133
Janowski, B. 105
Jaubert, A. 175
Johnson, A. R. 15, 81, 85
Jones, D. R. 110
Joyce, P. M. 98, 99, 107

Kaiser, W. C. 15
Karasu, C. 45
Kemp, B. J. 41, 60
Kessler, E. 6
Klausner, J. 17, 18, 21, 25–31, 34–36, 203
Klein, G. L. 108
Klenicki, L. 6
Knohl, I. 69, 92
Knoppers, G. N. 67, 95
Kraus, H. J. 133
Kuhrt, A. 50, 53
Kutzko, J. F. 98, 107
Kvanvig, H. S. 147, 148

Laato, A. 102
Lacocque, A. 103, 104, 191, 192
Lambert, W. G. 42–44, 53, 62
Lapide, P. 6, 10
Lauderville, D. 44
Levey, S. H. 34, 97, 100, 160, 161, 179
Lindars, B. 169
Longman III, T. 77
Luz, U. 6, 10

Maccoby, H. 6, 10, 21, 23, 30, 31, 34, 201
Mason, R. 95, 100
McGrath, A. E. 164
McWhirter, J. 89
Merrill, E. H. 108
Mettinger, T. N. D. 108, 113, 119
Meyboom, P. G. P. 42
Miller, P. D. 132
Mitchell, D. C. 204
Moltmann, J. 204
Moody Smith, D. 12
Morgenstern, S. 88, 162, 175, 178, 181, 186
Mowinckel, S. 13, 15, 16, 38, 41, 43, 44, 46, 49, 52, 53, 58, 69, 74, 85, 96, 122, 128, 152, 168, 178

Neusner, J. 4, 9, 10, 14, 17, 36, 122, 194, 209
Nickelsburg, G. W. E. 144
Niehaus, J. J. 41
Novak, D. 4–6, 15, 196, 201, 208
Novak, R. M. 180
Novaković, L. 189

Oakley, F. 41, 51, 54
Ochs, P. 6
O'Connor, D. B. 40–42, 50
Oesterley, W. O. E. 16, 76, 88, 89, 141, 156
Oswalt, J. N. 105, 108–10
Otzken, B. 72

Parpola, S. 54
Patai, R. 88
Peterson, D. 113
Prosic, T. 136, 137

Räisänen, H. 195
Redford, D. B. 41
Riegner, G. M. 5
Ringgren, H. 15, 16
Robert, D. L. 199
Robinson, T. H. 82, 137
Rooke, D. W. 69, 73, 123, 124, 133
Rose, W. H. 100
Rosenberg, S. 13
Rosenzweig, F. 204
Ruether, R. R. 7
Russell, D. S. 148, 150

Sandmel, S. 12, 13, 19, 21, 23–26, 28, 30–33, 35, 202
Schechter, S. 198
Scholem, G. 4, 90, 192, 207
Segal, J. B. 75
Segal, R. A. 39
Silverman, D. P. 40–42
Smalley, S. 22, 175, 186
Smith, C. 37

Smith, M. S. 16, 71
Soulen, R. K. 194, 195
Stannard, B. 53, 57–59
Stuhlmacher, P. 105

Tasker, D. R. 46, 57
Telchin, S. 199
Tollington, J. E. 100

VanderKam, J. C. 17, 125, 128, 138, 141, 200
Van der Toorn, K. 74, 75
Vermes, G. 9, 18, 21, 22, 24, 26, 28–30, 33, 129, 173, 178, 198
Von Soden, W. 42

Walton, J. H. 37, 103
Warner, M. 167, 170
Wegner, P. D. 13
Weisinger, H. 65
Wenborn, N. 6
Wigoder, G. 6
Williams, C. H. 159, 165, 169
Williamson, H. G. M. 98, 99
Winter, P. 25
Witherington III, B. 180
Wright, C. J. H. 117
Wright, D. P. 45, 46, 56, 57
Wright, N. T. 7, 16, 17, 159, 168, 179, 181, 185
Wyatt, N. 39, 46, 47, 56–59
Wyschogrod, M. 7, 194, 195

Yuval, I. J. 166